Faulkner: the Unappeased Imagination

Faulkner: the Unappeased Imagination

A Collection of Critical Essays

edited by

Glenn O. Carey

℞

The Whitston Publishing Company
Troy, New York
1980

To
Harry Modean Campbell

Foreword: Faulkner's "Clusters of Experience"

In *Conrad the Novelist*, Albert J. Guerard writes, "There are certain moments in our lives, or clusters of experience, to which the unappeased imagination returns again and again, endowing them with significances no one could have seen at the time."

Thus it is with the unappeased and creative imaginations of Conrad and Faulkner, for both writers took their "clusters of experience" and enriched them with multi-faceted meanings and significances. Faulkner acknowledged his indebtedness to such creative burgeoning during his interviews at the University of Virginia:

> The story can come from an anecdote, it can come from a character. With me it never comes from an idea because I don't know too much about ideas and ain't really interested in ideas, I'm interested in people, so what I speak from my experience is probably a limited experience. But I'm interested primarily in people, in man in conflict with himself, with his fellow man, or with his time and place, his environment.

What writers such as Faulkner further accomplish is to awaken our dormant and passive imaginations, causing us to return to "certain moments in our lives" that we now are able to comprehend anew, with meanings we earlier were unable to see. For the more we interpret the works of such highly creative writers, the more we become aware that our angles of vision have become deeper and broader, with greater understanding not only of these authors' clusters of experience but also of our own and of our fellow man's. Resultantly, the contributors to this book of critical essays on Faulkner have gone into his vast creative world, the Yoknapatawpha County of his unappeased imagination, and interpreted the significances they found there.

In selecting criticism about Faulkner's fiction, I am fortunate to have essays from the critics included herein, and it is especially heartwarming to include the 1947 interview of Faulkner as recorded by Harry Modean Campbell, an early pre-Nobel Prize Faulkner critic, whose book with Ruel E. Foster, *William Faulkner: A Critical Appraisal*, was pioneering in its scope. As Professor James W. Webb, formerly of the University of Mississippi and now Curator of Rowan Oak, has written, "This work still proves to be a sound treatment of the author. It still stands up well with the best of more recent studies of Faulkner."

Among those to whom I am indebted are the book's essayists for their patient and full cooperation, especially Melvin Backman, Edwin Moses, Sanford Pinsker and Woodrow Stroble. I also thank Stephen H. Goode for his wholehearted support, Barbara Reising, Carolyn Britt and Mary John Thurman for their kindnesses, Earle Labor and Margaret Carey for their understanding, and Meredith and Harry Campbell for their generous friendship.

                                                          Glenn O. Carey
                                                       Richmond, Kentucky

TABLE OF CONTENTS

Acknowledgements and Permissions

The editor gratefully acknowledges the following excerpts reprinted by permission of Random House, Inc.:

From *Absalom, Absalom!* by William Faulkner, copyright © 1936 by Random House, Inc.

From *As I Lay Dying* by William Faulkner, copyright © 1946 by Random House, Inc.

From *The Collected Stories of William Faulkner* by William Faulkner, copyright © 1950 by Random House, Inc.

From *Essays, Speeches and Public Letters of William Faulkner* edited by James B. Meriwether, copyright © 1965 by Random House, Inc.

From *A Fable* by William Faulkner, copyright © 1954 by Random House, Inc.

From *Flags in the Dust* by William Faulkner, copyright © 1973 by Random House, Inc.

From *Go Down, Moses* by William Faulkner, copyright © 1955 by Random House, Inc.

From *A Green Bough* by William Faulkner, originally published 1933, copyright © 1965 by Random House, Inc.

From *The Hamlet* by William Faulkner, copyright © 1940 by Random House, Inc.

From *Intruder in the Dust* by William Faulkner, copyright © 1948 by Random House, Inc.

From *Knight's Gambit* by William Faulkner, copyright © 1949 by Random House, Inc.

From *Light in August* by William Faulkner, copyright © 1950 by Random House, Inc.

The editor also gratefully acknowledges permissions for the following excerpts:

From *Marionettes* by William Faulkner, copyright © 1975 by Yoknapatawpha Press. Reprinted by permission of Jill Faulkner Summers (Mrs. Paul D. Summers, Jr.).

From "Kentucky: May: Saturday" by William Faulkner, copyright © 1955 by *Sports Illustrated* of Time, Inc. Reprinted by permission of Harold Ober Associates, Incorporated.

From *Mosquitoes* by William Faulkner, copyright © 1927 by Liveright Publishing Corporation. Reprinted by permission of Liveright Publishing Corporation.

From *Soldiers' Pay* by William Faulkner, copyright © 1926 by Boni and Liveright, Inc. Copyright © renewed 1954 by William Faulkner. Reprinted by permission of Liveright Publishing Corporation.

From *Faulkner's Narrative* by Joseph W. Reed, Jr., copyright © 1973 by Yale University Press. Reprinted by permission of Yale University Press.

From *William Faulkner: The Yoknapatawpha Country* by Cleanth Brooks, copyright © 1963 by Yale University Press. Reprinted by permission of Yale University Press.

From *The Rhetoric of Fiction* by Wayne Booth, copyright © 1961 by University of Chicago Press. Reprinted by permission of University of Chicago Press.

From *T. S. Eliot's Poetry and Plays* by Grover Smith, copyright © by Univeristy of Chicago Press. Reprinted by permission of University of Chicago Press.

From *The Faulkner-Cowley File* by Malcolm Cowley, copyright © 1966 by Viking Press. Reprinted by permission of Viking Press.

From *The Look of Things* by John Berger, copyright © 1974 by Viking Press. Reprinted by permission of Viking Press.

From *The Portable Faulkner* edited by Malcolm Cowley, copyright © 1946 by Viking Press. Reprinted by permission of Viking Press.

From *The Hero with the Private Parts* by Andrew Lytle, copyright © 1966 by Louisiana State University Press. Reprinted by permission of Louisiana State University Press.

From *Time and Reality: Studies in Contemporary Fiction* by Margaret Church, copyright © 1963 by University of North Carolina Press. Reprinted by permission of University of North Carolina Press.

From *Force and Faith in the Novels of William Faulkner* by Kenneth Richardson, copyright © 1967 by Mouton Press. Reprinted by permission of Mouton Publishers.

From *Southern Renascence* edited by Louis D. Rubin, Jr. and Robert D. Jacobs, copyright © 1966 by Johns Hopkins University Press. Reprinted by permission of Johns Hopkins University Press.

From *William Faulkner: Study in Humanism from Metaphor to Discourse* by Joseph Gold, copyright © 1966 by University of Oklahoma Press. Reprinted by permission of University of Oklahoma Press.

From *The Myth of Southern History* by F. G. Davenport, copyright © 1970 by Vanderbilt University Press. Reprinted by permission of Vanderbilt University Press.

From *The South in American Literature 1607-1900* by Jay B. Hubbell, copyright © 1954 by Duke University Press. Reprinted by permission of Duke University Press.

From *Eudora Welty* by J. A. Bryant, Jr., copyright © 1968 by University of Minnesota Press. Reprinted by permission of University of Minnesota Press.

From *The American Cowboy* by Harold McCracken, copyright © 1973 by Harold McCracken. Reprinted by permission of Doubleday and Company, Inc.

From *The Tragic Mask: A Study of Faulkner's Heroes* by John L. Longley, copyright © 1957 by University of North Carolina Press. Reprinted by permission of University of North Carolina Press.

From *Faulkner's "As I Lay Dying"* by André Bleikasten, copyright © 1973 by Indiana University Press. Reprinted by permission of Indiana University Press.

From *Faulkner's Women: Characterizations and Meaning* by Sally R. Page, copyright © 1972 by Everett/Edwards, Inc. Reprinted by permission of Everett/Edwards, Inc.

From *Collected Poems: 1909-1962* by T. S. Eliot, copyright © 1963 by Harcourt Brace Jovanovich, Inc. Reprinted by permission of Harcourt Brace Jovanovich,Inc.

From *The CEA Critic,* "The Biblical Background of Faulkner's *Absalom, Absalom!*" (36, 1974) by John V. Hagopian. Reprinted by permission of the College English Association.

From *CLA Journal,* "*Absalom, Absalom!* The Irretrievable Bon" (9, 1965) by Aaron Steinberg. Reprinted by permission of *CLA Journal.*

From *Modern Fiction Studies,* "What Happens in *Absalom, Absalom!*" (13, 1967), by Floyd C. Watkins; and "*Absalom, Absalom!* and the Negro Question" (19, 1973) by John V. Hagopian, copyright © 1967 and 1973 respectively by Purdue Research Foundation. Reprinted by permission of Purdue Research Foundation.

From *Mosaic,* "On *Absalom, Absalom!*" (7, 1973) by Cleanth Brooks. Reprinted by permission of *Mosaic.*

From *The Paris Review,* "The Art of Fiction XII: William Faulkner" (4 1956) by Jean Stein, copyright © 1956 by The Viking Press, Inc. Reprinted by permission of the Viking Press, Inc.

From *The Sewanee Reivew,* "*Absalom, Absalom!*: The Historian as Detective" (79, 1971) by C. Hugh Holman; and "Brother, Son and Heir: The Structural Focus of Faulkner's *Absalom, Absalom!*" (78, 1970) by M. E. Bradford. Reprinted by permission of *The Sewanee Review.*

The editor also gratefully acknowledges permission from *Arizona Quarterly* to reprint with revisions "Faulkner and His Carpenter's Hammer" (32, 1976) by Glen O. Carey, copyright © by *Arizona Quarterly.*

Faulkner in the Classroom—1947

by

Harry Modean Campbell

Editor's Note: The following interview notes were transcribed by Dr. Harry Modean Campbell at the University of Mississippi in the spring of 1947 during a visit to English classes by Faulkner and Phil Stone, the Oxford lawyer who helped his young friend Bill get started in his career. Dr. Campbell is currently Professor Emeritus of English at Oklahoma State University.

Faulkner: I think Eudora Welty's *The Robber Bridegroom* is a charming and fantastic story.

[*Campbell*: Praises *Native Son*, and Willa Cather, Elinor Wylie, Dreiser, Frank Norris.]

Faulkner: I write the way I do because I have to; I wish sometimes that I had a style different from the one I have.

Stone: Faulkner has a personal mannerism and not a style, and Faulkner misses greatness by fastening his material and his characters on to his personal mannerism as on to a kind of Procrustean bed. His style does not follow his subject matter as it should. Look at the difference between style of Balzac in *The Lily of the Valley* and in *Cousin Betty*. There's a difference in style in different Shakespeare plays, but Faulkner's is always the same.

Faulkner: A writer can't draw characters as simply as Nature can.

Stone: It is the characters in nature who are complex. The characters in literature cannot be made as complex as those in life and if this should be done, such characters would not be convincing.

Faulkner: I sometimes revise, sometimes not. I wrote *As I Lay Dying* without changing a word; that was a successful *tour de force*.

Stone: I don't believe this really happened, and I do not

think *As I Lay Dying* a *tour de force*. I do think it is the best novel Bill has written from the standpoint of modern technique. *The Sound and the Fury* is the splendid *tour de force*.

Faulkner: I don't know how my characters are going to develop when I begin to write about them. I can't control them if they become alive. If a character is nothing but a puppet, you can tell what he is going to do, but if he becomes alive he does his own talking. Sometimes you have no more control over him than you would have over an incorrigible child.

Stone: Very few of Faulkner's characters are alive and most of them are puppets. The language they use may be their language, but too often most of their ideas are the ideas of their creator.

Faulkner: I try to tell the truth of man, truth inside the heart. I use exaggeration, cruelty as tools. I am trying to show the truth, not the facts.

In *The Wild Palms* I used that technique as a mechanical device to bring out the story I was telling, which was the contrast between two types of love. One man gave up his freedom for a woman; the other gave up freedom to escape from a woman.

The best training for writing is to read, read, read; read everything—trash, classics, good and bad, and see how they do it. Just like a carpenter who works as an apprentice and studies the master. Thirty-five to forty-five is the best age for writing novels. Then the fire is not used up. The author knows more.

Stone: I do not think this true about novelists. I think Bill says it because in his subconsciousness, and only there, he realizes that he is fading out and that he has not developed much since he was forty-five.

Faulkner: Criticisms are tools of a trade. Critics work for money. It is best not to pay too much attention to printed criticism. There are a few men who are sound, who are scholars in the field, but not many. The present-day trend of writing—cheap stuff full of blood and thunder. What you write must uplift the heart; otherwise it is not great writing. People will read *Huck Finn* for a long time, but Twain's stuff is too loose; it is a series of events.

Stone: This is true but it is also true that all of Bill's novels are simply a collection of episodes. He has design in particular, but he lacks fundamental design and I doubt if he has ever really written a novel. Consequently, his short stories are much better than his novels.

Faulkner: For years I have read anything and everything. Now I read only a few favorites. I haven't read any new books of fiction in fifteen years. [*Campbell*: This couldn't be strictly true; he showed he knew a good deal about books written within the last fifteen years. He reads everything in the following list, probably once every twelve months:

> *Don Quixote*
> *Moby Dick*
> The Henry plays of Shakespeare
> Some of Balzac
> *The Brothers Karamazov*
> The Old Testament
> *Madame Bovary*
> *The Nigger of the Narcissus*
> *Vanity Fair*
> *Henry Esmond*
> *Pickwick Papers*

Strong influences on his writing:

> Conrad (*Campbell*: strong unconscious in-
>   fluence probably)
> The Russians
> The Old Testament
> Swinburne
> Melville
> Balzac (*Campbell*: perhaps, probably a lot
>   more than he is conscious of)]

Stone: He has read very little since 1930. This is quite natural with the professional writer. As to the new books of fiction, he may have skimmed through them, but I doubt if he has really read many of them. As to the best of older works, this may be true and is correct generally. Probably the strongest influences on his writing are Swinburne, Balzac and the Old Testament. This last is obvious when you consider his style.

Faulkner: My favorite Shakespeare plays are the Henry plays and *A Midsummer Night's Dream*. My favorite characters are Prince Hal and Falstaff.

Truth is what makes a book good for me. By truth I mean the things in man that make him bid for immortality—that he can be generous in spite of himself, brave when it is to his advantage to be cowardly, that makes him better than his environment and instincts tempt him to be.

Stone: I think the vague idea Bill has in mind when he speaks of truth is that spark of soul that runs through all humanity and that is its only hope. If this is it, then his statement is correct.

Faulkner: I write about the South because it is what I know. My viewpoints would be essentially the same if I lived in any other section. My picture of the South is therefore misleading and I regret this. I had to use the material I had . . . My purpose is to tell the story as best I can, let the chips fall where they may. I just try to tell the truth of man. I use exaggeration when I have to, and cruelty as a last resort. The area itself is incidental; the South is what I know best. I am sorry that this picture gives a wrong or distorted view. The fate of the South is the fate of the nation. The whole nation is too closely united for the South to have a fate of its own. I don't know what is going to happen in this country, but in my mythical county, Yoknapatawpha, the Snopes family is going to drive out the aristocracy.

Stone: Perhaps he is sorry that his picture of the South gives a distorted view. Anyway what he says is going to happen in his mythical county is actually happening all over the South.

Faulkner: I am primarily a poet and not a prose writer. A poet has to overemphasize.

Stone: This is largely true except the last sentence. I think what he means is the "fine excess" of which Keats spoke. In this sense he is correct. It is a pity that he did not take to heart the doctrine of Keats to the effect that art consists in a fine excess and not in singularity.

Faulkner: The Negro is spiritually tougher than the white man. He is able to survive on less than the white man is. . . he has learned moderation.

He has all the white man's virtues, some of them to a greater extent than the white man has: he probably has more sympathy with children, is kinder to them than white people are—Negroes seem to make better nurses; his affections for the old and helpless of his own race are keener than the white man's. The Negro's vices—drunkenness, gambling, lying, thievery—the white man has taught him. . .

If Christianity means anything there can be no color line in churches. . . I think separate schools are more practical.

[*Campbell*: The main criticisms of him are that his style is bad, that he loves brutality and blood for their own sake, that he is intolerant of criticism and even goes to the trouble to insult people who think well of his writing. He thinks he would enjoy most talking to his detective lawyer. One of the characters he is proudest of having created is Dilsey.]

Faulkner: I don't put my beliefs in my characters. I hope some psychological good will come out of my novels, that they will give the reader what the Greeks call catharsis. My best satisfaction is in being able to remember what I have written afterward and not be ashamed.

Stone: He has written some beautiful stuff and a little that is wonderful but never has he given what the old Greeks gave and I'm sadly afraid that he never will.

Faulkner: My two favorite books are probably *The Sound and the Fury* and *Go Down, Moses*. *The Sound*. . . still continues to move me.

I have faith in human beings as individuals, not as a race.

Darl had schizophrenia.

Stone: As to learning more from reading from books than you can from life, this is largely bunk. He started out in an ivory tower, and I think he would have stayed there if I had not caught him by the neck and pitched him into life. The raw material of art is always life and not art. Consequently this raw material alone will never be art. It is a good thing to read books to see how the other fellow did the trick but that is all the good it does a writer.

Faulkner: I think people haven't tried Christianity yet. Dilsey was the stabilizing influence in *The Sound*. . . Her strength came out of oppression. Temple proves that women are tougher than evil, that they can stand almost anything.

Stone: Why in the world didn't someone ask him about his sense of humor? I manufactured this for him almost out of whole cloth, and it is one of the best things he has. It has been my idea for a long time that if he would carefully write the three or four other unwritten books of the Snopes Saga it may turn out to be the greatest thing he has ever written and might establish him as the greatest of American humorists. Also it would be a profound social document on the present South. You know that we think the race problem on the South is secondary and that the real troubles of the South grow from the rise to power, influence and wealth of the poor whites.

Addie Bundren and William Faulkner

by

Melvin Backman

As I Lay Dying is a key work in the creative life of William Faulkner. This novel seems to have channeled some of the currents of troubled feelings which run through *Sartoris, The Sound and the Fury*, and *Sanctuary* (particularly the first version, written in the summer of 1929 immediately after *The Sound and the Fury* and just before *As I Lay Dying*). It is the thesis of this study that these troubling elements—the conflicting demands of life and art, Faulkner's double heritage, love and sex (specifically as experienced in incest), death and salvation—come together in the creation of Addie Bundren. It is the intent of this study to explore how these elements have contributed to the making of *As I Lay Dying* and, more significantly, what they tell us about the tensions operating in Faulkner's creative process. The tensions—relating primarily to his roles as artist and man—seem to have come to a head at this point in his life. In *As I Lay Dying* they clash and fuse in a strange and richly transmutative process, creating one of Faulkner's most poetic and moving novels.

Of all the characters in *As I Lay Dying*, Darl and Addie Bundren seem the closest to the author, as if they tapped the conflicting elements of Faulkner's own polarized being. The polarization was immediately connected with the new demands being made upon him by his marriage in June 1929 to Estelle Oldham, his childhood sweetheart who eleven years before, as the result of parental pressure, had rejected the aspiring poet for a promising lawyer. In those eleven years the failed poet had become a writer of short stories and novels, the most recent being *The Sound and the Fury*. Faulkner had not yet achieved any real recognition or financial gain as a writer. To make a living for his new family (there were two children by Estelle's previous marriage to Cornell Franklin), Faulkner took a night job as supervisor in the University power plant. There, in the fall of 1929, he wrote *As I Lay Dying*. The novel tells, in a sense, of the casting off of the poet for the sake of the family

family, a situation reflecting a comparable crisis for Faulkner at the
time. Marriage for Faulkner and for Addie Bundren represented a
"violating of aloneness," a threat to their authentic being; yet it
represented too a new kind of commitment to family, which Addie
would come to recognize as the "duty to the alive."[1] In an inverted
way, another correspondence between the situations of author and
character may be seen in the fact that Faulkner had taken over the
care of another man's two children, and that Addie gave two children, Dewey Dell and Vardaman, to Anse in order to make up for her
adultery and the bastard child.

The ambivalence that Faulkner apparently felt toward his
marriage and his art may have been compounded by his ambivalent
relationship to his ancestor and namesake, William Falkner, his
great-grandfather. The Old Colonel had been an energetic and imaginative man of action—reckless, violent, imperious, willful, flamboyant,
and successful. He had been a man of many talents: lawyer, planter,
writer, soldier, politician, businessman, and community leader. As a
Confederate hero, political leader, and builder of railroads, he had
been a dominant figure in the affairs of northern Mississippi from the
1840s through the 1880s.[2] He had left his mark on Mississippi, his
family, and particularly his great-grandson, William Faulkner. In
Faulkner's early years his ancestor served as the legend out of which
he shaped his life goals—to become a writer and soldier like the Old
Colonel. According to his brother Jack, Faulkner "more or less
consciously patterned his life after the Old Colonel's" (Blotner, 105).
But in the Twenties when Faulkner was an ex-soldier who had never
seen combat and was a failed poet and unrecognized novelist, the
differences in their accomplishments and circumstances probably
seemed huge and galling to the great-grandson. The two men were
alike in body, about five and a half feet tall, but the Butler artistic
heritage from his mother's side had, according to Blotner (p. 546),
supplanted some of the wildness of the Old Colonel in young Bill
Faulkner. In *Sartoris* this double heritage may be seen in the double
protagonists—Bayard Sartoris and Horace Benbow, reckless pilot and
frustrated poet—and in the novel's pendular movement from motion
to stasis. A related counterpoint in *The Sound and the Fury* is evident in the angry aggression of Jason as it contrasts with and opposes
the brooding, suicidal introspection of Quentin. A similar but somewhat different pattern in *As I Lay Dying* manifests itself in the
motion of Jewel and the stasis of Darl. Put in another way, this
clash of character, movement, and idea becomes the sibling rivalry
between Darl and Jewel, the struggle between the need to do and the

need to write:

> ... the immitigable chasm between all life and all print—that those who can, do, those who cannot and suffer enough because they can't, write about it.[3]

This "chasm" or rather this clash mirrors not just the opposing elements of Faulkner's heritage or even the ambivalent feelings of the artist toward himself but also a dynamic source of Faulkner's creative life.

These polarized elements, though somewhat disguised as in a dream, are central to an early autobiographical fantasy entitled "Carcassonne."[4] This is how "Carcassonne" begins:

> AND ME ON A BUCKSKIN PONY *with eyes like blue electricity and a mane like tangled fire, galloping up the hill and right off into the high heaven of the world.*
> His skeleton lay still. (895)

And this is how it ends:

> *I want to perform something bold and tragical and austere* he repeated, shaping the soundless words in the pattering silence *me on a buckskin pony with eyes like blue electricity and a mane like tangled fire, galloping up the hill and right off into the high heaven of the world* Still galloping, the horse soars outward; still galloping, it thunders up the long blue hill of heaven, its tossing mane in golden swirls like fire. Steed and rider thunder on, thunder punily diminishing: a dying star upon the immensity of darkness and of silence within which, steadfast, fading, deepbreasted and grave of flank, muses the dark and tragic figure of the Earth, his mother. (899-900)

In this early poetic fantasy may be found the seeds of *As I Lay Dying*. Addie the dying mother, Darl the mad poet, and Jewel the centaur—they are all there, buried deep, strangely fused and transmuted. While the poet's imagination galloped heavenward, like a Norman steed charging for Christ's sake against the pagan foe, the poet's body lay dying. There is another passage in "Carcassonne" which seems to connect with the title *As I Lay Dying*: "... *where I was King of Kings but the woman with the woman with the dog's eyes to knock my bones together and together*" (898). When Faulkner was asked to explain the title of *As I Lay Dying*, he referred to

the Eleventh Book of *The Odyssey* and quoted "the speech of ghost-
ly Agamemnon to Odysseus: 'As I lay dying the woman with the
dog's eyes would not close my eyelids for me as I descended into
Hades' " (Blotner, 634-635). In *As I Lay Dying* Faulkner reversed
the Homeric scene: it is the woman who lay dying, not the man,
although Addie Bundren and Clytemnestra both shared in the sin of
adultery.

The point, however, of the association between "Carcassonne"
and *As I Lay Dying* seems to rest not just on the correspondence of
the slow dying of the poet with the dying of Addie Bundren but on
Faulkner's splitting off the "galloping horse" from the Carcassonne
poet and fusing it to Jewel, so that the soaring flights of the poet's
imagination become the fierce, elemental energies of Jewel and the
spotted pony.

> When Jewel can almost touch him, the horse stands on his
> hind legs and slashes down at Jewel. Then Jewel is enclosed by
> a glittering maze of hooves as by an illusion of wings; among
> them, beneath the upreared chest, he moves with the flashing
> limberness of a snake. For an instant before the jerk comes
> onto his arms he sees his whole body earth-free, horizontal,
> whipping snake-limber, until he finds the horse's nostrils and
> touches earth again. Then they are rigid, motionless, terrific,
> the horse back-thrust on stiffened, quivering legs, with lowered
> head; Jewel with dug heels, shutting off the horse's wind with
> one hand, with the other patting the horse's neck in short
> strokes myriad and caressing, cursing the horse with obscene
> ferocity.
> They stand in rigid terrific hiatús, the horse trembling and
> groaning. Then Jewel is on the horse's back. He flows upward
> in a stooping swirl like the lash of a whip, his body in midair
> shaped to the horse. (12)

There is in Jewel's relationship to his horse an intense physical-
emotional rapport consisting of a savagery and affection that may be
connected with the whipping and petting his mother gave him as a
child. From the violent actions uniting man and horse explodes a
primitive kinetic power rendering emotion into immediate act. Jewel
generates motion and action—yet not in a restless sense, for having
been Addie's jewel from birth, he is remarkably secure in his emotional being. Darl's refrain—"Jewel's mother is a horse"—suggests
that Jewel's relationship to the horse serves as an unconscious displacement of his love for his mother and, as one may sense from the

incest?
special relationship…

description of Jewel's soaring on his buckskin pony, produces feelings of erotic release and exhilaration.

In terms of the unconscious the horse, according to Jung, "represents the lower part of the body and the animal drives that take their rise from there. The horse is dynamic power . . . it carries one away like a surge of instinct."[5] Jung relates the horse also to the mother archetype. From this perspective, one may interpret Jewel as embodying an elemental force for life, deriving from Addie. In terms of his family heredity and dynamics Jewel unconsciously embodies that part of Addie Bundren which was drawn to passionate action and which consequently set him against his brother Darl. Jewel and Darl represent the opposing elements within Addie that have been given separate life in the son she loves and the son she rejects. Since Addie is the ultimate source of the tension between the brothers as well as the matrix of the opposing ideas or forces of the novel, it is to her that one must go for an understanding of the family and of the novel itself.

Addie Bundren speaks directly to the reader only once—two-thirds of the way through the novel, just after Jewel has saved her from the water; yet this section is emotionally the most intense of the novel, psychologically the most complex, and philosophically the most dense. She begins with the time when she was an unhappy schoolteacher, whipping the children she taught, feeling badly frustrated and hating life, especially in springtime. And so she took Anse as a way out, only to discover another kind of unhappiness; she had merely exchanged unrelatedness and sexual frustration for a life that violated her essential being, for an awareness that in this world she could never truly express what she felt most deeply in her own being.

> And when I knew that I had Cash, I knew that living was terrible and that this was the answer to it. That was when I learned that words are no good; that words dont ever fit even what they are trying to say at. When he was born I knew that motherhood was invented by someone who had to have a word for it because the ones that had the children didn't care whether there was a word for it or not. I knew that fear was invented by someone that had never had the fear; pride, who never had the pride. I knew that it had been, not that they had dirty noses, but that we had had to use one another by words like spiders dangling by their mouths from a beam, swinging and twisting and never touching, and that only through the blows of the switch could

my blood and their blood flow as one stream. (163-164)

Her rejection of words seems rooted in her estrangement from others and in her need to reject people in order to preserve and draw from her own solitary being. Her distrust and repudiation of words are part of her private indictment of society, not just for its cant but for its inauthentic existence. Let Anse, she said, have his dead word *love*, and let Cora Tull have her dead words *sin* and *salvation*; but Addie insisted, "I would be I" (166).

Implicit in Addie's rejection of words is her rejection of Darl. When she found she was pregnant with Darl, she believed she would kill Anse:

> It was as though he had tricked me, hidden within a word like within a paper screen and struck me in the back through it. But then I realized that I had been tricked by words older than Anse or love, and that the same words had tricked Anse too. . . . (164)

She took out on the child the hostility to Anse and whatever feelings of rejection she had suffered in her earlier life. That she felt tricked by the word *love* and by Anse's "deception" contributed also to her negative feelings about the child. With strange irony Darl would become a man of words, the poet ridden by his sensibilities and too much awareness—a stranger in life. Yet in the deepest levels of his estranged being Darl was much like Addie, for both were loners, psychological orphans who had never had a mother; paradoxically, rather than serving as a bond, this similarity may actually have contributed to her rejection of him, since she drew strength from her estrangement, whereas he drew weakness from his. Curiously, never once in the novel did she speak to Darl; it is as though he did not exist for her. Nor did she ask for him at her deathbed; she asked only for Jewel and Cash. Certainly Darl's pathetic cry "I have no mother" voices the chief emotional lack of his life and determines his abulic state of being, as well as his relationship to Jewel. In fact, Jewel and Darl become what their mother gave and failed to give to them. Addie's adulterous passion for the Reverend Whitfield, which was motivated more by estrangement and defiance than by love, is metamorphosed into the passionate love invested in Jewel; it produces Jewel's direct, passionate, confident nature and his proclivity for action, heroic action. Jewel is her passion child, hers alone.

Darl Bundren is the unheroic spectator-antagonist to the Bundren family mission: to transport their mother to her final resting place. Yet he is also the novel's chief narrator, intuitively and clairvoyantly aware of all the hidden feelings, relations, and experiences which constitute the Bundren family. Despite the fact that Faulkner has made Darl expendable in terms of the family, the author is deeply drawn to this character—as may be evidenced in the striking beauty and power of Darl's language and in the pathos of his situation. It is Darl who really creates the novel because that is all he has—the rendering into verbal life of what he cannot be or do or love. In his sensibility and vulnerability, Darl is much like Quentin Compson; they are the expendables in their families. Moreover, the Bundren family, despite the difference in social status and milieu, provides a curious analogue in other ways to the Compson family. One notes certain correspondences: ineffectual fathers, rejecting mothers, pregnant daughters, favored sons, and idiot or childlike sons. The favored sons, Jason and Jewel, generate the energy and actions of their stories. There is, however, no Compson equivalent for Cash Bundren, who represents a steadying influence for the family. Cash may be one of the factors responsible for the Bundren's family remaining together—this family cohesion constituting one of the chief differences from the Compson family.

Since a major factor causing the breakdown of the family in Faulkner's novels is generally connected with incest, it seems logical at this point to examine how incest may figure in *As I Lay Dying*. Most critics do not perceive any incest at all; yet John Irwin, who has made a fascinating study of the seminal role of incest in Faulkner's novels, finds some evidence of an incestuous attraction between Darl and Dewey Dell.[6] It is my contention that, although such a brother-sister attraction may exist in *As I Lay Dying*, it is tenuous; the dominant attraction is between sons and mother. Jewel's attraction toward Addie is passionate but displaced onto the horse so that he is unaware of it. Darl's attraction is ambivalent—in that Addie's rejection of him has planted a deep resentment in him at the same time that it has created an intense need for Addie. The intensity of Darl's need seems related to Quentin's need for Caddy—the very similarity of names, Addie/Caddy, suggesting incestuous associations for the author. The incest relationship works consciously and obsessively on Quentin Compson in *The Sound and the Fury*, whereas it works unconsciously and ambivalently in *As I Lay Dying*.

To understand the full implications of the incest theme in *As I Lay Dying* one may have to go back to the incest relationship emotionally most charged for the author: that of Quentin and Caddy Compson, with Dalton Ames forming the third part of the oedipal triad. Yet the roots of this relationship were planted in the Father-Caddy-Quentin relationship of Quentin's boyhood and still further back in the Father-Mother-Quentin relationship of Quentin's childhood.

> When I was little there was a picture in one of our books, a dark place into which a single weak ray of light came slanting upon two faces lifted out of the shadow. *You know what I'd do if I were King?* she never was a queen or a fairy she was always a king or a giant or a general *I'd break that place open and drag them out and I'd whip them good* It was torn out, jagged out. I was glad. I'd have to turn back to it until the dungeon was Mother herself she and Father upward into weak light holding hands and us lost somewhere below even them without even a ray of light.[7]

It is a relationship which on the surface cannot be precisely described as oedipal, for, though Quentin wished to punish both his father and mother, his hostility was directed more against his mother than his father. She was the "dungeon." Quentin, cut off from the two of them, was lost with Caddy or the other children somewhere below in the darkness. What emerges most clearly from this dreamlike picture-memory is the feeling of a child's helplessness, of being adrift in dark and empty space, lost—a feeling which seems to underlie Quentin's lament: "if I'd just had a mother so I could say Mother Mother" (213). If this feeling represents Quentin's psychic reality, then one would expect him to reach out for a mother surrogate and to compensate in his fantasies and rationalizations for his psychic needs. This may explain why Quentin, as time and sex pushed Caddy out of his world, refused to let go of her, as if his regressive, incestuous clinging to her were his way of preserving identity and life, of holding at bay the nada threatening to engulf him. The cultural values he made use of in condemning her sexual promiscuity seem essentially rationalizations, for his tie to her and need of her constituted the basic reality of his being. Benjy, insulated from time by idiocy, represents the pure incarnation of that need. For Benjy, Caddy was always the tree of life; for Quentin she became the tree of knowledge. It was not only the sin of her sexual promiscuity which drove Quentin to suicide; it was also their irreversible separation which impelled him toward death.

The kind of death Quentin envisioned and chose for himself reflects the nature of his need and character. Death by water suggests the need to return to the oceanic security of the womb, as may be seen in the passages describing his anticipated death. The passages also point up his desire for resurrection at the same time as they state that his desire for resurrection would not be fulfilled:

> and I will look down and see my murmuring bones and the deep water like wind, like a roof of wind, and after a long time they cannot distinguish even bones upon the lonely and inviolate sand. Until on the Day when He says Rise only the flat-iron would come floating up. (*The Sound and the Fury*, 98)

> That's where the water would be, heading out to the sea and the peaceful grottoes. Tumbling peacefully they would, and when He said Rise only the flat irons. (139)

> When you leave a leaf in water a long time after awhile the tissue will be gone and the delicate fibers waving slow as the motion of sleep. They dont touch one another, no matter how knotted up they once were, no matter how close they lay once to the bones. And maybe when He says Rise the eyes will come floating up too, out of the deep quiet and the sleep, to look on glory. (144)

> Let us sell Benjy's pasture so that Quentin may go to Harvard and I may knock my bones together and together I will be dead in . . . . in the caverns and the grottoes of the sea tumbling peacefully to the wavering tides. . . . (216-217)

These descriptions of the body's disintegration after drowning and of a peaceful merging with the sea reveal, in addition to the need to escape into death, a schizophrenic quality to his thinking, as if the "I am" were already detached from the body and had become just a spectating eye. The passages correspond in letter and spirit to the passages in "Carcassonne" describing the poet's vision, as he lay in the dark garret, of death by water:

> It was dark. The agony of wood was soothed by these latitudes; empty rooms did not creak and crack. Perhaps wood was like any other skeleton though, after a time, once reflexes of old compulsions had spent themselves. Bones might lie under seas, in the caverns of the sea, knocked together by the dying echoes of waves. Like bones of horses cursing the inferior riders who bestrode them, bragging to one another about what

they would have done with a first-rate rider up. But somebody
always crucified the first-rate riders. And then it's better to be
bones knocking together to the spent motion of falling tides in
the caverns and the grottoes of the sea. ("Carcassonne," 897)

He lay still beneath the tarred paper, in a silence filled with
fairy patterings. Again his body slanted and slanted downward
through opaline corridors groined with ribs of dying sunlight
upward dissolving dimly, and came to rest at last in the wind-
less gardens of the sea. About him the swaying caverns and the
grottoes, and his body lay on the rippled floor, tumbling peacefully to the wavering echoes of the tides. (899)

These passages describing the pull toward death for both the Carcassonne poet and Quentin point up the need of a counter-force for life.
In *The Sound and the Fury* the forces for life are embodied primarily
in Dilsey (the mother-servant who feeds and comforts the children,
ministers to and holds together the disintegrating Compson family)
and paradoxically in Jason (the "provider" and anti-Christ figure
who runs on frenetic energy generated by anger, spite, and the bour-
geois need for respectability). The first force was no longer relevant
to Quentin, isolated and impaled as he was by youth's sexual crises;
the second was morally and personally repugnant to him. What
Quentin—and, in a sense, the author—needed was something akin to
the Carcassonne poet's *"buckskin pony with eyes like blue electricity
and a mane like tangled fire, galloping up the hill and right off into
the high heaven of the world"* ("Carcassonne," 899). It was a need
which would find fulfillment for the author in *As I Lay Dying*.

Through the transmutative magic of the creative process,
Faulkner in telling the story of the Bundren family has separated the
elements of the Carcassonne poet—bestowing the gift of the horse
upon the chosen son, Jewel, and planting the ontological self-ques-
tioning and the death-wish in the rejected son, Darl. By the force
and bias of Addie Bundren he has converted the sibiling rivalry into a
universal struggle of passion against mind, action against words, being
against non-being, and life against death. Addie is Jewel's and Darl's
source and maker in that the sons draw their sense of purpose and
self or non-purpose and non-self from her loving or rejecting of them.
Lacking a self and purpose of his own, Darl feeds compulsively on
the others, especially on Jewel, feeling and generating resentment.
These "lacks" induce a fundamental contradiction within him; he
multiplies "selves" by entering into the others' secret emotional
lives but cannot fill his own emptiness, cannot realize a self.

> I dont know what I am. I dont know if I am or not. Jewel
> knows he is, because he does not know whether he is or not.
> . . . And Jewel *is*, so Addie Bundren must be. (76)

Darl is a kind of Hamlet who cannot have his mother's love, who cannot act but broods on being and non-being, who is aware that "this world is not his world," "this life his life" (250). Darl wants ultimmately "to ravel out into time" (198). Jewel, as Darl knows, is a passion child who has what Darl lacks: Addie and being, the power to act, the power to get at life through the body, and the energy to convert stasis into motion—into life. Jewel has the buckskin pony.

It is an integral part of my thesis that Faulkner's need, at this stage in his life, to combat the Quentin-Darl component within himself compelled the creation of Addie Bundren. The author was seeking a figure of strength rather than of weakness, seeking the doer rather than the verbalizer, the realist rather than the illusionist, the stoic rather than the melancholist. Whatever estrangement and doubts and despair about existence Addie felt—"I knew that living was terrible" (163), "I knew at last what he [Father] meant" when he said "that the reason for living is getting ready to stay dead" (167)—she lived committed to life. She "believed that the reason for living was the duty to the alive" (166). She combines the exististentialist's assertion of will over despair with the individualist morality of the outsider, like Hester Prynne, in a narrow puritanical community. In fact, one might justifiably call *As I Lay Dying* Faulkner's *The Scarlet Letter*. Both novels portray a lonely woman of strength and pride who commits the sin of adultery with a minister in the woods, who conceives in sin, and yet who, through love of child and service to others, seems intended to win salvation.

Despite the authors' differences in time and place, Faulkner and Hawthorne share a true affinity, based on their related puritanical outlook, their ancestral background, and common life experiences. Both authors lived in the shade of their ancestors, felt bound to them by destiny and kinship, yet felt resistant to them in their own individual spirit. Hawthorne and Faulkner recognized that the need to make their own way and forge their own identities would necessitate a severing of the ancestral roots—a need which may psychologically have contributed to the change in their ancestral names from Hathorne to Hawthorne, from Falkner to Faulkner. However, it was only when these two writers returned to their roots that they found their true subjects and authentic voices. They were ultimately compelled to work out the ancestral curses by becoming the conscience of their family and people. Whereas the Hawthorne or New England curse derived from the blood of the condemned witches, the Faulkner or American curse derived from the blood of the slaves. For the major portion of his stories and novels, Faulkner would explore the Southern past in order to articulate the sin against a race, against humanity. But that development would come later in the 1930s and early 1940s; now in 1929, having completed *The Sound and the Fury* and the first version of *Sanctuary*, he was working through the clashing feelings engendered by his marriage. He was struggling to break out of the prison of self, yet to preserve his individual being and to keep the artist alive. Like Hawthorne, he had moved from the solitary introspective years of his twenties toward marriage and family in his thirties—both authors sharing in their need for woman, family, love and in their desire to serve.

So it was that Hawthorne and Faulkner created a Hester Prynne and an Addie Bundren: strong women isolated in body and spirit from their communities, impelled to love, to sin, and finally to atone. The women do what the men, Dimmesdale and Darl, cannot do: they save themselves by losing themselves—Hester in Pearl, Addie in Jewel. In Addie's case the instrument of her salvation would prove to be her bastard son, as Addie had prophesied:

> "He is my cross and he will be my salvation. He will save me from the water and the fire. Even though I have laid down my life, he will save me." (160)

Whatever degree of success Addie may have achieved in breaking out of the spiritual isolation and estrangement that Darl Bundren or Quentin Compson experienced may be measured by the love she implanted in Jewel. It is this love—at least, during the ordeals of water and fire—which has made the rider of the buckskin pony in *As I Lay Dying* into the "King of Kings" ("Carcassonne," 898). The transformation of Addie began at the birth of Jewel:

> With Jewel—I lay by the lamp, holding up my own head, watching him cap and suture it before he breathed—the wild blood boiled away and the sound of it ceased. Then there was only the milk, warm and calm, and I lying calm in the slow silence, getting ready to clean my house. (168)

It is the maternal nature of Addie's love which redeems, for Faulkner, her adulterous passion for the Reverend Whitfield—just as in

The Sound and the Fury it was only Dilsey who could provide re-demptive love. After the birth of Jewel, Addie began to clean house; but in *The Sound and the Fury* Quentin was still struggling, until his death, to wash out the stain of sexuality.

Faulkner's intense involvement with incest, particularly in the writing of *The Sound and the Fury* and *Sanctuary*, points up deeply conflicting feelings about love and sex in that stage of his life. Faulkner seemed unable to portray human sexuality as an in-tegral part of love; he seemed compelled to separate the two, reject-ing female sexuality as disturbing and shameful. At the bottom of Faulkner's attitude toward woman and love is a puritanical recoil from female sexuality—mixed with a somewhat Tolstoyan feeling for the maternal. But the mother that Tolstoy celebrated in nine-teenth century Russia could not be found by Faulkner in twentieth century America—except in a black mother-servant like Dilsey. Addie Bundren is a compromise figure: she must atone for her sexuality before she can qualify for salvation through love.

Despite Faulkner's emphasis on love and salvation in *As I Lay Dying*, the fact remains that the novel is the story of a prolonged, macabre journey of the stinking, decomposing corpse of the mother, tended by her family and surviving the ordeals of water and fire, toward her final resting place in the Jefferson cemetery. Some critics—for example, Bedient and Bleikasten—feel that *As I Lay Dying* is dominated by an apocalyptic, absurdist vision of the terror and meaninglessness of existence in a world where man is nakedly vulnerable to disaster, death, dissolution, and madness.

> In *As I Lay Dying* life is conceived as the antagonist, living is "terrible," the protagonist self is alone: a naked and isolated consciousness in a broad land. This nakedness, this dreadful isolation, is already a kind of defeat, a form of abjectness, so that the utmost to be expected from the mind in its continual conflict with the world is simply a capitulation without dis-honor: a surrender of everything, if need be, except pride.[8]

> *As I Lay Dying* is an almost timeless fable. The human beings it presents seem to date from before history; yet they have already been exiled from Paradise, and are already doomed and damned. The effects of the primal curse are indeed strongly felt, but Faulkner does not here, as in his other novels, raise questions about the origins of the malediction. What we are shown instead is the naked scandal of existence revealed through the extremes

of madness and death. The decomposing corpse dragged along
the road is the *memento mori*, a grim reminder of the radically
contingent and irremediably finite nature of man; death is, as
Addie soon learned, what invalidates all life.[9]

Death in *As I Lay Dying* is a scandal for the outsiders, because they
smell it and because the prolonged macabre funeral offends their
sense of decorum. Faulkner does not necessarily share their outrage;
on the contrary, he may be amused by it, for his own attitude to
death seems more grimly realistic. Certainly the Bundren family
exhibit little sense of outrage; they seem almost oblivious to the
corpse's decomposition. For them, Addie in the coffin is, in a very
real sense, still alive—inducing Vardaman to bore holes in the coffin
so that she can breathe, and moving Cash and Jewel to risk their
lives to save her. Darl would like to sacrifice himself for Addie too,
but he has no self.

No matter how outrageous and grotesque the Bundrens' behavior may seem to the reader, Faulkner's sympathy with the Bundren family remains constant. Moreover, he accords human dignity,
strength, and pathos—a kind of timeless quality—to Addie's death:

> She is looking out the window, at Cash stooping steadily at
> the board in the failing light, laboring on toward darkness and
> into it as though the stroking of the saw illumined its own
> motion, board and saw engendered.
> "You, Cash," she shouts, her voice harsh, strong, and un-
> impaired. "You, Cash!"
> He looks up at the gaunt face framed by the window in the
> twilight. It is a composite picture of all time since he was a
> child. . . . For a while still she looks down at him from the com-
> posite picture, neither with censure nor approbation. Then the
> face disappears.
> She lies back and turns her head without so much as glancing
> at pa. She looks at Vardaman; her eyes, the life in them, rushing
> suddenly upon them; the two flames glare up for a steady in-
> stant. Then they go out as though someone had leaned down
> and blown upon them. (47)

> Dewey Dell rises, heaving to her feet. She looks down at the
> face. It is like a casting of fading bronze upon the pillow, the
> hands alone still with any semblance of life: a curled, gnarled
> inertness; a spent yet alert quality from which weariness, ex-
> haustion, travail has not yet departed, as though they doubted
> even yet the actuality of rest, guarding with horned and penur-
> ious alertness the cessation which they know cannot last. (50)

Death comes for Addie Bundren as sleep follows travail and exhaustion—as a natural event. She does not die as one of the damned; having expiated her sin, she has made, in her own way, peace with her maker. Whatever unhappiness she may have endured and given (chiefly to Darl), she has, nevertheless, served her family faithfully—living and dying with her own kind of stoic integrity.

It is Cash—the first son to occupy a special place in Addie's emotional life—who takes over after Addie's burial and becomes the voice of sanity in the journey back to life. He strikes a balance between the extremes of Darl and Jewel. Although closest to Darl in age and sympathy, Cash belongs to those who own a self. His identity, a craftsman's identity, is drawn from his hands; his hands make his mother's coffin and place him among the doers rather than the verbalizers. He differs from Darl too in that he accepts life and plays his role in the working world of family and community. His sense of duty, stoicism and reticence point up his kinship to Addie; yet his stoicism emanates from a deeper part of his being and reflects an egolessness and quietism foreign to Addie. Less heroic than Jewel in the water and fire ordeals, Cash is, nevertheless, responsible too—in his own quiet, steady, literal-minded way—for bringing Addie Bundren to her final rest.

Addie's ghost is not laid until they bury her. Like the ghost of Agamennon, the "I" in the title is still alive. Her interior monologue establishes her as probably the novel's most alive and authentic character:

> And so when Cora Tull would tell me I was not a true mother, I would think how words go straight up in a thin line, quick and harmless, and how terribly doing goes along the earth, clinging to it, so that after a while the two lines are too far apart for the same person to straddle from one to the other; and that sin and love and fear are just sounds that people who have never sinned nor loved nor feared have for what they never had and cannot have until they forget the words. (165-166)

Dead or alive, Addie is still the emotional center of the Bundren family, holding it together, even to the comic finale.

Just as the stoic character of Addie Bundren works as a counterforce to despair and abulia, so do the novel's comic elements perform a comparable function. The final scene in *As I Lay Dying* points up the comic reversal of the tragedy of the disintegrating family—the principal subject of *The Sound and the Fury*. At the end of *The Sound and the Fury* the Compson carriage—dilapidated, drawn by old Queenie, and bearing only Luster and Benjy—does not make it to the Jefferson cemetery. But the Bundren wagon, having survived fire and flood, completes its long trek to the cemetery; then the Bundrens, having buried their corpse and picked up a second Mrs. Bundren, set out with family intact on the homeward journey back to life. The Bundren story concludes with a joke, not to belittle Addie but to affirm the continuity of life—so that the ludicrous, bumbling Anse emerges as comic symbol of persevering mankind.

Implicit in *As I Lay Dying* is the recognition of the absurd, but, unlike Camus in *The Stranger* or *The Plague*, the author does not protest against death's role in the scheme of existence. In the character of Addie he achieves a stoic acceptance of death, and in Cash a limited but sane vision of life. Darl he has put away. Yet it is Darl, the extension of Quentin Compson and the Carcassonne poet, who has tapped the deepest source of the author's being: the threatened artist. In that sense, the "I" in the title *As I Lay Dying* refers to Faulkner himself. Addie and Darl may be said to represent the opposing poles of the struggle between life and art. It is this struggle that underlies *As I Lay Dying* and has involved the author deeply and ambivalently. The conscious thrust of the novel is toward Addie, the unconscious toward Darl. The conscious thrust, despite the death of Addie and the madness of Darl, is toward life and sanity; the unconscious thrust toward death and madness.

Although Darl Bundren may be an extension of Quentin Compson, his emotional deprivation is deeper, his situation more isolated, his state of mind more unbalanced, his vision more poetic and ontological. Quentin's suicide is like a romantic ritual carried out by a quixotic narcissist-idealist. There are no options, no cultural rationalizations for Darl. Darl is naked man seized and put away. Yes, more than Quentin, Darl is our brother.

> Darl is our brother, our brother Darl. Our brother Darl in a
> cage in Jackson where his grimed hands lying light in the quiet
> interstices, looking out he foams.
> "Yes yes yes yes yes yes yes yes." (244)

Darl is the madness that society imprisons, yet it is principally Darl's brooding poetic vision combined with Addie's force that makes *As I Lay Dying* into "something bold . . . and austere" ("Carcassonne," 899) and tragicomical. In one sense both Darl and Addie, despite their mutual antagonism, represent creative forces for their author: she for life, he for art. Taken together, Darl and Jewel and Cash and Addie constitute the fused and struggling elements of life and art.

Notes

[1] *As I Lay Dying* (New York: Random House, 1964). This edition will be used for all references to *As I Lay Dying*.

[2] Joseph Blotner, *Faulkner: A Biography* (New York: Random House, 1974), pp. 3-58, 105, 151, 187, 361, 441, 546, 717.

[3] William Faulkner, *The Unvanquished* (New York: Random House, 1938), p. 262. These are the thoughts of Bayard Sartoris, son of Colonel Sartoris (the character based on Faulkner's great-grandfather), at the time when he was being incestuously tempted by his stepmother. Since Bayard was not a writer, the thoughts would seem to be Faulkner's.

[4] According to Blotner (pp. 501-502), probably early 1926. For the text of "Carcassonne" see *Collected Stories of William Faulkner* (New York: Random House, 1950), pp. 895-900.

[5] C. G. Jung, *Modern Man in Search of a Soul* (New York: Harcourt, Brace, 1933), p. 25.

[6] John T. Irwin, *Doubling and Incest/Repetition and Revenge* (Baltimore: Johns Hopkins University Press, 1975), p. 53. Irwin's work is an invaluable source for commentary on incest in Faulkner.

[7] *The Sound and the Fury* (New York: Vintage, 1954), p. 215. This edition will be used for all references to *The Sound and the Fury*.

[8] Calvin Bedient, "Pride and Nakedness: *As I Lay Dying*," *Modern Language Quarterly*, XXIX (March 1968), p. 63.

[9] André Bleikasten, *Faulkner's AS I LAY DYING* (Bloomington: Indiana University Press, 1973), pp. 132-133. This is the best critical study available on *As I Lay Dying*.

Knowledge and Involvement in Faulkner's The Wild Palms

by

William Price Cushman

William Faulkner believed that the worth of a man's life depends in large measure upon his relationship to the world around him. Involvement stems from the kind of knowledge with which he perceives the world. Faulkner depicts this mental process in major characters of several of his novels. For example, Thomas Sutpen's "design" is so abstract and rigid that he is totally uninvolved with humanity. Jason Compson's ratiocinative turn of mind, revealed in the clear, rational prose of his section of *The Sound and the Fury*, accompanies a cold detachment from even his family. Addie Bundren disapproves of verbal articulation because it requires analytical powers that discourage commitment. Quentin Compson's obsession with time as an external, mechanical end rather than as an internal, subjective medium is symptomatic of his rigidity and his separation from reality. On the other hand, characters such as Dilsey are serenely and intuitively involved. Faulkner has faith in the heart and in intuition, but he is deeply suspicious of the head, of ratiocination, and of skilled articulation.

A detailed analysis of *The Wild Palms* has not been attempted in terms of the theme of knowledge and involvement. Within its narrative lie several patterns which indicate the amounts and kinds of knowledge available to the three major characters, the tall convict, Charlotte Rittenmeyer, and Harry Wilbourne. An examination of this network produces insight into some of the principal thematic concerns of the novel. These motifs are practical knowledge (having to do with functioning in the everyday world), the nature of one's relationship to the world around him, and, most important, the resulting extent and nature of one's involvement. In *The Wild Palms* the quality and significance of man's existence depends upon fluid interaction with the world. From this issue also comes the paradoxical vision of the novel: life with involvement is pain, but life without it is nothing.

Knowledge may take several forms, but, whatever the form, it is ultimately the awareness the individual has of his relationship with reality. Men may perceive sensuously, imaginatively, or ratiocinatively. They vary widely in their capacity to retain what they know and in their use of it. The range of cognizance is quite large: at a fairly shallow level a person has objective information, while at a more profound one he has insights about himself and his position in the world. A study of perception in *The Wild Palms* reveals that the extent and kind of one's comprehension affects his ability to function competently. A fluid, serene, dynamic relationship between man and the world—involvement—makes effectiveness possible. A fragmented, tense, static view of reality has the opposite result. *The Wild Palms* shows graphically what a vital and potent force man can be. It also demonstrates, however, that involvement is without ultimate significance unless it is meaningful as well as practical, that is, unless it produces active participation in the struggles of human existence, as well as survival in a hostile universe.

The novel has a very strange structure. It is composed of two stories, "Wild Palms" and "Old Man," which are closely related thematically but completely separate in plot and characters. It has ten chapters, five from each story. "Old Man" has been the more popular, appearing alone as a work in some editions. Most commentary on the novel has had as its principal objective the justifying of the bizarre structure by explaining the thematic relationships between the stories. However, the characters' mind-sets are sometimes briefly mentioned. Olga W. Vickery observes the convict's uses of language.[1] Joseph J. Moldenhauer is aware that Harry is very introspective while the convict is not.[2] Floyd C. Watkins emphasizes the flaw of the convict: his refusal to put his very considerable talents to work by becoming involved in the world.[3] Margaret Church acknowledges that Harry and the convict have "conscious" and "intuitive" senses of reality, respectively.[4]

One may analyze in detail each of the three major characters in terms of knowledge and involvement if he treats *The Wild Palms* as the novel that it is. These two subjects, viewed systematically, penetrate to the heart of what the novel is about. Almost all critics—if they have considered both stories at once—have examined the tall convict on the one hand and Charlotte and Harry together on the other, treating them, so to speak, as a matched pair. The fact is, however, that the two lovers are as different from one another as they are from the convict. It is important, therefore, that they be studied as individuals.

The tall convict, Charlotte, and Harry compose an interesting and profound set of contrasting kinds and amounts of knowledge, abilities to get along in the world, and degrees of involvement. The tall convict has incredibly little factual information about the world; nevertheless, the fluid (that is, adjustable, not rigid), intuitive manner in which his mind operates provides him with a practical involvement through which he is able to live with remarkable effectiveness. On the other hand, since he is responsive rather than creative, his involvement is not true commitment. Charlotte's mental processes are similar, but she is creative rather than merely responsive; therefore, she is more capable of a meaningful life. But even Charlotte refuses what Faulkner perhaps felt is man's most important obligation: commitment to family. Charlotte is close to nature insofar as she conceives three times; but in two different ways she rejects the responsibilities produced by her own fertility. Harry is the only one of the three who undergoes substantial change. For most of "Wild Palms" he furnishes ample contrast to the convict, for he is fragmented, detached, ratiocinative, unable to function well in the world. He is never fully involved with anything—even Charlotte—until her pregnancy, suffering, and death. Under the force of these events he becomes committed for the first time. Examination of knowledge and involvement in *The Wild Palms* casts into stark relief its dismal vision: life for man is a struggle; yet the very qualities which enable him to live powerfully lure him at the same time to avoid the struggle.

The mental processes of the three characters reveal a startling discrepancy between the amount of information each has about the practical world and his or her ability to function effectively in that world. Within this framework the tall convict has no formal training (education) and incredibly little practical information, but he can do almost anything. Many critics have marveled at the convict's achievements, but few have emphasized the ignorance out of which those achievements are born. His lack of knowledge about the Mississippi River is remarkable. In the first place he has never even seen it: "for the first time he looked at the River within whose shadow he had spent the last seven years of his life but had never seen before; he stood in quiet and amazed surmise . . . ."[5] Not only has the convict never been around the river itself, but apparently he is unacquainted with streams and creeks of all sizes. For example, the narrator implies that the tall convict does not know the name of even a paddle: ". . . the tall one, when he returned to the surface, still retained what the short one called the paddle" (p. 143). Also, the convict "had never learned to swim . . ."(p. 234). His lack of knowledge about the animal world is unusual for a native of his rural area. He cannot distinguish bucks from does, for "he had never seen one [a deer] of any kind anywhere before except on a Christmas card . . ." (pp. 230-231). He does not even recognize the skin of an alligator: "he saw the hide nailed drying to the wall . . . knowing it was a hide, a skin, but from what animal . . . he did not know . . ." (p. 255). In the face of such ignorance the man's achievement is truly sensational. He not only survives the fierce and powerful flood waters, but he protects as well the woman and her baby. He saves the skiff and returns it to the state. He does swim, and he fights and defeats alligators with no weapon but a knife.

Harry Wilbourne has extensive training but can do almost nothing. Harry's education is emphasized. He has paid a great price, in money, time, and work, to attain what society considers an ultimate of all formal knowledge—the M. D. degree. By contrast his inability to function in the everyday world is as astounding as the convict's miraculous achievements. Faulkner keeps Harry's inability to act effectively constantly in the reader's mind, often in such quiet ways as the parenthetic element in this sentence: "And she told the doctor about watching him [Harry] cleaning (or trying to clean) a mess of fish at the kitchen steps . . ." (p. 9). Seldom can he act easily and naturally. In their train compartment Charlotte tells him to lock the door, but "he had never been in a drawing room before and he fumbled at the lock for an appreciable time" (p. 60). Another parenthetic remark provides commentary upon Harry: the heater at the mining camp in Utah "burned gasoline; when a match was struck to it . . . it took fire with a bang and glare which after a while even Wilbourne got used to . . ." (pp. 182-183). Also in Utah "he would walk . . . among but mostly into the [snow] drifts which he had not yet learned to distinguish in time to avoid, wallowing and plunging . . ." (p. 207).

Charlotte closely resembles the tall convict: as in his case, no mention is made of how she never receives any formal education. Nevertheless she lives naturally and productively in the everyday world. She easily finds jobs. She can sculpt and paint. She can read and cook. Unlike Harry but like the convict, she is able to overcome a language barrier. She communicates with the miners in Utah (pp. 200-201).

The kind of knowledge the convict has of the world enables him to act. He intuitively knows his environment. The convict's frequent instinctive perceptions define his intuitive mental processes. For example, the great courage which he displays in attacking the alligator with only a knife is not calculated courage at all: "not even thinking this since it was too fast, a flash; it was not a surrender, not a resignation, it was too calm, it was a part of him, he had drunk it with his mother's milk and lived with it all his life . . ." (p. 258). When the Cajun tells him to leave, the convict tries to reflect, to reason, upon the meaning of his life at the Cajun's camp, but his mind simply does not function deliberatively: "thinking (this a flash too, since he could not have expressed this, and hence did not even know that he had ever thought it) . . . (and he had done well here—this quietly, soberly indeed, if he had been able to phrase it, think it instead of merely knowing it . . ." (p. 266). The convict seems to be conscious of this correspondence of which he is capable and to have outright faith in it. When the woman asks what the Cajun's warning means, the convict replies simply, "I dont know . . . . But I reckon if it's something we ought to know we will find it out when it's ready for us to" (p. 267). When he is on the last leg of the long journey back to Parchman, he exhibits the same calm confidence—this time in his ability to intuit the point at which he wants the hired boatman to leave them: "He didn't know how he would know but he knew he would . . . and sure enough the moment came . . ." (p. 336).

By contrast Harry never acts spontaneously and "naturally"; intuition never guides him. Rather he thinks, reflects upon his actions. As a result he is detached from reality; that is, he is uninvolved. His chief subject of ratiocination is the purpose and nature of his venture with Charlotte. The discussion with McCord (pp. 131-41) before departing for Utah illustrates the painful detail in which Harry assiduously thinks about how he should live. He has decided, calculated, that he has been confined all his life and that he will break his shackles. The problem is that he never once *felt* the bonds (so far as the narrator tells). Only when Charlotte enters his life and imposes her will upon him does he decide to rebel. The rebellion comes from his head rather than from his heart. Thus he tells McCord that his living with Charlotte has given him "the wisdom to concentrate on fleshly pleasures—eating and evacuating and fornication and sitting in the sun . . ." (p. 133). This passage demonstrates forcefully that Harry's method of knowing is completely topsy-turvy. Because his motivation is rational, he has formulated a design, a calculated abstraction, and is trying to follow it. He thinks that by going through the stereotyped motions of rebellion one can truly rebel. His complaint about their "respectability" in Chicago is not that their life there was not meaningful but that it was not cast in the mold of amorality and rebellion: "We lived in an apartment that wasn't bohemian, it wasn't even a tabloid love-nest . . ." (p. 134). The means have become the end. Harry's ratiocinative mental processes prevent involvement and lead him into a serious misunderstanding of values.

Charlotte's perception of reality and her relationship to it are similar to those of the convict and different from those of Harry. She never thinks, reflects, or analyzes. Her impulsiveness and urgency best illustrate her intuition. Soon after arriving at the lake in Wisconsin, for example, Harry, McCord, and Charlotte see a buck on the beach, "its head up, watching them for an instant before it whirled, its white scut arcing in long bounds while Charlotte, springing from the car . . . ran to the water's edge, squealing. 'That's what I was trying to make!' she cried. 'Not the animals . . .: the motion, the speed' " (pp. 99-100). In Chicago her puppets and marionettes are "begun continued and completed in one sustained rush of furious industry . . ." (p. 91). Rather than analyzing she just lives the total sweep of her life. Thus the relationship between her method of knowing and her actions is a very close one. This integration produces the same working involvement that enables the convict to function smoothly.

The tall convict's perception of time and the significance he assigns to its passage also contribute to his being able to act effectively. For him the measuring of the passing of events is a means and never an end; unless there is a need for calculating time, he never thinks about it. Only once, when the birth of the woman's child is imminent, does time become his "itch" (p. 169). He hurries in an effort to reach some sort of high ground before the unpredictable waves of flood water strike again. This emergency is an appropriate occasion for temporal concern. He feels the anxiety in order that the baby may be delivered in a safe place. Throughout the rest of the novel he merely seeks his goals of saving the woman, saving the boat, and returning to Parchman. He goes as well and as fast as he can. The point is that hurry is never an end in itself, a dead-end that would produce tenseness and fragmentation. Rather, concern with time is a means to an end, integrating the convict with the events of his life.

In Harry's career, by contrast, measuring the passage of events is an end in itself, separating him from their meaning; that is, he expends so much consciousness analyzing and calculating time and thinking of ways to use it that he is unable to become involved in the incidents whose passing it charts. For example, during his first visit to the Rittenmeyers' house "at ten oclock Wilbourne said he must go" (p. 42). The implication is that he makes the remark not because he wants to go or thinks Charlotte wants him to, but because ten o'clock is the "time to go." Harry's decision in Wisconsin to make a calendar is revealing, for, like time, it is outside him; he views it as an object, as something separate from himself. It is completely unrelated to Charlotte's and his condition and to their activities at the lake. Supposedly Harry makes the calendar so that Charlotte and he will know when winter has arrived and they must leave the lake. The tall convict would merely correspond with nature at this point: he would stay until the weather became cold.

Like the convict, Charlotte is concerned far more with living life than with measuring its passage. Whereas Harry feels that he must "make everything last so there wont be any gaps between now and six oclock . . ." (p. 51), Charlotte worries only that she will not have enough time to do all she wants: "quick, quick. We have so little time . . . in fifty years we'll both be dead. So hurry. Hurry" (p. 210). Rather than depend on Harry's calendar in Wisconsin she responds to the weather exactly as the convict would: at first she swims early in the morning, but as the mornings become cooler, she swims later in the day. Thus she is far more effectively tuned to the passage of time than is Harry, whose calendar turns out to be inaccurate by twelve days!

Still another demonstration of the tall convict's subjective involvement is his intuitive knowledge of the meaning and role of the cost, or price, that man must pay for desired ends. The point is significant in the same way the matter of time is, for it shows that the convict lives and perceives in a "natural" correspondence with the world instead of in analytical detachment from it. The characteristic is best illustrated by the sequence of jobs he secures during the long trip back to Parchman from Cajun country. The money he earns from these jobs is, as it should be, the means to an end, not an end in itself. The first job brings him six dollars. He spends it all on food, his goal of returning to Parchman with woman, baby, and skiff never diminishing (p. 333). After his next job he spends "the whole sixteen dollars" (p. 335) on food and goes on. He rolls dice to augment the earnings from his final employment. One of the convicts later asks, "How much did you win?" The convict's reply indicates conclusively that his emphasis is in the proper place: " 'Enough,' the tall one said. It was enough exactly . . ." (p. 336). It was exactly enough, that is,

to get him and his party to Parchman. For the convict the money has
meaning solely in its capacity to enable him to return just as time has
meaning only as he tries to reach dry land for the woman's child-
birth.

Again Harry is exactly the opposite of the convict and stands
precisely juxtaposed to him: just as Harry is concerned with time itself instead of with the meaningful events that time should contain,
so is he a slave of cost instead of the meaning that price can buy. Because of Harry's ratiocination time and cost stand as barriers between
him and the world—barriers that make involvement impossible. In
contrast to the way the convict uses food for strength to live, Harry
says during his seclusion in Wisconsin, "I'm happy now . . . . I know
exactly where I am going. It's perfectly straight, between two rows
of cans and sacks, fifty dollars' worth to a side" (p. 100). Instead of
"living" at that beautiful spot "he now thought constantly of the
diminishing row of cans and sacks against which he was matching in
inverse ratio the accumulating days . . ." (p. 111). In Harry's value
system time and cost (whether it be monetary or whatever) have become the ends to be served rather than the means to the end of viable living.

Like the tall convict, Charlotte attaches far more importance
to the worth of an experience than to its cost. In a calm and self-
assured way she knows the prices exacted by the world for conse-
quential living; without carping she is always willing to pay the price
and to aim recklessly for the highest experiences available. She believes, for example, "that love and suffering are the same thing and
that the value of love is the sum of what you have to pay for it . . ."
(p. 48). Charlotte never has patience with Harry's querulousness
about cost: "Then what does it matter what it cost us . . .? Isn't it
worth it, even if it all busts tomorrow and we have to spend the rest
of our lives paying interest?" (pp. 87-8).

Although the convict and Charlotte are impressive evidence of
what a potent force man can be when he can act effectively, the
novel exacts another requirement for a worthy, purposeful existence;
that is, it delineates two kinds of involvement—superficial and profound. The convict and Charlotte are realists, while Harry is not one.
However, the fact that a person is able to function in the world does
not mean that he willingly will accept a relationship or that he actively will seek it. *The Wild Palms* seems to say that only for him who
voluntarily participates in the struggles of men is life of ultimate significance.

The convict is never profoundly involved, a fact that is revealed, for example, by distinguishing between instinct and intuition. Heretofore, in the examining of the characters' capacity to act, the two terms have been virtually interchangeable, for they both are irrational mental processes. There is, however, an important difference between them. Intuition implies direct insight, an active creativity; instinct is unimaginative, responsive. A person with strong instincts is unlikely to enter willingly into the trials of humanity. The convict's perceptions are far more responsive than creative, resembling the effective but dull instinct of animals. His first fight with an alligator shows this kind of knowledge. Actually Faulkner makes very plain the close relationship between the convict and the animal world. There are, for example, the terms of his friendship with his mule (p. 241). His memory is like that of an animal: he is able to remember and adapt (pp. 150-51), but until he experiences something he never knows it. The other convicts, whom the tall one wants so desperately to rejoin, are carefully likened to animals. Five times within fourteen pages (pp. 28-30, 61-72) the narrator uses the verb *herd* in portraying the guards' handling of the men. Four times within five pages (pp. 65-9) he uses *crawl* to describe the movement of the vehicle in which the men are riding. They are "immobile, patient, almost ruminant, their backs turned to the rain as sheep and cattle do" (p. 67). Creatures such as these, whether they be human or animal, are not significantly involved.

The distinction between intuition and instinct is lost on the purely ratiocinative Harry (until after the catastrophe when he begins to change), but Charlotte is intuitive in the fullest sense. So, although the mental processes of Charlotte and the convict are very similar as opposed to that of Harry, they are, nevertheless, profoundly different from one another. Charlotte's intuition is revealed partly by her "knowing" far in advance the suffering with which she will have to pay for her venture with Harry, but it is indicated more fully by the creative, artistic bent, which is the touchstone of her character. Throughout "Wild Palms" her love of "making things" is kept before the reader's eye: "That's what I make . . ." (p. 41), "Jesus, we had fun, didn't we, . . . making things . . ." (p. 287), "I told you how I wanted to make things, take the fine hard clean brass or stone and cut it . . . into something fine, that you could be proud to show . . ." (p. 47). Her art is creative rather than imitative. When, in Wisconsin, McCord jokingly suggests that she salt the tail of the deer so it will pose for her, Charlotte quickly replies, "I dont want him to pose. That's just what I dont want. I dont want to copy a deer. Anybody can do that" (p. 102). She is almost never inactive; in Chicago, for instance, when she can no longer find work, she turns to reading and cooking with energy and ability (p. 92). During all of these times she works with a "quality of irresistible driving . . . tense and concentrated" (p. 90).

The kind of use to which a character puts his senses distinguishes practicality from profound involvement. The convict uses his capacity to see, hear, and smell, but he uses it very practically—to help him achieve his assigned tasks. Charlotte's senses, on the other hand, stimulate creative, artistic activity in her. Her spirit is exhilarated by the sights, sounds, and smells of the world. Harry's detached objectivity is reflected by the fact that he is twenty-seven years old before he knows that he is color blind! In the last chapter, however—after Harry's relationship to reality changes markedly—there are over forty references to his seeing, hearing, smelling, tasting, and feeling the world around him. His sudden desire to be a painter indicates that his senses are stimulating creativity within him.

The convict's relationship to society shows clearly that his only interest in involvement of any kind is practical; left to his own desires, he would shun all responsible relationships. Because of this fact some doubt is cast upon Olga W. Vickery's useful study of the intuition-ratiocination relationship, for she believes that in his desire to return to Parchman "the convict takes on certain aspects of the civilized man" and "takes his place in society," a progression that culminates in his return to prison.[6] She principally supports this opinion with the fact that the convict improves steadily in his ability to communicate verbally after returning to prison. He demonstrates throughout his story, nevertheless, disinterest in all components and aspects of any fully developed society. His only concerns are to carry out his mission—a mission that was forced upon him—and to return to the prison, to his world of the known, the secure, in which he can escape all responsibility. This disinterested attitude is manifested by sometimes startling unawareness. There is the matter of observing sites passed by the skiff; he often fails even to look out of the boat (pp. 146, 157, 273). In the latter stages of the journey he fails to notice a city (p. 276); he does not bother to learn the name of the town in which he gets a job (p. 332); he passes a trestle that he recognizes from his frantic battle with the flood, but he looks at it "even without interest . . ." (p. 336).

Charlotte, on the other hand, becomes involved with other human beings, interacts with them, and is willing to commit herself to them. Harry first meets her at a party. She is a close friend to McCord and later to the Buckners in Utah. She is concerned about and can communicate with the miners. However, this standard of fruitful living points to Charlotte's flaw, the cause of her downfall. While she can relate in almost all respects, she cannot make and hold the most permanent and total commitments of all—those of marriage and family. Therefore, even she falls short.

Language is another valuable gauge of the kind of knowledge that permits involvement: in *The Wild Palms* ability to articulate varies inversely with ability to act. While the convict is in the wild fighting the flood and while he is in the viable but hard world that is society, that is, while he is forced by his orders into a certain kind of involvement, he is very inarticulate. In fact, he virtually does not verbalize at all. While he is a "doer," in other words, he is not a "talker." The point is that verbalizing necessarily demands analytical knowledge that must be accompanied by the very detachment that breaks down fluidity and subjectivity. Real involvement was experienced by primitive man who was "drawn to dwell beside the water, even before he had a name for water . . ." (p. 155). And it is the kind that the convict has on his mission. When he tries, for example, to reflect upon the meaning of his life at the Cajun's camp, he is "thinking (this a flash . . . since he could not have expressed this, and hence did not even know that he had ever thought it) . . . (and he had done well here—this quietly, soberly indeed, if he had been able to phrase it, think it instead of merely knowing it . . ." (p. 266). Upon returning to the sterility of the prison (a dead and meaningless "society"), however, "suddenly and quietly, something—inarticulateness, the innate and inherited relectance for speech, dissolved . . . the words coming not fast but easily to the tongue as he required them . . ." (p. 332). Indeed, rather than being an indicator of significant living, as Mrs. Vickery believes, these linguistic skills appear to be the precise opposite.

As with the tall convict, Charlotte's use of langauge provides evidence that she has a perception of reality that transcends mere analysis. She is not a "talker"; she has no long intricate speeches. Her lack of articulation is accentuated during periods of crisis when she sometimes lapses into passionate but almost incoherent tirades. She has serene confidence in her ability to do without verbal communication. The necessity of telling the Polish miners that they are working for a corrupt firm, for example, tests Charlotte's communicative skills in a serious way, for the Poles cannot speak English. Harry is completely helpless before the milling mob, but Charlotte calmly tells them the story by means of pictures. Faulkner underscores the significance of her feat by giving the scene a tone of mystery: he says, for example, that she produces her drawing implements "from somewhere" (p. 200) and that "(she had never seen Callaghan [the villain], he [Harry] had merely described him to her, yet the man was Callaghan) . . ." (p. 201).

Before the involvement he attains as a result of Charlotte's death Harry's speeches are shrill, analytical, and frequent. He is a talker, not a doer. His decision to remain in jail, however, is described in terms that are obviously reminiscent of the tall convict. For instance, the decision is made before he is able to "think it into words . . ." (p. 323). Harry's relationship to the world in this final scene is subjective, joining him to the reality he seeks rather than separating him from it. The words come only after the comprehension is complete; they are secondary. For the first time Harry's method of knowing signals involvement.

The portrayal of the prison, the ultimate goal of the convict and the scene of the end of the novel, places still further stress upon the convict's dull, responsive method of knowing and his desire to avoid profound involvement. It also casts doubt upon Mrs. Vickery's belief that the prison represents a fully developed society.[7] The other prisoners already have been likened to animals. Moreover, the convict's means of finding his way back to Parchman are much like those of animals finding their way home over great distances. The periodic references to his later telling the story almost always indicate the sterility of his comfort there. He is "safe, secure, riveted warranted and doubly guaranteed by the ten years they had added to his sentence . . ." (p. 164). In addition, he is usually lying down, "his body jackknifed backward into the *coffinlike* space between the upper and lower bunks . . ." (p. 242, my italics).

Just as the tall convict voluntarily chooses prison, so does Harry; Harry's decision has, however, precisely the opposite significance. In rejecting escape, which was offered him, he is electing to accept in his own mind his involvement with Charlotte. In rejecting suicide, which would be easy with Rittenmeyer's pill, he is choosing to continue the involvement, even though Charlotte is dead. Since the meaning of Harry's being in prison is different from that of the convict, his condition there is similarly different. For the first time in the novel he is there not dependent on words, and he intuits a concept as fluidly and subjectively as Charlotte ever does—and the words do not come until after the perception (p. 323). Rather than lying in a "coffinlike" space like that of the convict he stands at the window (p. 313). Rather than lazily smoking with his comrades as the convict does he at least looks at that "bright star" in the "dying west" and thinks of Charlotte, who had loved "making things" (p. 324).

Although the convict is in many respects admirable, he fails the final test of the quality of a man's existence. In saving the woman and her baby and in returning the boat to its owners he displays devotion to duty, physical courage, and capacity to function effectively in the world. His successes stem from his method of knowing the world. However—also because of the way he perceives the world —he chooses uninvolvement in the difficult struggle that is man's search for life and meaning. *The Wild Palms* portrays, therefore, a bleak vision. Faulkner has charted his pessimism according to man's power to acquire and retain knowledge. The qualities which enable the convict to endure the injustices of society and the awsome power of nature, his animal-like intuition, adaptability, and singleness of purpose, are the very ones that prevent his accepting a responsible role in society; that is, those qualities naturally encourage him to seek familiarity and security and prevent his having initiative or foresight. Hence, there is a final, terrible paradox. Although society is cruel and unjust and although nature is a formidable antagonist for man, his life can have meaning and, indeed, remains real only when he does not seek, as does the otherwise noble convict, to escape the struggle with them.

NOTES

[1]Olga W. Vickery, *The Novels of William Faulkner: A Critical Interpretation*, rev. ed. (Baton Rouge: Louisiana State Univ. Press, 1964), pp. 156-66.

[2]Joseph J. Moldenhauer, "Unity of Theme and Structure in *The Wild Palms*" in Frederick J. Hoffman and Olga W. Vickery, eds., *William Faulkner: Three Decades of Criticism* (East Lansing: Michigan State Univ. Press, 1960), pp. 305-322.

[3]Floyd C. Watkins, "William Faulkner, the Individual, and the World," *Georgia Review*, 14 (1960), 238-47.

[4]Margaret Church, *Time and Reality: Studies in Contemporary Fiction* (Chapel Hill: Univ. of North Carolina Press, 1963), p. 244.

[5]William Faulkner, *The Wild Palms* (New York: Random House, 1939), p. 73. References to this volume are to the Vintage Edition; subsequent ones appear in the text.

[6]Vickery, p. 160.

[7]Vickery, p. 157.

"*Carry on, Cadet*":
Mores *and Morality in* Soldiers' Pay

by

Duane J. MacMillan

William Faulkner probably wrote *Soldiers' Pay*[1] in a small ground-floor apartment at 624 Orleans Alley in New Orleans during the early spring months of 1925. He had intended to book steamer passage to Europe, but after spending some time with William Spratling (with whom Faulkner would collaborate on *Sherwood Anderson & Other Famous Creoles* [1926]) he rented the apartment between St. Anthony's Garden and St. Louis Cathedral and set to work on his novel. During March through June the twenty-seven-year-old Faulkner also contributed several stories and sketches to the New Orleans *Times-Picayune*: he had already published a collection of poems, *The Marble Faun*, the previous December. *Soldiers' Pay* (or *Mayday*, as Faulkner had originally entitled it) was his first piece of extended prose fiction—his first novel. Faulkner and Spratling finally sailed for Europe on July 7, 1925, aboard the freighter, *West Ivis*.

Critical attention has focussed on Sherwood Anderson's influence on Faulkner at this time. Because the two men were friends together in New Orleans and because Anderson recognized talent in his young companion and wished to assist him in breaking into print, the older writer used his influence with his publishers on Faulkner's behalf.[2] Horace Liveright agreed in late August to bring out the book and *Soldiers' Pay* was officially published February 25, 1926. Reviews of the book tended to place it in the post-war tradition of *What Price Glory?*, a collaborated play by Maxwell Anderson and Laurence Stallings, and C. E. Montague's novel, *Disenchantment*.

During the half-century since its publication *Soldiers' Pay* has continued to attract sporadic critical interest because of its position in the Faulkner canon (no over-all critique can ignore it) and because *Soldiers' Pay* prefigures works which were to come. A less important reason for its continued consideration is the recurring popularity of the war-novel genre. The published criticism in English[3] falls roughly into three slightly overlapping categories: numerous brief passages ranging from a few lines to a few pages within the context of longer articles and books; reasonably short commentaries, also usually part of more comprehensive undertakings; and, finally, eight or nine full-length essays devoted to the study of this novel in some depth.[4] The book has been judged an apprentice work. It contains patches of the purplest prose; characterization is often limited, ambiguous, or downright confusing; thematic development is uneven and obscured by authorial intrusions, seemingly irrelevant literary allusions, and loosely patterned repetitions of phrases, images, and situations; there are so many kaleidoscopic loose ends in the novel that it is difficult to see how it all hangs together; it is in but not of the post-war *fin de siecle* tradition. Too often *Soldiers' Pay* appears to be a kind of disorganized seed-bed from which ideas, themes, and characters ripen to maturity in later works but which itself might have benefited in 1926 from editorial pruning.

All this must be acknowledged and may justify designating *Soldiers'Pay* as "minor Faulkner"; but this does not necessarily mean artistic failure or bad literature. There is a core of thematic strength and meaning in *Soldiers' Pay*, as yet unexplored in published criticism, which establishes a viable pattern of unity within the book itself, enhances the literary value of the novel, and links it securely with the truly great works in the canon. The central theme is sketchily prefigured in the implications of the first chapter; but it is explicitly stated by Reverend Mahon at the beginning of the second: "There are certain conventions which we must observe in this world. . ." (p. 57). In order to prevail the race must first endure; in order to endure there are certain conventions incumbent upon humane beings, whether they exist in a Christian, a pagan, a war-time, or a peace-time society.

The "conventions" which Faulkner discusses in *Soldiers' Pay* are of two kinds: the petty, superficial, and unimportant acts one performs in order to function with a minimum of conflict in any given, organized society (Faulkner views these conventions ironically); and the deeper, vital, basic principles of man's self respect, responsibility, and humanity, without which all societies are doomed. Those conventions which Faulkner considers worthy of emulation are in no way to be confused with or attributed to traditional conformity or institutionalized *mores* and religion. Faulkner is ever suspicious of the McEacherns, the Hineses, the Grimms, and the Cora Tulls—those who permit tradition and environment to define their responses to life. What Faulkner suggests in *Soldiers' Pay* is that, given the contingencies which life forces upon us, we are required to acquit ourselves with decency and deference to "the old verities" which Faulkner extolled at Stockholm in 1950. It is noteworthy to find the foundations of such a philosophy in Faulkner's first novel: it supports the idea that the non-Yoknapatawpha works were cut from the same bolt of cloth from which he fashioned *Absalom, Absalom!*, *The Sound and the Fury*, *As I Lay Dying*, *Light in August*, and *Go Down, Moses*.

In *Soldiers' Pay* the two fragments from the "Old Play" (pp. 7, 46) initiate the idea of conventions, particularly as they apply to military life. The first epigraph suggests that irrespective of whether or not Mercury is clean-shaven, the important thing is that he has used conventional or "issue" equipment. The second fragment illustrates the very practical precautions one must take before beginning a cross-country flight. The difference in degree of importance between a smooth check and a full petrol tank points up the precise dichotomy between the two types of conventions Faulkner is discussing. Military regulations imply that a very special kind of conventional behaviour can satisfy both insignificant and vitally important actions; but it is doubtful that Faulkner expects such epigraphs to be taken absolutely "straight." His characteristic view of formalized and trivial conventions is usually ironic; he suggests that the inherent nobility or ignobility of men's actions is ultimately far more important and lasting than conformation to mere tradition—military or civilian. The underlying irony of the passages is implicit in Faulkner's use of "Mercury," the Roman god of eloquence, skill, and speedy messages, in connection with the returned flier. Donald Mahon (Jones calls him "Mercury's brother" [p. 135]) is the direct antithesis to these characteristics: he has returned from the fields of Mars almost mute, practically immobile, and with dying mind. Both quotations conclude with "*Carry on, Cadet*" (italics added). This phrase is echoed at least nine times by Donald (pp. 172, 182, 183, 184, 246, 279) as he suggests that Joe carry on reading, talking, or working—filling up time until Donald can die. Because "we all gwine dat way, some day" (p. 296), these references imply that everyone is literally "filling up" time until death; one must attempt to "carry on" adequately in all circumstances.

The opening of Chapter V is a vivid explication of how people are required to "carry on' in a military environment: when Dewey Burney defaults on his human responsibility, death follows tragically and instantaneously for the innocent and guilty alike. It is true that "in wartime one lives in today. Yesterday is gone and to-morrow may never come" (p. 173). Madden constantly asks, "What do you expect of me?" (Julian, Joe, and Cecily ask the same question, at different times, in peace-time America). The only functional answer is that one must live by certain agreed-upon rules or chaos and anarchy result. Faulkner points up the ironic discrepancies in the shallow, useless conventions which one adopts in order to "get along" in organized societies. France and the American South have totally different sets of picayune rules which operate superficially on its members; but underlying these *mores* must be a common ground of dignity, responsibility, and self-respect.

When rules suddenly or arbitrarily change, one is caught off guard. The stystem becomes vulnerable to both sentimentalism from within and parody from without on the superficial level, and to annihilation on the more serious level. Hence the soldiers do not "fit" into a peace-time society: strangers in a strange land, they do not "know the dance steps," and are accordingly faulted and alienated— ironically in the same way as the uninitiated Lowe and the "jelly-beans" are excluded from the experiences of Joe, Donald, Green, Madden, and the other returned soldiers. When peace-time conventions are applied to servicemen, or *vice versa*, hilarious or bitter satire is possible—and Faulkner uses a heavy hand, especially in Chapters I and V. The discrepancies between the two systems are skilfully exemplified in the unstated ironic horror evinced when a civilian says to Joe, "Just be quiet, soldier, and we'll look after you. Us Americans appreciates what you've done" (p. 16). The differences between real war experiences and the ignorant placations of such platitudes are obvious: they represent the same polarity of values manifested between shaving with "issue" and acting honourably and nobly under stress. Yet this does not change the *donnée* of the situation: in each instance one must "Carry on, Joe," and maintain one's basic humanity.

The world of Charlestown into which Donald is re-introduced, literally "back from the dead," displays sharp contrasts with "devastated France" and the passenger train of Chapter I. In Charlestown it is spring; life is burgeoning, people generally behave in a predictable, socially acceptable manner called "civilized"; institutional religion is an observed and observable constituent of life; hospitality is extended and accepted. The majority of people give popular lip service and assent to the petty conventions of life (those *mores* comparable with the "issue" gear in the military): but they often regard such social

graces as more important than the underlying, vital rules of humanity. Charlestown is composed primarily of shallow, egocentric people
like Mrs. Burney, Mrs. Saunders, Mr. Rivers, Mrs. Worthington, and
Dr. Gary. It is "incumbent upon" men and women like Reverend
Mahon, Margaret Powers, and Joe Gilligan to maintain the really important conventions of life in that same environment.

When Januarius Jones meets Reverend Mahon, two or three
observations can be made: the minister has been privately grieving,
mentally comparing the gorgeous April morning with the war experiences of his "lost" son. After acknowledging the casual illusion of
the church spire's "fall" against the scudding clouds, Mahon attempts
to place the phenomenon within a traditional, viable, serious reference. When Jones deliberately discredits "Sunday" Christians, the
rector promptly rebukes him. Jones tries to excuse his flippancy, but
the good rector pursues the issue by stipulating: *"There are certain
conventions which we must observe in this world: one of them being
an outward deference to that cloth which I unworthily, perhaps,
wear. And I have found this particularly incumbent upon us of
the—what shall I say—?"* (p. 57, italics added). Baldly stated, the man
of God has instructed the goat-eyed academic that there are certain
rules of conduct which must be observed. Reverend Mahon's use of
"outward deference" towards his collar (particularly since he is an
Episcopal minister, and since nowhere else in the novel is he especially concerned with perfunctory social graces) suggests to the perceptive reader a possible allusion to the Episcopal Catechism's definition
of the Sacraments: they are regarded as "outward and visible signs of
inward and spiritual graces." There may be an analogy between
Mahon's diction and the two kinds of conventions here under discussion It is important that the priest and the scholar set good examples
for the rest of society on at least two counts: they are the leaders,
the "officers" of that society (indeed, Mahon is a "soldier of the
cross"); they are also the intellectual leaders whose responsibility it is
to ensure the survival and proliferation of moral, ethical conduct. In
his chastisement of Jones, Mahon is delivering a short exemplum on
the parable of the talents. (Faulkner would continue to draw on the
Christian-Episcopal "lumberyard of experience" throughout his
canon: *cf. The Sound and the Fury, Light in August, A Fable, etc.*)
The majority of people in Charlestown never see beyond Reverend
Mahon's collar, but he recognizes fully the kind of virtue for which it
stands. In addition to his first rebuke, Mahon "corrects" Jones on at
least three other occasions: two instances are cases of mere tactless,
tasteless bad manners (pp. 70, 75) and Mahon treats them lightly; the

third is more serious and Mahon reacts accordingly and decisively. Jones attempts to belittle Donald's forthcoming marriage and the rector says, "You have retained several of your youthful characteristics, Mr. Jones. . . . One in particular: that of being unnecessarily and pettily brutal about rather insignificant things" (p. 254). (Reverend Mahon is less direct, perhaps, than is Joe in dealing with Jones [*cf*. p. 288], but both the priest and the soldier are fully aware when the scholar has transgressed more than superficial matters of good taste: they both recognize the innate difference between social propriety and ignoble conduct.) Jones eases the embarrassment of this first encounter with Reverend Mahon by beginning to quote an Horatian ode which the cleric completes.[5]

That Reverend Mahon is not much concerned with the petty trivialities of "popular" social conventions is further evidenced by his deliberate toleration of Donald's youthful behaviour. The boy was allowed to come and go at all hours of the day and night, eat when and what he liked, attend school at his discretion, and wander anywhere that suited his fancy. It is difficult to imagine such conduct being sanctioned by the majority of Mahon's congregation—especially where "the minister's boy" was concerned.

But *Soldiers' Pay* does more than simply compare war-time and peace-time conventional or unconventional behaviour. A major problem dealt with in the novel is that of the military man forced into civilian situations and the resulting effects on all those concerned. Such a "multiple focus" makes possible opportunities for comparison, juxtaposition, and irony. It also attests to Faulkner's artistic prowess and sophistication early in his literary career. The conductor's seemingly innocuous statement, "I can't bring a train into Chicago with the whole army drunk on it" (p. 12) is a case in point. The trainman is outraged that the soldiers' indecorous behaviour may prove embarrassing for him personally (a thoroughly selfish attitude): his exaggerated "whole army" is an index of his concern. Conversely, the tiny group of battered veterans and Julian Lowe make a sad and grim sampling of the entire army.

Petty and superficial military conventions are more rigorously detailed and evident than those of civilian life—and they are more meticulously followed. As a result there is a kind of perverse security inherent in the military establishment:

And so here was Green in bars and shiny puttees, here was

> Madden trying to acquire the habit of saying Sir to him, here
> was Tom and Dick and Harry with whom both Green and
> Madden had gambled and drunk whiskey trying to remember
> that there was a difference not only between them and Green
> and Madden, but that there was also a difference between
> Madden and Green. (p. 173)

Due deference must be shown to the bars and puttees exactly as towards Reverend Mahon's collar, for they symbolize that code of ethics and human nobility which alone can sustain life. In the military life regimentation of behaviour can often be the sign of the grace exemplified by Madden when he refuses to enlighten Mrs. Burney regarding Dewey's infamy (pp. 185-186), or to relate the actual details of Dick's death to Margaret at the dance (p. 210). It also is the sign of fortitude in combat as is shown when Green refuses to verbalize his fears that he may be killed (p. 176), or of the conventions necessarily adopted by Margaret and Richard in their marriage (p. 163). Military conventions are not often viable in peace-time situations: when the soldiers at the dance try to use their "outworn conventions" they fail to make conquests and they delude themselves that the girls really do not enjoy the new dances; among themselves, however, the soldiers act with mutual understanding and decency. Joe Gilligan is from the beginning totally aware of the differences between the war-time and peace-time *milieux* and of the differences between merely superficial, unimportant behaviour and serious, grave actions. He jokingly tells Lowe that "home" in America they "don't want to offend no savage customs" (p. 24). He later explicates his position regarding Donald to Margaret: "you know damn well that I can help him—if I don't let a whole lot of don'ts stop me. And if I know I'm right there ain't any don'ts or anything else going to stop me. . . . I mean, you and I know what to do for him, but if you are always letting a gentleman don't do this and a gentleman don't do that interfere, you can't help him. Do you see? (pp. 40-41).

The two kinds of social conventions apparent in Charlestown are analogous to those suggested by the "Old Play" fragments. There are the "regular issue" conventions which enable the community to function smoothly and there are those which are more vital and must be taken more seriously. Dr. Gary is recognized as a socially acceptable "catch" (p. 167) even though he lacks any modicum of sympathy or compassion where Donald and his father are concerned (his antithesis is the humane specialist from Atlanta: *cf.* p. 285). At the dance Gary's "partner was young and briefly skirted: you could see that she danced with him because it was the thing to dance with Dr. Gary—no one knew exactly why" (p. 199). Similarly "conventional"

characters are the young Baptist minister (p. 278); Julian Lowe (in
civilian dress) when he writes to Margaret that "Mother says for me
to go in business and make money if I expect a woman to marry me
so I am going to start in to-morrow. . ." (p. 277); Mr. Saunders, who
wants his daughter to do right by the family's reputation in town
(pp. 115, 141); and Mrs. Saunders, who momentarily drops her social
veneer before Margaret and then demands an explanation for Cecily's
"coming down" *en dishabille* (p. 267). All these characters are
caught up in superficialities, in words rather than acts (like Cora Tull
of *As I Lay Dying*): they confuse propriety with humanity, *mores*
with morality.

In this respect, Cecily Saunders is, indeed, her parents' daughter. She often seems entirely superficial, callous, self-centred, and
foolish. She tells George Farr that she will marry Donald because it is
"expected of her" (p. 87), and even when she accepts Farr's proposal
(p. 215) she is overtly conscious of what is socially acceptable on
such occasions. (This scene is neatly parodied when Jones queries
Cecily about the kind of proposal she would like to hear [p. 266] .)
Her behaviour at the dance is socially faultless (p. 190), but unforgiv-
able by any humane standard, as is her attempt to mask her own
irritation at mistaking Jones for Donald (p. 141). Seen in this light, it
is not difficult to agree with Januarius Jones in his opinion of Cecily:
"What makes you so beautiful and disturbing and so goddammed
dull? . . . You are a shallow fool, but at least you can do what you
are told" (pp. 227, 229).

There is, however, more to Cecily Saunders than this brief description suggests. Her final elopement may not simply be an example
of her pragmatic choosing the procedure easiest and most opportune
for herself, nor a mere sign of futile last-minute honesty because of
her pregnancy. At the first luncheon at the manse Cecily twice covers
gaucheries by Jones and Reverend Mahon (pp. 71, 72), and the tone
of these passages suggests that Cecily's behaviour is prompted not by
"social conventions" but by genuine concern for her "Uncle Joe"
Mahon. Later, Cecily deliberately parodies and satirizes "polite" conversation with Jones when they are with Emmy on the verandah
swing (p. 92) so that she can embarrass Jones in retaliation for his
malicious behaviour at the dining table (p. 74). But there are more
positive instances wherein Cecily shows herself to possess some depth
of character. On at least six occasions she shows more perception and
humanity than Jones would apparently allow. While bantering with
and avoiding the embrace of Jones, Cecily says to him, "You're a
funny sort of man, aren't you? . . . I wouldn't put anything past

you—if you thought you could get any fun out of it" (p. 91). This is a shrewd judgment of Jones's character, on their *first* meeting. At another luncheon, this time at the Saunders's, Cecily recognizes Jones's potential power over her with acumen and maturity: she reconsiders her position "with that vast tolerance of their men which women must gain by giving their bodies . . . that the conquering male is after all no better than a clumsy, tactless child" (p. 220). In the same episode Cecily tells Robert to run along and cease questioning Jones concerning his war experiences. She says, "Don't you see that real soldiers never like to talk about themselves?" (p. 219). This statement is not only a deliberately ironic jibe at Jones (who was never a "real soldier" of any sort); it must also modify to some degree the impression Cecily gives through her inane comments at the dance (pp. 189 ff.). During Cecily's last heated argument with her mother over Donald, Mrs. Saunders puts stock in Aunt Callie Nelson's gossip but Cecily not only recognizes the tale for what it is, she also realizes the probable cause of Aunt Callie's comments (p. 259). This suggests sophistication and maturity not seen in her mother.

With these vignettes of Cecily's behaviour in mind, her final "confession" to Reverend Mahon and her elopement are, if not a convincing portrayal of sincere regret and personal honesty, at least cause for looking at her character with an open mind. The day on which she elopes Cecily rushes past Margaret Powers to enter the minister's study: "she stared at the other woman's shadowed face for a long moment. Then she said Thank you, thank you, suddenly, hysterically, and ran quickly into the house" (p. 275). Cecily is apparently thanking Margaret for the compassion and understanding which she extended to Cecily in her bedroom during the interview which Margaret had thought "hopeless" because of Cecily's adopted "conventional" behaviour (p. 266). Perhaps this strange amalgam of selfishness and maturity in Cecily results from an inexperienced author's lack of a clear focus on his character: it is more likely, however, that in Cecily Saunders Faulkner was developing a more three-dimensional character than those who, like Jones, see her only as a stereotyped "flapper." Furthermore, it is well to keep in mind that in his very next novel, *Mosquitoes*, Faulkner has a character (the novelist, Dawson Fairchild), say, "In life, anything might happen, in actual life people will do anything. It's only in books that people must function according to arbitrary rules of conduct and credulity" (*Mosquitoes* [1927], p. 149). As a multi-dimensional character, Cecily contributes a degree of aesthetic excellence not often awarded

Soldiers' Pay.

For Reverend Mahon, Margaret, and Joe "conformity" simply masks their underlying humane consideration for each other and for Donald rather than indicating any support of Charlestown's "respectability." Both the rector and Mr. Saunders attempt to expedite the engagement through normal, decent channels (each personally aware of the utter futility of the arrangement) with mutual respect (pp. 116, 256). Out of sincere kindness towards the rector (and *not* out of deference to Charlestown's gossips) Margaret smokes only in the back garden and Joe comments ironically on her losing her "good name" (p. 104). The minister covers his private amusement with "public" disapprobation of Joe's fighting with Jones by saying, "But boys will fight, eh Joe?" (p. 316). On a previous occasion the cleric muses momentarily whether or not he should have forced his son early in life to conform to a socially acceptable type (p. 68): this suggests, at least, that Reverend Mahon is completely aware of the dichotomy in the choice he made, much like Joe's "gentlemanly don'ts" alluded to above. Several references to young Donald's possessing the innocence and innate purity of a faun (pp. 69, 82-83, 125) imply that in letting his son grow up outside the bounds of conventional respectability, the minister made the correct choice. Even Jones, the potential sybarite—when he does not deliberately contravene them for his own selfishness—pays some deference to both kinds of conventions and, more importantly, recognizes their respective merit and value. He politely and instinctively defers to his host's dessert preference, but (of greater consequence) he understands and sympathizes with Reverend Mahon's reasons for raising Donald as he did (p. 69) and this in part accounts for Jones's genuine magnanimity toward Cecily (p. 229). Nevertheless, Jones is well aware of the limitations and abuses of social conventions:

> 'we, the self-styled civilized peoples, are now exercised over our minds and our arteries instead of our stomachs and sex, as were our progenitors and some of our uncompelled contemporaries.'
> 'Uncompelled?'
> 'Socially, of course. Doe believes that Doe and Smith should and must do this or that because Smith believes that Smith and Doe should and must do this or that.' (p. 64)

Such "compelled observance" of convention—expecially where

Donald is concerned—is, in part, responsible for Reverend Mahon's stoically bitter comment: "As I grow older, Mr. Jones, I become firmly convinced that we learn scarcely anything as we go through this world, and that we learn nothing whatever which can ever help us or be of any particular benefit to us, even" (p. 69).

The most serious, vital, and *moral* convention deliberately adopted by and acted upon by Reverend Mahon (whose character is progressively strengthened by Faulkner as the book moves towards its inevitable conclusion) is manifested in his attitude towards the wounded Donald and his imminent death. This particular convention provides the key to the thematic, structural, and philosophical heart of the novel. It also provides a basic principle of unity for such diverse patterns as images of nature, references to enduring Negroes, and differences in tone. A clue to the importance of this idea rests inherent in Faulkner's original title for the book, *Mayday*. This title implies that the centre of Faulkner's interest may not have been in "soldiers' pay" *per se*, but in either the cyclical continuity of the seasons regardless of man's periodic folly (this is what the mockingbird is singing about in the magnolias [pp. 283, 316]), or in a subtle allusion to *"m'aidez"*—the international distress call on wireless radio. Ironic and grim death is omnipresent amidst vibrant life. But if individuals behave decorously and humanely, with simple dignity and responsible observation of the principles of life which Faulkner extols, then life is worthwhile. Out of the Waste Land existence of trench warfare and Charlestown comes the promise of eternal spring with its proverbial hope and deliriums of wheeling sparrows. In terms of Reverend Mahon's rather unconventional Episcopal faith, God may see the little sparrows fall, and Donald may be one of these sparrows; but the world turns on its axis and the delirious Georges and Cecilys will endure long enough to produce the necessary Donalds, Joes, and Margarets. In this sense, *Soldiers' Pay* suggests what the individual, the family, and the community must do in order to "carry on" when the wounded veteran returns—from whatever "war." If the reader accepts the idea that Reverend Mahon truly believes that his son will regain his health, then, as Cleanth Brooks holds, the minister is guilty of a kind of "wilted, tolerant, sentimental morality."[6] However, where anyone else is concerned, Reverend Mahon does not seem deficient in perception, understanding, or charity. This is evidenced by his dealing with the rest of his flock, his treatment of Emmy, his understanding of Joe at the end of the novel, and even in his actions towards Jones on several occasions. Given the situation of Donald's returning home, what *does* one *do*? *Soldiers' Pay* proposes that in order to "carry on" with any degree of human decency, it behooves the group around Donald to adopt a certain kind of attitude regarding his condition—the "convention" of pretending that, given time, Donald will get well. Reverend Mahon initiates and sustains this effort, thus permitting and assisting his son to die in relative peace and dignity. The terrible old woman's question, "Can't something be done for him?" (p. 31) is ultimately answered for Donald and, by extension, for all the "soldiers" who must be "paid" in the currency of one realm or another, through compassion, courage, and *caritas*. Only once or twice does the rector's human fallibility let his conduct toward the boy lapse from his assumed attitude: considering the rector's personal attributes and the kind of upbringing he had given his son, these lapses deepen and make more poignant the cleric's character rather than obfuscate it.

Contrary to much critical opinion, several incidents in *Soldiers' Pay* suggest that Reverend Mahon is every bit as aware of the others in the community that Donald is dying, but that he institutes the best possible means for carrying on at this most difficult time. Very early in the novel Reverend Mahon explains to Jones that the "hand of Providence" is evident in horticulture for "it enables man to rise and till the soil, so that he might eat": horticulture provides a viable convention for living (pp. 63-64), and one is reminded of the Episcopal harvest hymn, "Work for the Night Is Coming." He enlarges upon this idea to Margaret (p. 108); but with Jones the minister directly ties the convention to Donald's death: "why should death desire only those things which life no longer has use for? Who gathers the withered rose?" (p. 67).[7] In reply to Jones's charge that "We purchase our salvation as we do our real estate. Our God . . . must have dignity," the rector asserts, " 'No, no. You do them injustice. . . . Only the ageing need conventions and laws to aggregate to themselves some of the beauty of this world. Without laws the young would rieve us of it as corsairs of old combed the blue seas' " (p. 58). As early as Mr. Saunders's first meeting with Donald, it is perfectly clear that Donald's condition is terminal: " 'Did anyone have to tell you about him?' 'My God, no! Anybody could look at him. It made me sick' " (p. 177). Nothing in *Soldiers' Pay* suggests that Reverend Mahon is less perceptive than Mr. Saunders. When the boy loses his sight, his father silently begs Joe to maintain the convention of Donald's convalescence: "The rector gazed at Gilligan. Don't say it, his eyes seem to plead. Gilligan's glance fell" (p. 167). Dr. Gary brutally acknowledges Donald's blindness and only then does the minister say that he had been expecting it (p. 168). Later in poignant juxaposition to the April life sprouting around them, Reverend Mahon says,

" 'Wait until next month. He will be stronger then. This is a trying month for invalids. Don't you think so?' " (both his gardening and pastoral experience would surely have taught him otherwise), and Margaret replies, " 'Yes,' she would tell him, looking out at the green world, the sweet, sweet spring. 'Yes, yes' " (p. 285). On at least three occasions Margaret and Joe assist the cleric in maintaining the illusion of Donald's returning health (pp. 118, 154, 168). But the effort to sustain this convention is trying for all concerned. The minister temporarily forgets his "front" at the dining table while trying to think of a way to tell his son that Cecily is not going to marry him (p. 272). While planning "engagement details" with Mr. Saunders, Reverend Mahon *twice* thinks to himself: "This was Donald, my son. He is dead" (p. 256). This scene not only makes a wry comment on the superficial conventions of marriage-planning but also points up the fact that the rector knows full well that his son is about to die. Reverend Mahon's attitude toward the matter is not characterized by lack of perception or sentimentality, but by simple compassion, charity, and love.

Looking beyond the immediacy of the Mahon family, one can see how Faulkner uses satire and parody to stress his attitude towards petty, trivial conventions in general and towards romantic love in particular. Parallel situations and complimentary character roles are used effectively towards this end: *e.g.*, Joe Gilligan makes a good mouthpiece for poking fun at the military side of life and Januarius Jones fulfills a similar function for the civilian; Margaret is a war-time bride as Cecily is a peace-time bride; Julian Lowe and George Farr are surprisingly alike as romantic comic lovers; Joe and Jones might be similarly linked, *etc.* Numerous examples of this "literary convention" range from the absurdly funny to the pathetically ironic; but in every case Faulkner strikes through the sham facades to point out more worthy and viable verities underneath. For example, when Julian says on the train that he cannot drink rot-gut whiskey, Joe replies, " 'Why, sure you can. Listen: think of flowers. Think of your poor gray-haired mother hanging on the front gate and sobbing her gray-haired heart out. Listen, think of having to go to work again when you get home. Ain't war hell? I would have been a corporal at least, if she had just hung on another year' " (p. 10). Joe wryly points up the difference between the commitments made by Madden, Donald, and Green, and that of the conductor and the salesman who stayed home, "minding the store" (p. 11). A vivid contrast underlies Joe's comment: "all the old bunk about knights of the air and the romance of battle, that even the fat crying ones outgrow soon . . ." and Julian's daydream: "To have been him! he moaned.

Just to be him. Let him take this sound body of mine! Let him take
it. To have got wings on my breast. . . ." (pp. 41, 45). This dichotomy is repeated, in effect, in the "movie war" described at the
dance (pp. 188-190). Romantic love is parodied by George Farr's
mooning after Cecily, by the various proposed and actual "duels" of
honour between Julian and Joe, George and Jones, and Joe and
Jones; but especially by the hilariously adolescent *billets-doux* from
Julian to Margaret. Even Jones's rutting has a reality about it that is
missing from Julian Lowe's love letters which are signed, "Your sincere friend" (p. 187). The vast difference between social convention
and real love is aptly demonstrated in the scene between Joe and
Margaret in the woods, where young Robert Saunders symbolizes the
superficiality of petting, holding hands, and kissing (pp. 164-165).

Faulkner suggests that when conventions become ends in
themselves, or are used selfishly or self-indulgently—such as expiating
Julian's romantic disappointment, permitting Cecily to be a social
butterfly, or allowing Mrs. Burney to become a grim social parasite—
then conventions deserve to be exposed as stupid, foolish, and useless. Wider implications of "carrying on" in an acceptable manner are
symbolized in Faulkner's use of seasonal cycles, various references to
Negroes enduring through simple fulfillment of repeated tasks,
wheeling flights of pigeons and sparrows,[8] and the implication that
people like Cecily and Emmy are part and parcel of the "Sex and
Death" business of the world at large. More subtly he suggests an
interesting relationship between Donald and young Robert Saunders
who unknowingly manifests many attributes of the pilot's youthful
experiences.[9] An additional *leit-motif* regarding the alleviations and
amelioration of grief over an extended period of time is implied by
Margaret's loss of Richard (p. 163), which fades as George's temporary loss of Cecily does (p. 213), as even Reverend Mahon tells Joe
that his loss of Margaret will fade into some sort of proper perspective (p. 318).

One final structural difficulty must be examined: it concerns
Donald's brief vision of his past when he was fatally wounded, and
Reverend Mahon's intuited perception of his son's "summons" just
before he expires. Brooks gives a good explication of the problem
when he calls into question the artistic efficacy of the doctor's remarkable prognosis (pp. 154-155) and the literary merit of Donald's
"flashback" and its relationship to the rector (pp. 292-294).[10] Donald's temporarily regaining his memory, however, should not seem all
that remarkable, for it is foreshadowed at least three times in the

novel. When Cadet Lowe first meets Donald on the train, they have a drink together:

> 'Nose down,' murmured Lowe. The man looked at him with poised glass. He looked at the hat on Lowe's knee and that groping puzzled thing behind his eyes became clear and sharp as with a mental process, and Lowe thought that his lips had asked a question.
>
> 'Yes, sir. Cadet,' he replied, feeling warmly grateful, feeling again a youthful clean pride in his corps.
>
> But the effort had been too much and again the officer's gaze was puzzled and distracted. (pp. 27-28)

A few pages later, time that is regulated by watches and calendars is shown to be irrelevant to Mahon for he is temporarily outside chronological time. He is in a kind of natural eternity and suspended animation (p. 32). During Donald's final vision he accomplishes the act of memory attempted earlier with Lowe. While in his cockpit there is an ambivalence between "sun-time" and "watch-time" for the young aviator: he is temporarily "out of time," flying in pure, golden sunlight not unlike that contemplated by Reverend Mahon (pp. 56-57), or the moon-light tryst described by Emmy (p. 127). Donald marvels at the amount of fuel he has taken on ("Empty your bladder and fill your petrol tank, Sir" [p. 46]). And when he is hit, "his trained hand nosed the machine up smartly" (p. 294), which suggests that his first effort at remembering had been triggered by Lowe's toast, "Nose down." The whole concept of Donald's attempting to remember is explained by the doctor:

> 'He is practically a dead man now. More than that, he should have been dead these three months were it not for the fact that he seems to be waiting for something. Something he has begun, but has not completed, something he has carried from his former life that he does not remember consciously. That is his only hold on life that I can see.' (pp. 154-155)

Donald's temporary restoration to lucidity is artistically effective on three counts: he is thus permitted to meet his death as a knowing, live man and not as a vegetable, with dignity and the fortitude which his father was afraid that he had not taught the boy; it allows Reverend Mahon to experience once since Donald's return, "This *is* Don-

ald, my son. He is *alive"* : but most important of all, it enables the
boy to drop back into chronological time so that—dying in time—he
joins the natural cycle of birth and death described immediately following his last "That's how it happened" (p. 294). Neither the doctor's heightened perceptivity nor Reverend Mahon's hearing Donald's
"call" to his bedside should, in the context of *Soldiers' Pay*, elicit
much surprise. There are at least fifteen different instances wherein
characters (most often Margaret and Joe) instinctively and intuitively
realize knowledge with which they have not been normally acquaint-
ed. Not all the examples are of equal merit or import, but their number alone indicates that for the characters of this novel, the phenomenon is not unusual.[11]

The final three pages of the novel recapitulate the major
themes, images, and philosophical problems posed by *Soldiers' Pay*.
The lyric intensity and ironic ambivalences of these passages have
been commented on by most critics but it is wrong to criticize the
book because no final resolutions are explicitly delineated. Art never
gives answers to life: at best it simply redefines questions. In
Soldiers' Pay Faulkner does not stipulate specific conventions to be
used in individual social contexts; but he does satirize useless superficialities and formalized empty traditions. Moreover, Faulkner advo-
cates certain principles or conventions for honourable, responsible
conduct: they are his reiterated criteria of "love and honour, and
pity, and pride, and compassion, and sacrifice." As they walk together in the spring evening, Joe awkwardly tries to "do something"
for Reverend Mahon who has done all he could for Donald: Joe
decides to stay on at the manse. But the rector both sees through the
soldier's "convention" and genuinely appreciates the motives behind
the proposed sacrifice: " 'Not at all. I won't have it. You have
already done all you can' " (p. 317). Then, just as Lowe had "known
all the old sorrows of the Jasons of the world" (p. 31), Joe "knew
suddenly all the old sorrows of the race" (p. 317), and he pours out
his heartache to the minister. The rector comforts Joe by suggesting
that God is Circumstance and that "the Kingdom of God is in man's
own heart" (p. 317). Here is a partial answer to two questions and
themes repeatedly raised in the novel. From the train conductor of
Chapter I to Margaret's and Joe's final parting at the station, characters ask: "What do you want? What do you expect? What can I do?
(*cf.* pp. 12, 16, 51, 52, 53, 59, 85, 174, 216, 253, 264, 302, 307).
There is no God but Circumstance—the way things are—the *donnée*
of life itself. How man acquits himself—honourably or dishonour-
ably, selfishly or unselfishly, as a Powers or as a Burney—depends on

man's own heart. He alone controls his response to life; he alone is responsible for his actions. Circumstance is also defined as "luck" which has been a *leit-motif* throughout the novel. There is no more use in complaining of "bad" luck than there is on depending upon "good": there is neither malevolence nor benevolence in Fate. Man must act accordingly if he is to make the best use of his time here on earth. In order to "carry on" effectively, it behooves man to adopt certain conventions. When these conventions are of the right kind and spring from the right motivations, then the "soldiers" are "paid" and man can continue to endure in order that he may some day, perhaps, prevail. Within this context, the final scene in *Soldiers' Pay* frames the novel and harkens back to the opening of Chapter II. The spire on the Negro church recalls the illusion of the falling spire against the clouds. But the spire, itself a convention, only appears to fall. Its ruin only seems imminent. In reality it endures against the storms and changes wrought by the seasons, an apt outward and visible sign for that inward and indomitable spirit of man. The Negro spire has been adopted and adapted from the white man's tradition—hence the tilt in the construction—offering a different convention for living, but ultimately advocating the same kind of salvation:

"Carry on, Joe."

Notes

[1]William Faulkner, *Soldiers' Pay* (New York, Boni and LIveright, Inc., 1926). All subsequent references are to this edition and will appear in parentheses immediately following quotations.

[2]If Faulkner did not deliberately set out to confuse this issue for his own amusement, he certainly seems to have altered the story with each retelling. *Cf.* William Faulkner, "Sherwood Anderson," *Atlantic*, CXCI (June, 1953), 27-29; William Faulkner, *Lion in the Garden: Interviews with William Faulkner, 1926-1962*, eds. James B. Meriwether and Michael Millgate (New York, Random House, 1968), p. 218; William Faulkner, *Faulkner at Nagano*, ed. Robert A. Jelliffe (Tokyo, 1956), pp. 54-56; William Faulkner, *Faulkner at West Point*, eds. Joseph L. Fant and Robert Ashley (New York, 1969), pp. 104-105. Among the critics, reasonable views are offered by Michael Millgate, *The Achievement of William Faulkner* (New York, Random House, 1964), p. 18, and Joseph Blotner, *Faulkner: A Biography* (New York, Random House, 1974), I, 400-442. See also:

Richard P. Adams, "The Apprenticeship of William Faulkner," *Tulane Studies in English*, XII (1960), 123-125; Robert Coughlan, *The Private World of William Faulkner* (New York, 1953), pp. 49-50; Irving Howe, *William Faulkner: A Critical Study* (New York, Random House, 1951), p. 16; H. Edward Richardson, *William Faulkner: The Journey to Self-Discovery* (Columbia, 1969), p. 133; William Van O'Connor, "William Faulkner's Apprenticeship," *Southwest Review*, XXXVIII (1953), 1-14; and Carvell Collins, "Faulkner and Anderson, Some Revisions," paper delivered at the Modern Language Association's Annual Meeting (Chicago, December 28, 1967).

³One regrets the lack of adequate translations of some foreign language studies and critiques, notably Mario Materassi's two pieces: "Le prime prose narrative di William Faulkner," *Paragone*, XVII, No. 196, 74-92; and "Le immagini in *Soldiers' Pay*," *Studie Americani* [Roma], IX (1963), 353-370.

⁴Important essays are offered by Cleanth Brooks, "Faulkner's First Novel," *Southern Review*, II, 4 (Autumn, 1970), 1056-1074; John T. Frederick, "Anticipation and Achievement in Faulkner's *Soldiers' Pay*," *Arizona Quarterly*, XXIII, 243-249; Irving Howe, *op. cit.*, pp. 17-19; Robie Macauley, "Afterword," in William Faulkner, *Soldiers' Pay* (New York, 1968), pp. 225-234; H. Edward Richardson, "The Decadence of Faulkner's First Novel: The Faun, the Worm, and the Tower," *Etudes Anglaises*, XXI (1968), 225-235; Robert M. Slabey, "*Soldiers' Pay*: Faulkner's First Novel, " *Revue des Langues Vivantes* [Bruxelles], XXX (1964), 234-243; Olga W. Vickery, "Faulkner's First Novel," *Western Humanities Review*, XI (Summer, 1957), 251-256, reprinted in her *The Novels of William Faulkner* (Baton Rouge, 1964), pp. 1-7; Edmond L. Volpe, *A Reader's Guide to William Faulkner* (New York, 1964), pp. 49-56; and Margaret Yonce, "Faulkner's 'Atthis' and "Attis': Some Sources of Myth," *Mississippi Quarterly*, XXIII, 3 (Summer, 1970), 289-298.

⁵It is Book I, Ode XXII which they quote—with a couple of word inversions and, most probably, a typesetter's error: "loac" for "loca."

⁶*Op. cit.*, p. 1061.

⁷Given the rector's vocation and the rather overt symbolism of the rosebush, it is not difficult to link Donald with Christ, who said, "I am the Rose of Sharon. . . " (Canticles 2;1). Although there seems to be no deliberate pattern of religious symbols in *Soldiers' Pay* (as there is, *e.g.*, in *A Fable* [New York, 1950]), there are many instances which are often highly suggestive. For a fairly complete survey of such allusions, see George K. Smart, *Religious Elements in Faulkner's Early Novels: A Selective Concordance* (Coral Gables, 1965).

⁸Faulkner uses the phrase "a delirium of sparrows" or variations thereof several times in *Soldiers' Pay* (*cf.* pp. 57, 61, 88, 105, 123, 185, 244, 252), plus several allusions to pigeons flying about or perching on the church spire (*cf.* pp. 180, 181, 184, 282). The birds symbolize the natural freedom of cyclical growth, death, and rebirth: "And so April became May. There were fair days . . .

so early flowers bloomed and passed and later flowers bloomed to fade. . . .
Leaves grew larger and greener . . . birds sang and made love and married and
built houses in them. . . . while pigeons held their own crooning rituals of aud-
ible slumber in the spire . . ." (pp. 281-282). It is worth noting that the natural,
burgeoning cycle heralds Cecily's conception and climaxes in an image of sparrows (p. 244). Both Cecily and Emmy (p. 110) are associated with sparrow imagery. What is important is that the two girls are part of the natural cycle of fertility and regeneration. It is not for nothing that Faulkner has Emmy seduced by
Jones at precisely the same time as Donald's body is put into the earth in the
midst of a regenerative rain: "Sex and Death: the front door and the back door
of the world. How indissolubly are they associated in us!" (p. 295).

[9]One of the more subtle touches in *Soldiers' Pay* is Faulkner's skilful
linking young Robert Saunders with Donald Mahon in order to suggest the con-
tinuance of repeated generations. Reverend Mahon cites the difficulty they had
to get young Donald to wear a hat or tie (pp. 68, 83); Mrs. Saunders says the
same thing about her son (p. 230). Both Donald and Robert use the woodland
pool for truant skinny-dipping. Donald is regularly described as a young faun
(pp. 69, 82-83, 125); both boys are limned in almost identical terms: "His body
was the color of old paper, beautiful as a young animal's" (p. 159); "Because he
was beautiful, with his body all brown and quick, so still. . . (p. 274). Finally,
Robert is linked securely to Donald by the latter's death; for Aunt Callie, who
had been Donald's nurse, comforts Robert, the next generation's avatar to learn
about death (pp. 298-299).

[10]*Op. cit.*, pp. 1062-1064.

[11]Margaret realizes that Donald is going blind (p. 37); Joe knows Mahon
is dying (p. 39); Joe foreshadows Cecily's attitude to the engagement (p. 40);
Joe knows that Margaret is married but is without a husband (p. 42); Joe instinctively "enters" Julian's dream (p. 47); Margaret intuits that Julian is an only
child (p. 54); Margaret knows that it will be Mrs. Saunders who will oppose the
marriage (p. 119); both Margaret and Joe recognize that making love in the
woods is "not for them" (p. 164); Madden anticipates Dough's unspoken request
(p. 102); Margaret twice knows that Joe is about to propose to her and stops
him (pp. 164, 251); Margaret realizes that Cecily is eloping (p. 275); Reverend
Mahon "hears" Donald call (p. 292); the rector realizes that Margaret is leaving the manse for good (p. 300); both Joe and Margaret instinctively recognize
that they cannot elope (p. 307).

Comedy in The Town

by

Edwin Moses

For all its wealth of comic incident, *The Town* has not generally been regarded as a successful comic novel. Cleanth Brooks, for
example, claims that by "avoiding the central novel of the trilogy,
one would lose nothing very essential, though he would forego some
incidental comedy that is interesting on its own account,"[1] and
Edmond Volpe sees the novel as "a failure because its stories are not
thematically unified."[2] A more generous appraisal of the novel, and
Faulkner's handling of comedy in it, is Michael Millgate's: "When
Faulkner incorporates this short-story material ["Centaur in Brass,"
"Mule in the Yard," "The Waifs"] into *The Town*, he distributes the
relatively self-contained comic episodes in such a way that they
operate within the book's aesthetic pattern as discrete, static
elements set off against the flow of narrative which contains them,
while in social and thematic terms they serve as reminders of what
Snopesism means in practice and are ironically counterpointed
against the irrelevance and ineffectuality of Gavin Stevens's anti-
Snopes crusade."[3] If the comic elements are primarily ironic, however, in the sense that they emphasize Gavin's failure, then *The
Town* becomes surprisingly reminiscent of *Sanctuary*, in its picture
of a mechanical society, epitomised by Flem Snopes, which grinds
down the noble aspirations of the individual. Olga Vickery's reading
supports this view: "The conscious moral life of the community
triumphs over the instinctual life of its individuals. . . . Hence Flem's
victory and Gavin's despairing anguish at the end of the novel mark
not only the death of Eula but also the illness of human society."[4] If
one sees the central issue of the book as the conflict between Flem
and Gavin, then the dark interpretation naturally follows; for Gavin
is a pretty frail reed, ill adapted to fight the Snopeses of the world on
pragmatic battlegrounds. If on the other hand one reads the novel as
essentially a *Bildungsroman*, "outlin[ing] Gavin's education in the
nature of women and reality,"[5] then the issue becomes how much
Gavin actually learns, how valuable his education is in itself, and thus
how much it weighs against Flem's pragmatic triumphs in determin-

ing the coloration of the novel.

But these elements, though certainly important, leave too much unexplained to be regarded as the sole organizing principles. *The Town* was published seven years after Faulkner's famous statement, in the Nobel speech, that "man will not merely endure: he will prevail." Faulkner's public utterances are never to be accepted on faith as unvarnished truth, and of course his literary works must ultimately speak for themselves, but nevertheless the Nobel statement should alert the critic to the possibility that Flem's triumph in *The Town* is more apparent than real. It is important to remember, too, that *The Town* is part of a trilogy, in the last novel of which Flem's downfall becomes explicit; so one might reasonably expect to find the seeds of his destruction in *The Town*, lest his fate in *The Mansion* seem mechanically imposed rather than organic. A third consideration is structural: not only does Faulkner interpolate comic stories which have nothing directly to do with Gavin Stevens, he *ends* the novel with one—the incident of the four Snopes Indians. If the focus had actually been on Gavin, the logical ending would have been his discovery (Ratliff's interpretation, anyway) of Eula's motive for committing suicide (357). Any responsible interpretation of *The Town* needs to take account of the terms in which Faulkner chose to achieve closure; for the ending of a conventional novel cannot be "incidental" or irrelevant unless one postulates a complete breakdown of the novelist's art.

The fundamental unifying principle of *The Town*, and the primary source of comedy, is the eternal collision between illusion and reality. The terms as I use them here include but are not limited to Northrop Frye's definition in his essay on comedy: "Illusion is whatever is fixed or definable, and reality is best understood as its negation: whatever reality is, it's not *that*."[6] Reality, as in *The Hamlet*, is the complexity, unpredictability, intractability of things as they are. Nature loves "concupiscent uproar and excitement," according to Gavin, and realists like Ratliff and old Het enjoy uproar and excitement, the general unruliness of things, of any sort. Reality is bordered in *The Town* by two different kinds of illusion: Flem's commitment to the "cold stability of currency" instead of the "wild glory of blood," and Gavin's romantic idealism. Both are potentially destructive. Quentin Compson, of course, was an early victim of the disparity between his romantic vision of life and reality, and Gavin avoids the same fate (whether by literal suicide or not) through his ability, with the help of Ratliff, to bridge the gap and accept the reality which Eula's suicide finally reveals to him. He is capable, that is, of change and adaptation, of at last becoming somewhat attuned to things as they are. But for Flem, the cold stability of currency translates easily into the cold stability of the grave. Periodically throughout *The Town* he is engaged in fending off the incursions of reality, mostly with money (in such comic episodes as "Centaur in Brass," "Mule in the Yard," and "The Waifs," to use the short-story titles), and in this novel he succeeds. The very persistence of reality, however, revealed especially by the placement of "The Waifs," signals his eventual downfall. When money loses its power to bring about a predictable pattern of cause and effect, as finally it must, Flem dies at Mink's hands. The degree to which he is out of tune with the process of life is further suggested by the fact that Linda's maturation presents him with a crisis. Linda, in Gavin's words, is "that female thing or creature which becomes (you cannot stop it; not even Flem Snopes could) a woman—woman who shapes, fits herself to no environment, scorns the fixitude of environment" (284). The rhetoric about women aside, Gavin's perception that Flem would stop the very process of growth if he could is perfectly accurate. He keeps Linda in Jefferson to prevent her from marrying, thereby becoming a blocking figure in a drama whose hero is not a specific suitor, but simply life itself.

Gavin is not so much a deliberate blocking figure as one who bumblingly gets in the way of the process of life through not quite understanding what is going on, with results miscellaneously good, bad, and indifferent. Yet the role he plays, especially in his dealings with Manfred DeSpain and Matt Levitt, in one ironic sense resembles Flem's. He does not want Eula or Linda for himself in any literal way, and therefore avoids being a rejected suitor (another perpetual loser in comedy), but rather tries to make them and their lives fit his preconceptions of what they should be. What the blocking figure does socially—locks people into a rigid role, with the object of safeguarding his own status in the world—Gavin attempts in philosophical terms, with the equivalent object of safeguarding his romantic conception of reality. So that Flem and Gavin should sometimes seem to be on the same side is not at all surprising. For his social purposes, for instance, Flem would have liked a daughter "homely and frightened from birth and hence doomed to spinsterhood"—a perpetual virgin, that is—whereas Gavin's conception of ideal womanhood seems to be the equally virginal and unobtainable love-object of courtly romance.[7] Both dreams run counter to the inexorable pressures of things as they are, and both men become gulls therefore in comic dramas identical in their essentials, however much they differ in tone and detail. Gavin, a man of genuine good will, learns from the social disasters he encounters, adapts as best he can to reality, and becomes, if never exactly heroic, at least admirable and likeable; Flem, rigid to the last in his denial of life, remains the victim of a cosmic joke more grim than funny. The similarities are nevertheless deep-rooted enough to give the novel an essential unity which it has often been accused of lacking. The point is that the comic material, both the "interpolated" short stories and the social comedy involving Gavin Stevens, is far from incidental; it is so central that analysis of its form and function provides probably the most fruitful single approach to *The Town*.

Such an analysis, necessarily somewhat summary, follows, with the proviso that approaching a complicated novel from a single point of view is likely to make it seem, not more unified than it actually is, but less diversified in character and incident and tone. To talk about comedy in *The Town* and mention Ratliff only incidentally, for instance, seems almost patently a distortion of the novel. But however funny his comments, Ratliff plays primarily a choral role in this drama, and for an excellent reason: he is so completely attuned to things as they are, as opposed to Flem and Gavin, that he never resists reality sufficiently to produce conflict. And he is too well balanced between detachment and involvement to allow himself to be acted upon. On the one occasion when he intervenes directly to forestall one of Flem's plots—the attempt to take over Wall Snopes's grocery—his action is so pragmatic, so quietly effective as to be almost invisible. In *The Hamlet* Ratliff underwent a thorough initiation in the ways of Snopeses, and so was central to that novel; having learned his lesson, he becomes peripheral to the action of *The Town*.

As Ratliff is a sophisticated realist, so Chick Mallison is an innocent one: a "mirror which obliterated all except truth," Faulkner said, "because he didn't know the other factors existed."[8] If there is any really incidental comedy in *The Town*, it occurs in such incidents as the rabbit hunt, with its series of escalating indemnities paid to Aleck Sander for jumping into the frozen creek, and in Faulkner's sporadic attempts to make of Chick a naive narrator on the order of Huck Finn. ("I thought the story would be more interesting as told through the innocence of a child that knew what he was seeing but had no particular judgment about it.")[9] A description of one of Montgomery Ward Snopes's pictures as showing "the Seine river bridges and ks whatever they are" is hardly the stuff of which classic comedy is made; apparently Faulkner never quite decided what he wanted to do with Chick. Margaret Mallison and her husband are realists who function primarily as foils to Gavin—as a standard against which to measure his quixotic flailings. Maggie, according to Gavin himself, exemplifies a healthy balance between order and impulse, respectability and the willingness to deny it, and nothing in the novel suggests otherwise. The Mallison family and Ratliff collectively represent the implicit norm of *The Town*, and thereby play an important role, but they are too sane and well-balanced to function as more than the ground against which we observe the figure of the dramatic action.

Faulkner is a master of symbolic incident, unobtrusive because completely integrated, which quietly reinforces his meanings. So, for instance, Flem begins his systematic theft of the power plant brass by stealing the safety valves. He thereby creates a dangerously unstable situation, simply because he is not attuned to the pressures—in this case, one hundred pounds per square inch—of reality. (Such an interpretation of the incident in isolation would be strained, but in fact Faulkner is alerting the reader to a pattern which runs all through the novel.) If Flem Snopes is unlikely to be the one killed in the resulting explosion, that too is typical: neither will he be facing Tom Tom Bird's butcher knife. But what Flem fails to realize, and never learns, is that the attempt to coerce a predictable pattern of events out of the intractable stuff of human needs, follies, obsessions, is precisely analogous to removing those safety valves. Wrenched out of shape, reality tends to snap back violently (and often hilariously), and even Flem cannot always manage to stand clear of the inevitable catastrophe. In his attempts to manipulate Tom Tom and Tomey's Turl, Flem plays on economic and social motives (the only ones he really understands), telling each that the other wants him fired, but what he forgets is the emotional factor: that Tom Tom has a young wife of whom he is fanatically jealous, and that Tomey's Turl is a local Don Juan. And this is what sets in motion the brief, violent bedroom farce which destroys Flem's plot and results in the brass being dumped into the water tank. That anyone in his right mind would deliberately throw away a load of valuable brass presumably startles Flem to the roots of his being. But then who in his right mind would attempt to sell French postcards in Jefferson, Mississippi? Flem is constantly in arms against the ubiquitous irrational.

Montgomery Ward Snopes, as shabby a sinner as ever walked the streets of Jefferson, ultimately owes his downfall to his flouting of a superficial social reality, according to Gavin Stevens: it is unrealistic to retail cosmopolitan vice among rural Baptists. But the actual events suggest that Gavin, out of tune with more basic realities, has contented himself with at best a half-truth. Morally Flem and Montgomery Ward may be interchangeable, but in their approaches to manipulating their environment they are diametrically opposed. Flem tries to minimize the unpredictable effects of irrationality by appealing to self-interest, which is governed by reason: if the vice-president of a bank removes his own money from it, for instance, it is only reasonable to follow suit. Even his manipulation of Linda, which depends on her emotional response to his simulated devotion, involves setting up a situation in which her reaction follows logically and predictably from his action. But Montgomery Ward's livelihood depends upon the dark, irrational aspect of the human psyche, which motivates all those furtive nocturnal excursions to his darkroom. (That what is in fact a dark room should be disguised as a photographic darkroom is another neat symbolic touch.) He uses self-interest—the fear of getting caught—as an ordering and stabilizing principle, and for a time maintains an uneasy balance. But inevitably the pressure of things as they are becomes too great: Grover Cleveland Winbush, the very walking symbol of law and order, gives in to prurient impulse at exactly the wrong moment; the vacated darkness produces its thieves; and the urgent demands of Uncle Willy's drug habit lead the inquiry directly to Montgomery Ward's door. If chance seems to play too significant a role in this chain of events, the proper rebuttal is simply that life is an extraordinarily chancy business, and that failure to take that into account leads to disaster. By manipulating the evidence against Montgomery Ward, Flem tries—as he typically does—to eliminate chance altogether, and this time he succeeds. He obliterates the pornography business as a social reality, in that only a few insiders ever learn of its existence; but the dark ungovernable impulses it represents and feeds on remain a fundamental reality, just as Mink, in exile at Parchman, remains alive, unbribable, implacable.

"Mule in the Yard" is the funniest and most characteristic comic episode in *The Town*; related in manner and tone to "Spotted Horses," it gives the same joyous sense of "dust and uproar," the swirling confusion which inheres (even though it usually lies out of sight under the decent surface of things) in life. Again Flem brings matters under control, this time by means of a simple bribe, but again the episode has ironic overtones which suggest that his success is temporary and illusory. For as opposed to Montgomery Ward, I. O. Snopes is in his essentials a cut-down version of Flem himself. A modest entrepreneur, he depends in his dealings with the railroad

upon a rigid and predictable pattern of cause and effect: a mule dies
on a sharp curve, and the railroad produces sixty dollars. That pattern breaks down when human carelessness and unpredictability
bring about Mr. Hait's accidental death. Like Flem, I. O. reveals himself as utterly out of tune with the process of life, not only by killing
mules for a living, but by his fear and hatred of them. He typically
appears in Jefferson in the dust of his drove "at a panting trot, his
face gaped with forlorn shouting and wrung with concern and terror
and dismay" (236).[10] And people who are out of tune with life tend
to get trampled by it, as Henry Armstid does in "Spotted Horses"
and as I. O. does here: "He was lying flat on his face, the tail of his
coat flung forward over his head by the impetus of his fall, and old
Het swore there was the print of the cow's split foot and the mule's
hoof too in the middle of his white shirt" (240). As with Flem (in
the earlier and cruder stage of his development), I. O.'s only reality is
money, his demand for which in Mrs. Hait's yard, as life swirls gid-
dily and dangerously all around him, is ludicrous, a classic example
of inappropriate response—or rather of failure to respond to his surroundings at all:

> And Mr Snopes too, the mules running all over him too, he
> and Mrs Hait glaring at each other while he panted:
> "Where's my money? Where's my half of it?"
> "Catch that big son of a bitch with the halter," Mrs Hait
> said. "Get that big son of a bitch out of here," both of them,
> old Het and Mrs Hait both, running on so that Snopes's pant-
> ing voice was behind them now:
> "Pay me my money! Pay me my part of it!" (239)

Long after it has become apparent that neither is operative, he clings
forlornly to logic and justice. He must, he thinks, own either the
mule or the ten dollars Mrs. Hait paid him for the mule. In one of the
funniest lines of the book, Mrs. Hait reveals the blithe ease with
which she has broken down this argument:

> "Honey," old Het said to Mrs Hait, "what did you do with
> that mule?" Uncle Gavin said there was one slice of bread left.
> Mrs Hait took it and sopped the last of the gravy from her
> plate.
> "I shot it," she said. (256)

The setting of this scene is profoundly revealing, for while I.O. walks
off alone into the darkness, the two realists, old Het and Mrs. Hait,
share a companionable meal; afterwards "old Het sat back on the

box with the empty skillet in her hand and sighed with peaceful and happy relaxation" (256). The scene is prophetic, calling up a vision of Flem, in *The Mansion*, sitting by himself in his dim house while the real business of life goes on around him.

The appearance of the four Snopes Indians is an especially ominous portent, and not only because the episode occurs at the end of the novel. A particularly disreputable Snopes returns in the guise of his children to haunt Flem, for one thing, just as Mink reappears in *The Mansion*. And the fact that these are children, a new generation, evokes the sense that the unruly, the irrational, the primitive perpetually renew themselves and therefore perpetually threaten. To attempt to deny or escape from them is simply to deny an essential aspect of life, but in fact there is no escape. Mrs. Widrington walls her dog off from life—"the only time it wasn't sneering out through the Cadillac window, it was sneering out through a window in the house where it—they—lived" (362)—yet somehow, inexplicably, it disappears, and all the money and respectability in the world can never alter the fact that its gnawed bones lie at the mouth of the children's cave. They break into the bottling plant, again inexplicably, "because no door was open nor window broken"; it is as if they had passed through the very walls themselves. The Dewitt Binfords, who propose to turn an honest profit by boarding them, early learn the hazards of trying to fit them into an orderly social routine, for their strange powers stem, not merely from the arbitrary demands of the tall tale, but from the fact that they represent a powerful and basic aspect of the human psyche: they are unruly and ungovernable instinct personified. Small wonder then that Dewitt Binford, a civilized man, can never hope to slip up on them in the dark, their native element, and surprise them in their sleep, or drug them with sleeping pills in soda pop. Nor can one exploit them for his own purposes, as Doris Snopes, himself so slightly civilized as to have a certain affinity for them, discovers by nearly being incinerated. There remain two expedients: to wall oneself off from them, as Dewitt and his wife do (but the incidents of the dog and the bottling plant have revealed what flimsy and temporary protection walls afford), or to accept them for what they are, as Ratliff does. In *The Hamlet* Ratliff learned all about the darkness within; that he has forgotten nothing is revealed by the evident equanimity with which he contemplates and talks about the children's doings, and by the calmness he displays when he sees them off at the station.

Flem insulates himself as best he can by paying for the dog, and by sending the children out to Frenchman's Bend, which represents a forlorn attempt to put his past definitively behind him. Frenchman's Bend is a place where federal officers vanish, through which "strange Negroes absolutely refuse to pass . . . after dark," and which breeds violent and intractable men like Mink Snopes. The past is never past; Flem can ignore it or wall himself off from it as much as he pleases, but it bears inexorably down on the present. The macabre and violent quality of the humor in this final scene of *The Town* suggests all the more clearly the fate in store for Flem.

While Flem remains fatally committed to illusion, Gavin makes at least some progress in the direction of reality. According to Faulkner, in *The Town* Gavin "had got out of his depth. . . . He got into a real world in which people anguished and suffered, not simply did things which they shouldn't do."[11] Nevertheless he continues conscientiously to try to cope with experience, and the very fact that he remains in somewhat random motion paradoxically allies him with reality, even though he fails almost completely to understand it. The comedy involving Gavin inheres in the discrepency between the real and his ideal; this gulf makes him funny but never contemptible.

The arrival of Gavin's first crisis is signalled by the clatter of DeSpain's cutout: the raucous unmistakable challenge, which sounds "just like laughing," of things as they are. An automobile in this context makes a particularly appropriate symbol, since its very presence on the streets of Jefferson flouts Sartoris' attempt to insulate the town against the realities of progress and change. The following exchange of provocative incidents reveals the extent to which Gavin is overmatched; the fact that, as Charles Mallison says, "he just dont know how to make the kind of trouble that a man like Manfred de Spain will take seriously" (58). The retaliation involving the rakehead is a peculiarly innocent gesture, undisturbing, without symbolic overtones, whose effect is limited to the physical mishap it brings about. DeSpain simply has his tire fixed and goes on his way. But Gavin's conception of the world, which is what DeSpain's ironic corsage attacks, is not so easily patched up. As Gavin himself comes to realize, the rakehead evokes his juvenility and assails his self image (he later thinks bitterly of himself as having acted like a vicious boy); the flowers are an image of the idealistic romantic concept of women; and the prophylactic jeeringly asserts the brute sexual reality. DeSpain, like Eula, ultimately becomes a casualty of one of the battles Flem wins in the course of his losing war, but he is a formidable realist nevertheless, a natural force who matches Eula so well that, as Ratliff puts it, "they never no more needed to waste time

understanding one another than sun and water did to make rain"
(99-100). So naturally Gavin—aside from the literal fact that he has
never learned to use his fists—is the one who gets knocked down in
the fight at the dance, just as I. O. Snopes rather than Mrs. Hait or
old Het gets knocked down by the mule.

The most poignant and revealing of Gavin's confrontations
with reality, comic in the sense that it involves a ludicrous reversal
of traditional roles, occurs in the scene with Eula in his office. But
Gavin, as he cries "Don't touch me!" and backpeddles around the
room, is really a pathetic figure, almost comparable to Quentin
Compson in the scene with Caddy in the creek. Faulkner reveals Gavin's hysterical fear of life as lived in part by using the office door
symbolically: Gavin, like Flem, attempts to wall himself away from
reality. When Eula enters the office she has to ask Gavin twice to
close the door, in order to shut out the cold; while from her point of
view the room contains warmth and life, from Gavin's it contains the
death of his dream. Then she asks him to lock the door, but Gavin,
by now feeling completely trapped, opens it instead. Eula once safely outside, "the cold invisible cloud leaned in again," and "again I
closed it"; he remains in the office alone, immured in the chill and
sterile purity of his vision. Reality bears down hard on him, though.
He reaches his nadir when, thrashing about aimlessly and frantically,
he brings the suit against DeSpain, and is reduced to appealing piti-
ably to his father: "What must I do now, Papa? Papa, what can I do
now?" (99)

The comedy stemming from Gavin's dealings with Linda is
gentler, less raucous, lower-keyed, simply because the reality of
Linda *happens*, by virtue of her youth and social position, to correspond more closely with his vision of her. For the moment illusion
and reality almost merge, though the problem is that what Gavin
would like to think of as Linda's essential attributes (virginity and
innocence, primarily) are in fact incidental and transient. Matt Levitt
is hardly the threat that Manfred DeSpain was; his fists and cutout
similarly represent things as they are, of course, but time for the moment protects Gavin, and Matt can no more debauch Linda than
Mink, from Parchman, can assassinate Flem. So for different reasons,
Gavin as much as Flem would prefer that Linda never grow up, and
for a long time he tries to keep her in a childhood world of ice cream
and poetry books (Herrick is a perfect choice; Donne seems risky).
This attempt to resist the process of life is what leads him into the
elaborate comic machinations (ducking down alleys and into door-
ways, bribing Chick to send books and messages) which he regards as

necessary to protect Linda's reputation. In one sense his later attempts to send her away to college reveal considerable courage and integrity, for leaving home normally signals, and contributes to, the end of childhood. But the fact that for Gavin himself universities have invariably served as *refuges* from the process of life raises the possibility that he has some subliminal, wistful expectation that this might hold true for Linda too. This is supported by his feeling, after he has become somewhat reconciled to reality, that a university is no longer the right place for her to go.

Despite his busy attempts to form Linda to his idealistic image of her, and thus to maintain a world in which he himself can live, there is some evidence that during the middle part of *The Town* Gavin begins to sense the futility of the course he is committed to, and so falls half in love with death. A man in his thirties, he describes himself as "the gray-headed bachelor, avuncular and what old Negroes called 'settled,' incapable now of harm, slowed the blood and untroubled now the flesh by turn of wrist or ankle, faint and dusty-dry as memory now the hopes and anguishes of youth" (217). And later he twice terms himself an "old man"—he is "only a few years from forty" (317). But this describes wish, not reality. Without his vision of unsullied timeless love he is, like Quentin Compson, nothing; and while time and reality have impinged steadily on his romantic idealism, he has not yet achieved a new vision, based on reality, capable of sustaining him. Two scenes just before Eula's suicide reveal him in this perilous transitional vacuum. He pictures himself first as

> the old man, standing there while there rises to you, about you, suffocating you, the spring dark peopled and myriad, two and two seeking never at all solitude but simply privacy, the privacy decreed and created for them by the spring darkness, the spring weather . . . (317)

He has come to recognize the cyclical, regenerative process of life, that is, but thinks of himself not only as incapable of playing a part in it, but as so alienated as to be suffocated by it. The other scene occurs after Eula has made him swear to care for Linda:

> It would even be quite cold by dawn, daybreak. But even then not cold enough to chill, make hush for sleep the damned mockingbird for three nights now keeping his constant racket in Maggie's pink dogwood just under my bedroom window. So the trick of course would be to divide, not him but his racket,

the having to listen to him: one Gavin Stevens to cross his
dark gallery too and into the house and up the stairs to cover
his head in the bedclothes, losing in his turn a dimension of
Gavin Stevens, an ectoplasm of Gavin Stevens impervious to
cold and hearing too to bear its half of both, bear its half or
all of any other burdens anyone wanted to shed and shuck,
having only this moment assumed that one of a young abandon-
ed girl's responsibility. Because who would miss a dimension?
Who indeed would be better off for having lost it, who had
nothing in the first place to offer but just devotion, eighteen
years of devotion, the ectoplasm of devotion too thin to be
crowned by scorn, warned by hatred, annealed by grief. That's
it: unpin, shed, cast off the last clumsy and anguished dimension, and so be free. (334-335)

Devotion to his dream no longer sustains him, but he is not yet
reconciled to the pain of life. So if he cannot simply die—pass into
that perpetual chill dark where no bird ever sings—then he should
somehow be able to live, assume the responsibilities and bear the
pain which that involves, and yet remain inviolate in his essential self.
This is all very romantically phrased, and he cannot yet translate it
into a workable philosophy of life, and yet in his bumbling and
prolix fashion Gavin is approaching a vital truth, one which all of
Faulkner's comic heroes have to learn: that in order to accept and
live fully in the real world, one must be simultaneously detached
from it and involved in it.

Gavin therefore is psychologically prepared for the transition
which Eula's death triggers in his outlook. What occurs is a kind of
exorcism, oddly reminiscent of the theory propounded by Whitfield
in *The Hamlet*. In order to be cured of sodomy, the theory goes, a
man has to be convinced emotionally, by eating of the animal's flesh,
that the partner of his sin is dead. The evidence that Eula, the pure
and worthy object of his idealistic devotion, is an illusion has been
staring Gavin in the face for eighteen years. But only after her death
can he accept her as what she was: a vital woman, trapped in an
impossible marriage with in impotent man, who at last took her life
because she was bored. Finally he can cast his dream aside and look
to the pragmatic requirements of the living.

Gavin has generally been regarded as ending his career in *The
Town* as a failure. For instance, Vickery says that Flem makes Gavin
"compound his hypocrisy" by helping with the monument.[12]
Millgate says that "it is one of the most pointed ironies of the novel
that whenever Stevens achieves some form of positive action he does

precisely what will assist Flem Snopes: his failure as an opponent
of Snopesism is more radical even than Ratliff's had been in *The
Hamlet*, and a good deal more culpable"; and that "at the end of
the book he seems only to have succeeded in deracinating"
Linda.[13] But these arguments are largely moot or irrelevant. Nowhere in the trilogy does Faulkner imply that a responsible man
should fight every one of Flem's schemes on principle, simply because Flem is wicked. Therefore what purpose would be served by
a quixotic attempt to interfere with Flem's harmless monument,
which will inevitably be completed anyway, or by proclaiming to
the world that Eula was a whore, which is no more true than that
she was a saintly wife? A man who felt compelled to make such
gestures would be indistinguishable from the "vicious boy" who
strewed tacks in front of DeSpain's auto. Nor could there be any
purpose in Gavin's simply withdrawing, sulkily ignoring the whole
monument project, when facilitating it will get Linda more quickly out of Flem's clutches, for in this situation the well-being of the
living is the *only* significant issue. Gavin's lie to Linda about her
paternity may or may not be wise, but the point is that he is willing to make a pragmatic decision based on what he takes (accur-
ately, I think) to be Linda's psychological needs, rather than ad-
hering rigidly to the truth for the sake either of principle or of
spiting Flem. And to fault him for sending Linda to New York on
the basis of what ultimately happens to her there is worse than
irrelevant, when one considers that a central theme of the novel is
that reality is complex, unpredictable, never guarantees anything,
and that to demand guarantees, as Flem does or as Gavin does in
the earlier stage of his development, is ultimately self-destructive.

Ratliff teases Gavin for sending Linda to New York in
search of dreams—"I thought that-ere was a varmint you hunted
anywhere" (350)—and he is quite right to do so, for Gavin displays
here a certain solemn earnestness which seems basic to his character. But he does get her away from Flem's life-denying influence,
and the fact that the dreams he envisions for her involve her
growth into a mature sexual relationship indicates that he has
finally reconciled himself to life as lived. The movement from
bondage to freedom—from Flem, from illusion—is a fundamental
principle of comedy, and if neither Gavin's nor Linda's deliverance
is exactly definitive, it is important to remember that "there is no
permanent defeat and permanent human triumph except in
tragedy."[14] In *The Town*, though, the arc is really upward for
Gavin and Linda, while Flem's apparent upward arc is all illusion.

Notes

[1]Cleanth Brooks, *William Faulkner: The Yoknapatawpha Country* (New Haven: Yale University Press, 1963), p. 216.

[2]Edmond Volpe, *A Reader's Guide to William Faulkner* (New York: Noonday Press, 1964), p. 317.

[3]Michael Millgate, *The Achievement of William Faulkner* (New York: Random House, 1966), pp. 236-37.

[4]Olga Vickery, *The Novels of William Faulkner* (Baton Rouge: Louisiana State University Press, 2nd ed., 1964), p. 182.

[5]Brooks, p. 217.

[6]Northrop Frye, *Anatomy of Criticism* (Princeton: Princeton University Press, 1957), pp. 169-70.

[7]See Brooks's chapter on *The Town* for an interesting discussion of Gavin's relationship to the courtly love tradition. I think Brooks is right in regarding Gavin as being committed to a pure, timeless, life-denying love, and go on that assumption in this essay.

[8]Frederick L. Gwynn and Joseph L. Blotner, ed., *Faulkner in the University* (Charlottesville: University of Virginia Press, 1959; 2nd ed., New York: Vintage, 1965), p. 140.

[9]*Faulkner in the University*, p. 116.

[10]William Faulkner, *The Town* (New York: Random House, 1957). This edition will be used for all references to *The Town*.

[11]*Faulkner in the University*, p. 140.

[12]Vickery, p. 188.

[13]Millgate, p. 240.

[14]Susanne Langer, *Feeling and Form* (New York: Scribners, 1953), p. 349.

"Barn Burning": A Definition of Evil

by

Edmond L. Volpe

"Barn Burning," published in 1939, is one of Faulkner's finest short stories and one of his most profound. In a sensitive exploration of the troubled psyche of a child, Faulkner defines the nature of evil. The story is deceptive in its apparent simplicity. It is easy to misunderstand the moral significance of the boy's emotional conflict if we fail to recognize metaphor as metaphor, ignore the subtlety of Faulkner's narrative technique and miss the implications of the imagery. On the surface, the young boy's emotional struggle seems to be equated with a conflict between an aristocracy representing ethical order and a sharecropper, Ab Snopes, representing moral entropy.

The protagonist is the youngest son of Ab Snopes. The child's given name is Colonel Sartoris. In the opening scene, in which the boy's emotional conflict is identified, the justice declares: " 'I reckon any boy named for Colonel Sartoris in this country can't help but tell the truth, can they?' " (4)* As Faulkner's narrator defines the boy's anxiety, he is trapped between the "old fierce pull of blood" and a thrust towards justice and truth. The external correlatives of the moral forces tearing the boy in two would therefore seem to be his father, the sharecropper, and De Spain, the aristocrat. Ab Snopes is a barn burner, a violent, destructive man. De Spain's plantation house, on the other hand, provides the child an objective image for the moral thrust generating his rebellion against his father. His immediate reaction to the sight of the house is to compare it to a symbol of justice, the courthouse. The white, ante-bellum manor evokes in the boy a surging sense of dignity and peace, and he feels certain, for a moment, that it must be safe from the malevolent touch of his father.

---

* Page references in parenthesis from *Collected Stories of William Faulkner* (New York: Random House, 1950).

The opposition of sharecropper and aristocrat suggests social as well as moral implications. And, in fact, certain elements in the story support the possibility. Ab makes the valid point that De Spain's house is built with "nigger sweat" as well as the white sweat of the sharecropper. Ab views himself, the narrator seems to suggest, as a continually violated victim of an unjust socio-economic system. He "burns with a ravening and jealous rage." (11) The "element of fire," the narrator authoritatively informs us, speaks to "some deep mainspring" of Ab's being "as the element of steel or powder spoke to other men, as the one weapon for the preservation of integrity, else breath were not worth the breathing, and hence to be regarded with respect and used with discretion." (7-8)

"Barn Burning" however is not really concerned with class conflict. The story is centered upon Sarty's emotional dilemma. His conflict would not have been altered in any way if the person whose barn Ab burns had been a simple poor farmer, rather than an aristocratic plantation owner. The child's tension, in fact, begins to surface during the hearing in which a simple farmer accuses Ab of burning his barn. The moral antagonists mirrored in Sarty's conflict are not sharecropper and aristocrat. They are the father, Ab Snopes, versus the rest of mankind. Major De Spain is not developed as a character; his house is important to Sarty because it represents a totally new and totally different social and moral entity. Within the context of the society Faulkner is dealing with, the gap between the rich aristocrat and the poor sharecropper provides a viable metaphor for dramatizing the crisis Sarty is undergoing. Ab Snopes is by no means a social crusader. The De Spain manor is Sarty's first contact with a rich man's house, though he can recall, in the short span of his life, at least a dozen times the family had to move because Ab burned barns. Ab does not discriminate between rich and poor. For him there are only two categories: blood kin and "they," into which he lumps all the rest of mankind. Ab's division relates to Sarty's crisis and only by defining precisely the nature of the conflict the boy is undergoing can we determine the moral significance Faulkner sees in it. The clue to Sarty's conflict rests in its resolution.

In the story's climactic scene, Ab Snopes orders his wife to hold her son to prevent him from warning De Spain that Ab intends to burn his barn. Sarty fights free of his mother's arms and rushes to the manor house. After De Spain passes him on the horse, he hears shots ring out and at once begins to think of his father as dead. The nature imagery which Faulkner introduces in the concluding paragraphs of the story does not suggest that Sarty's rebellion has meant a triumph for morality and justice. In the chill darkness, on the crest of the hill, the boy sits with his back towards home, facing the woods. His fear and terror of his father are gone. Only grief and despair remain. By aligning himself with De Spain, the boy destroys his father and gains his freedom. At the story's end, he moves into the future without looking back, responding, independent and alone, to the call of the "rapid and urgent beating of the urgent and quiring heart of the late spring night." (25) The imagery suggests a feeling of unity with the world of nature, a sense of wholeness as if the boy, at last, has found himself. The quiescent, enveloping nature imagery contrasts sharply with the threatening, rigid, metallic imagery which Faulkner uses to convey the child's sense of his father as a living force. The contrast clearly indicates that Sarty's struggle is against the repressive and divisive force his father represents. The boy's anxiety is created by his awakening sense of his own individuality. Torn between strong emotional attachment to the parent and his growing need to assert his own identity, Sarty's crisis is psychological and his battle is being waged far below the level of his intellectual and moral awareness.

Faulkner makes this clear in the opening scene with imagery that might be described as synesthesia. The real smell of cheese is linked with the smell of the hermetic meat in the tin cans with the scarlet devils on the label that his "intestines believed he smelled coming in intermittent gusts momentary and brief between the other constant one, the smell and sense just a little of fear because mostly of despair and grief, the old fierce pull of blood." (3) The smells below the level of the olfactory sense link the devil image and the blood image to identify the anxiety the father creates in the child's psyche. Tension is created by the blood demanding identification with his father against "*our enemy* he thought in that despair; *ourn! mine and hisn both! He's my father!*" (3) Sarty's conflict is played out in terms of identification, not in moral terms. He does not think of his father as bad, his father's enemies as good.

Faulkner develops his story on two levels of consciousness. He employs an adult narrator to translate the boy's tensions and interpret the moral significance of his anxiety. But the dramatic scenes, the characters and situations are objectifications, as in a nightmare, of the boy's psychological and emotional tensions. In the carpet-cleaning scene, for example, Sarty's dread of his father and his fear of the consequences of Ab's treatment of the rug give rise to a tableau as eerie as the opening scene of *Macbeth*. The child works at the woodpile, covertly watching his two bovine, weird sisters minister over the bubbling lye-filled pot. Over them stands the rigid black-suited figure of the father. The child's sense of despair and helplessness against the implacable force of the father is projected in the figure of the mother, appearing momentarily in the doorway, her face and eyes filled with despair.

Sarty's anxiety cannot be viewed simply as an Oedipal identification with the mother against the father. On the wagon, he repulses his mother. His eyes are focused upon his father striking the mules. In all the scenes, the mother remains a peripheral figure in the boy's consciousness. Like the stopped hands of the inlaid clock which was her dowry, the mother is a figure without life or power. In contrast, the image of the father, always in rigid black, looms in his consciousness as a terrifying, threatening force. The physical descriptions Faulkner provides us of Ab are always presented through the eyes of the boy. Blackness, metallic imagery, cold violence dominate these descriptions.

In the second major scene, Ab leads Sarty up the slope away from the family at the campfire. The child looks up at the towering figure of his father "against the stars but without face or depth—a shape black, flat, and bloodless as though cut from tin in the iron folds of the frockcoat." (8) Ab strikes his son on the side of the head "hard without heat, exactly as he had struck the two mules at the store, exactly as he would strike either of them with any stick in order to kill a horsefly." (8) These images of cold violence and indifference to inflicted pain convey the child's sense of his father's emotional frigidity. Ab's cold violence is not an expression of hatred or anger. Violence is a tool, used upon his son as upon the mules—to make them do his bidding.

Ab unjustly accuses Sarty of intending to betray him at the hearing, but he correctly recognizes that his son is moving out of childhood, developing a mind and will of his own and is no longer blindly loyal. In instructing the boy that everyone is the enemy and his loyalty belongs to his blood, Ab's phrasing is revealing: " 'Don't you know all they wanted was a chance to get at me because they knew I had them beat?' " (8) Ab does not use the plural "us." It is "I" and "they." Blood loyalty means total identification with Ab, and in the ensuing scenes, Snopes attempts to make his son an extension of himself by taking him to the De Spain house, rise up before dawn to be with him when he returns the rug, accompany him to the hearing against De Spain and finally make him an accomplice in the burning of De Spain's barn.

The moral import of Ab's insistence on blood loyalty is fully developed by the satanic imagery Faulkner introduces in the scene at the mansion. As they go up the drive, Sarty follows his father, seeing the stiff black form against the white plantation house. Traditionally the devil casts no shadow, and Ab's figure appears to the child as having "that impervious quality of something cut ruthlessly from tin, depthless, as though sidewise to the sun it would cast no shadow." (10) The cloven hoof of the devil is suggested by Ab's limp upon which the boy's eyes are fixed as the foot unwaveringly comes down into the manure. Sarty's increasing tension resounds in the magnified echo of the limping foot on the porch boards, "a sound out of all proportion to the displacement of the body it bore, as though it had attained to a sort of vicious and ravening minimum not to be dwarfed by anything." (11) At first Sarty thought the house was impervious to his father, but his burgeoning fear of the threat the father poses is reflected in his vision of Ab becoming magnified and monstrous as the black arm reaches up the white door and Sarty sees "the lifted hand like a curled claw." (11)

The satanic images are projected out of the son's nightmarish vision of his father, but they are reinforced by the comments of the adult narrator. Sarty believes Snopes fought bravely in the Civil War, but Ab, we are told, wore no uniform, gave his fealty to no cause, admitted the authority of no man. He went to war for booty. Ab's ego is so great it creates a centripetal force into which everything must flow or be destroyed. The will-less, abject creature who is his wife symbolizes the power of his will. What Ab had done to his wife, he sets out to do to the emerging will of his son. Ab cannot tolerate any entity that challenges the dominance of his will. By allowing his hog to forage in the farmer's corn and by dirtying and ruining De Spain's rug, he deliberately creates a conflict that requires the assertion of primacy. Fire, the element of the devil, is the weapon for the preservation of his dominance. Ab's rage is not fired by social injustice. It is fired by a pride, like Lucifer's, so absolute it can accept no order beyond its own. In the satanic myth, Lucifer asserts his will against the divine order and is cast out of heaven. The angels who fall with Lucifer become extensions of his will. In the same way, Ab is an outcast and pariah among men. He accepts no order that is not of his blood.

All centripetal will, Snopes can have no feeling for any other being. He is incapable of recognizing what Faulkner in *Absalom, Absalom!* describes as each person's sense of self, the "I Am" of his being. In the crucial scene on the slope, the narrator interprets

Sarty's resistance to his father's description of "they" as the enemy: "Later, twenty years later, he was to tell himself, 'If I had said they wanted only truth, justice, he would have hit me again.' " (8) Sarty's resistance constitutes a recognition of an entity beyond his father, a correlative of his own emerging sense of individuality. The truth and justice "they" the enemy want is nothing more than acknowledgment of their rights as individual entities. Ab would have hit Sarty again because such a statement would have been a challenge to Ab's will, identical with the challenge of the enemy. The "they" referred to in this passage are simple farmers, not aristocrats. Sarty is struggling to be himself. He responds with such intensity to the sight of De Spain's house not because it corresponds to some innate moral sense but because he sees it as an entity, powerful and completely isolated from his father's will. The mansion makes him forget "his father and the terror and despair both." (10) The surge of joy has the effect of diminishing the terrifying image of Ab to little more than a "buzzing wasp." The "they" who belong to the house he feels certain, must be safe from his father, their barns "impervious to the puny flames he might contrive." (10)

In the ensuing scenes, Ab moves inexorably to a collision with De Spain that must terminate in barn burning. Sarty's increasing anxiety as he watches Ab respond to the challenge De Spain represents corresponds to the escalating threat to his own identity that Ab poses as he forces the boy to submit to the pull of blood by making him his accomplice. When De Spain fines Snopes an extra twenty bushels, Sarty tries to stave off the barn burning by insisting to Ab that they will not pay. He will hide the bushels. Sarty's daydreams express a hope that somehow his father will change. In the field plowing, his bare feet in the rich soil, he dreams that Ab has accepted the fine. Acceptance would mean that Ab has acknowledged the integrity of an order beyond his own and is willing to live with it rather than striking out with his destructive violence. If that were true, if his father were indeed changed, then the boy's own terror and grief would be at an end, the *"being pulled two ways like between two teams of horses"* (17) would cease.

At the hearing of Ab's suit against De Spain, the boy momentarily feels defiant and even exultant. He believes his father is charged with barn burning, and Sarty knows Ab is innocent. His cry, protesting his father's innocence, expresses the desperate hope that Ab's innocence is proof that he has changed. The fear and terror immediately return. Ab's suit, Sarty recognizes, is an assertion of will that must end in barn burning. After the hearing, the child again insists to his father that they do not have to pay even the ten bushels. Ab's statement that they will wait until October to see what happens lulls the child's anxiety and the following scene has the quality of an idyll. For the first time, Ab appears human. The terrifying images of rigidity and blackness are gone. The boy listens to his father telling a story at the blacksmith's. At lunch, Ab divides the food with his two sons. During the slow afternoon they loiter along a fence watching the horse trading.

This peaceful interlude ends abruptly that evening with the mother's anguished cry. Again, Sarty sees the figure of his father stiff in the black suit "as though dressed carefully for some shabby and ceremonial violence." (20) When Ab orders him to get the oil from the barn, Sarty responds to the pull of blood, at the same time dreaming of running away and never returning. But he does return. When he dares, for the first time, to express opposition to his father, he is made a prisoner. The scene is right out of a child's nightmare. Ab grabs Sarty by the back of the shirt and holds him helpless with just his toes touching the floor, thrusting him into the bedroom and ordering the boy's mother to hold him. Ab will not allow the aunt to hold the struggling child. Sarty must fight free of the grasp of Ab's surrogate, the terrified creature whose will has become an extension of Ab's. By warning De Spain, Sarty identifies himself with an entity other than his father, and only by violating his blood does he gain his freedom. Whether Ab is actually killed we do not know. The detail is unimportant. For Sarty, Ab is dead. Significantly, the boy feels grief but no guilt. He has destroyed the crushing force that threatened his awakening identity and, at last, the fear and terror are gone. His nightmare ended, Sarty, appropriately, falls into a dreamless sleep, from which he awakens whole and at peace, ready for the future.

Throughout Faulkner's fiction, the crimes people inflict upon their fellow men derive from gradations of the inhumane ego-blindness that achieves its apotheosis in the satanic Ab Snopes of "Barn Burning." One of Faulkner's primary interests is in exploring the complex combinations of social and psychological forces that produce blindness to the individuality and rights of others. One of his major preoccupations, for instance, is the psychological and moral impact of such social concepts as white supremacy. The insensitivity to the equal humanity of others that such an abstraction produces is explored with great dramatic power in *Absalom, Absalom!* The central figure in that novel is Thomas Sutpen, whose imperious will is almost as destructive and powerful as that of Ab Snopes. Sutpen's will is harnessed to his grand design which is a synthesis of the myths, codes, and aspirations of Southern society. In contrast to Ab, whose will is absolute, a given, operating for and of itself, Sutpen's is exercised for a purpose and has its roots in humanly identifiable psychological and social forces. The effects, however, are the same. Sutpen leaves in his wake numbers of violated, mutilated egos, the way Snopes leaves the ashes of burned barns. In Sutpen's history of insensitivity is reflected the crime of the South—the blindness of white Southerners to the humanity of the blacks.

The many grotesques who populate Yoknapatawpha county are frequently victims of the kind of psychological tyranny that threatens Sarty or they are victims of rigid religious and social concepts that warp their personalities and turn them into obsessed creatures, incapable of acknowledging the individuality of their fellow human beings. The victim becomes the violator; the sins of the father are visited upon the children, and evil remains a constant in the history of mankind. The antithesis to the implacable satanic will that finds its avatar in Ab Snopes is Faulkner's code of the heart—a sensitivity to others that amounts to empathy. The young hero who articulates that code and attempts to practice it is Ike McCaslin in "The Bear" of *Go Down, Moses*, which was published a few years after "Barn Burning." Ike's conflict with his heritage has strong affinities with Sarty's battle to free himself from the crushing force of his father's will. Ike also battled the fierce pull of blood, blood which taints him with the sins of his fathers. In the woods, Ike discovers his natural self, his individual being, and at twenty-one, he attempts to cut himself off from his social heritage by renouncing his patrimony. In effect, Ike duplicates Sarty's act in killing his father to gain his moral freedom. Ike sees himself as the new Adam, but Faulkner recognizes him as only human. The old fierce pull of blood is too strong. Ultimately, Ike fails. He re-enacts the sin of his fathers by rejecting a girl with black blood. The new Adam is not born in Faulkner's fiction.

Intruder in the Dust: *A Re-evaluation*

by

Patrick Samway, S. J.

In 1955, in Japan, William Faulkner said that a writer is not really writing about his social and cultural environment, but that he is telling a story about human beings in terms of that environment and thus any work must reflect the background out of which it emerges.[1] If a writer tells a story to explore the sociological background, then he is writing propaganda. The novelist is concerned with people, with man in conflict with himself, and in this way with his environment. In the same year in Manila, Faulkner enlarged on his conception of the task of the writer, using some of the ideas he had previously expressed in his Nobel Prize speech:

> The writer must believe always in people, in freedom; he must believe that man must be free in order to create the art; and art is in my opinion one of the most important factors in human life because it has . . . been the record of man's rise from his beginnings. It is the writer's duty to show that man has an immortal soul.[2]

Thus Faulkner took his art seriously and did not use the novel form, as Dos Passos often did, as a channel for political thought. When he wanted to express himself politically, he wrote letters, short treatises, or essays which would deal specifically with civil rights problems.

Faulkner's overall approach to civil rights was moderate, too moderate for James Baldwin, who maintained "it is easy enough to state flatly that Faulkner's middle of the road does not—cannot—exist and that he is guilty of great emotional and intellectual dishonesty in pretending that it does."[3] Faulkner repeatedly said that the race problem was basically an economic problem and that children of both races normally feel free to intermingle: "It's only when the child becomes a middle-aged man and becomes a part of the economy that latent quality [of prejudice] appears."[4] He said that he opposed any evils in the South that would perpetuate segregation and, at the same time, he opposed forces from outside the South which would use legal or police compulsion to eradicate the evils overnight. He was against compulsory segregation in much the same way he was against compulsory integration. The Northerners, according to Faulkner, really know little about the South; they have a popular image of decadent people who through inbreeding and illiteracy are a kind of juvenile delinquent with a folklore of blood and violence.[5] He believed that the races should mix in order to preserve their freedom:

> And if we who are still free want to continue so, all of us who are still free had better confederate and confederate fast with all others who still have a choice to be free—confederate not as black people nor white people nor blue or pink or green people, but as people who are still free, with all other people who are still free; confederate together too, if we want a world or even a part of a world in which individual man can be free, to continue to endure.[6]

Writing for *Ebony*, Faulkner said that if he were a Negro he would want his fellow blacks to be "inflexibly flexible" and build on the decency and patience that have been part of their heritage for over three hundred years.[7] Patience is not a passive quality, but an active weapon which can bring about peaceful unity.

Faulkner's novel *Intruder in the Dust* concerns race relations in the South and it is often thought that one of the main characters, Gavin Stevens, represents Faulkner's views. In an oblique way, Faulkner addressed himself to the problem of whether or not one should regard Gavin as his spokesman on one of the typescript pages of the original draft:

> These characters and incidents are fictional, imaginative, and—some will say—impossible. In which case let them be accepted not as the puppet-play of a whodunit but as the protagonist pattern of a belief that not government first but the white man of the South owes a responsibility to the Negro, not because of his past since a man or a race if it be any good can survive his past without having to escape from it (and the fact that the Negro has survived him in the way he has is his proof) but because of his present condition, whether the Negro wishes it or not.

Faulkner saw *Intruder* as involving fiction and morality; the focus is on the white man's obligation to the Negro because of the Negro's present condition. If the work were solely a racial tract, however, then there might be some justification for the identity of Gavin and Faulkner. But, why would Faulkner want such a bewildering spokesman when he proved that he could be quite effective by himself? If Gavin were Faulkner's spokesman, then one would also expect that he dramatize Faulkner's views as well as articulate them. Yet, little or nothing in Joseph Blotner's biography of Faulkner even suggests that Gavin's experiences parallel any of Faulkner's. In fact, Faulkner was critical of Gavin and believed as an amateur Sherlock Holmes he was out of his depth.

In a review of Erich Maria Remarque's book, *The Road Back*, Faulkner wrote something about character study that might well apply to Gavin:

> It is a writer's privilege to put into the mouths of his characters better speech than they would have been capable of, but only for the purpose of permitting and helping the character to justify himself or what he believes himself to be, taking down his spiritual pants. But when the character must express moral ideas applicable to a race, a situation, he is better kept in that untimed and unsexed background of the choruses of Greek senators.[8]

As Faulkner hinted to Malcolm Cowley, Gavin assumes center stage in the last third of the novel and becomes the South's, not Faulkner's, liberal spokesman.[9] Though Chick listens to Gavin's words, he does not, as Olga Vickery maintains, "accept all Gavin's ideas as he occasions their transmutation into an acceptable form which can encompass both their angles of vision, the idealist and the realist."[10] While it cannot be denied that some of Gavin's views are close to those articulated by Faulkner, Gavin never strays from being a fictional, dramatic character. If anything, Faulkner satirizes Gavin as the Southern spokesman.

Gavin firmly believes, as does the larger Jefferson community, that Lucas Beauchamp is guilty of killing Vinson Gowrie; he is perplexed as to why Lucas had to shoot a Gowrie of all people. When Gavin and Chick Mallison walk into town the evening after the murder, Gavin discusses the simple ways of the country people. He notes they move into town to be close to human activity and rarely question life's deeper realities; in his opinion, a vocabulary of clichés often sustains them. When they meet Mr. Lilley, the representative *par excellence* of the town, Gavin interprets Mr. Lilley's philosophical stance to Chick: "He has nothing against what he calls niggers. If you ask him, he will probably tell you he likes them even better than some white folks he knows and he will believe it."[11] As a store owner, Mr. Lilley knows that Negroes steal small items occasionally and all he requires is that they continue to act like niggers, a position which paraphrases an earlier comment by Chick regarding Lucas: "They're going to make a nigger out of him once in his life anyway" (p. 32). Like Gavin, Mr. Lilley has no doubts about Lucas' guilt; yet he harbors no ill feelings towards Lucas and would probably contribute money to help pay his funeral expenses. Gavin seems to understand Mr. Lilley's position so well that he accepts it and makes no overt criticism about it.

Gavin is presented not as a man with shrewd insight or a penetrating philosophy and he brings no real sense of history to the racial problems he discusses. When confronting Lucas in the jail cell, he intimidates Lucas by constantly proclaiming Lucas' guilt. He reflects, too, Mr. Tubbs' position when Tubbs says he has a wife and two children and though he is the jailer, he does not want to get into a middle position between Lucas and the Gowries. Mr. Tubbs believes a quick lynching might have solved the problem. As a lawyer, Gavin is clear about his position: "I dont defend murderers who shoot people in the back . . ." (p. 60). On the other hand he admits, just by going to the cell, that he has taken the case, one that will be quickly expedited. Gavin wavers a little at the beginning, a sign, perhaps, that his words do not convey all that he thinks about Lucas.

When Gavin finally allows Lucas to talk about the murder, he interrupts him on a point of protocol, chastising him for not referring to a white man by a proper title. With laconic wit, Lucas responds by questioning whether he is to call each Gowrie "Mister" as they drag him out of the jail. Gavin does not really accept Lucas' version about Vinson Gowrie and another man storing lumber in order to later haul it away; he prefers to believe that Lucas called Vinson into the woods, told Vinson about the stealing, was called a liar, and then shot Vinson in the back. Lucas pleads that he has no friends; he wants to hire Gavin as a lawyer and not accept his services for free. In his haste, Gavin would even like to forget about buying tobacco for Lucas, something that Chick is more hesitant to do. Faulkner has clearly demonstrated the positions of the opposing forces and just as he dealt with triune forces in *A Fable*, so too, he is beginning to show three views here in the jail cell.

Later in Gavin's office, Gavin remains unyielding and even suggests, in an off-hand way, that Lucas was actually shooting a tin can or a mark on a tree. He does not realize how close to the truth he is. Gavin cannot take the risk of going out and digging up Gowrie's grave; he feels secure in knowing that Lucas is locked up in jail. Chick tries to argue with Gavin, as Lucas did previously, and gradually fathoms the meaning of words and vocabulary as he confronts Gavin on Gavin's level; Chick knows his uncle's voice is filled with "significantless speciosity." This knowledge is a turning point for Chick and he does not really consult with Gavin again until after Gowrie's grave has been dug up. Only after the exhumation, not before as in the case of Chick, does Gavin change his stance; he admits that truth often comes out "of the mouths of babes and sucklings and old ladies—" (p. 106). Gavin even exerts some leadership by suggesting that the strategy they use should include driving to Harrisburg and consulting with the District Attorney. And he encourages Miss Habersham to sit by the entrance to the jail so she can be seen by the townsfolk and help ward off any trouble.

It is only after Gavin has dropped Miss Habersham off at the jail that he begins to get closer to Chick, although Chick is aware of his "naive and childlike rationalising" (p. 122). Chick hopes that Gavin will not side with his mother and when Chick finally utters at the hopelessness of the situation, "You're just my uncle," Gavin replies he is worse than that, "I'm just a man" (p. 122). Gavin knows after Montgomery's body is discovered, it "took an old woman and two children . . . to believe truth . . . told by an old man in a fix deserving pity and belief, to someone capable of the pity even when none of them really believed him" (p. 126). Once this new relationship with Chick has been established, Gavin delivers his reflections on the place of the Negro in the South as he drives out to the graveyard with Chick on May 9th.

Gavin's ultimate philosophical conclusion comes at the end of the novel (with an interesting comment on Lucas' crucifixion [also mentioned earlier on page 138] especially in light of the Christ-motif Faulkner was developing in *A Fable*):

... Lucas' life the breathing and eating and sleeping is of
no importance just as yours and mine are not but his unchal-
lengeable right to it in peace and security and in fact this earth
would be much more comfortable with a good deal fewer
Beauchamps and Stevenses and Mallisons of all colors in it if
there were only some painless way to efface not the clumsy
room-devouring carcasses which can be done but the memory
which cannot—that inevictible immortal memory awareness of
having once been alive which exists forever still ten thousand
years afterward in ten thousand recollections of injustice and
suffering, too many of us not because of the room we take up
but because we are willing to sell liberty short at any tawdry
price for the sake of what we call our own which is a consti-
tutional statutory license to pursue each his private postulate
of happiness and contentment regardless of grief and cost even
to the crucifixion of someone whose nose or pigment we
dont like and even these can be coped with provided that
few of others who believe that a human life is valuable simply
because it has a right to keep on breathing no matter what
pigment its lungs distend or nose inhales the air and are willing
to defend that right at any price, it doesn't take many three
were enough last Sunday night even one can be enough and
with enough ones willing to be more than grieved and shamed
Lucas will no longer run the risk of needing without warning to
be saved. ... (pp. 243-244)

Just as Gavin is convinced that solipsism and extreme forms of personal solitude will not advance the cause of civil rights, he knows
that three people are enough to start the process of justice and re-
store belief in the dignity of human life. Unfortunately, Gavin does
not sustain his philosophical mood, but resumes by treating Lucas in
a much lighter vein, almost, many critics believe, as if he were a
stereotype. To seek a resolution, one where the emotional and
psychological energies can be submerged for a while, Gavin willingly
meets Lucas half-way and puts the emphasis on the correct fee that
Lucas owes him. Lucas had taught Chick that one does not pay for
hospitality and here Lucas teaches Gavin and Chick that one does
pay his legitimate debts especially when the concerned parties have
entered into a contractual relationship. Thus, this novel has a type of
resolution, hinting that in microcosm the race problems can be adequately dealt with, something that Faulkner had not achieved in his
earlier novels.

Though Gavin presents a rather persuasive conclusion to his
argument concerning the future of the civil rights movement in the

South, he has an unfortunate start by characterizing Lucas and the other blacks in the South as "Sambo." Gavin never speaks in a derogatory manner about Sambo; in fact, he is very much aware of the Negro's racial heritage and part of Gavin's philosophy is to build a solid interracial society based partly on the positive qualities and attributes Negroes have exhibited over the decades. The main problem is not Gavin's Sambo-slur, but his level of abstraction rooted neither in first principles nor in the immediate experience of Chick or the other characters in the novel. No common denominator is achieved in attempting to communicate his views and this undercuts the effectiveness of his pronouncements.

Gavin's views are centered on his contention that New England and the South are the two regions in this country where homogeneous people live. The Negro, he adds, possesses this homogeneity, too, though Gavin does not predicate this initially. At least in the South, the blacks and whites should confederate and the white man should swap with the Negro "the rest of the economic and political and cultural privileges which are his right, for the reversion of his capacity to wait and endure and survive" (p. 156). In addition the South should continue to defend its homogeneity from any interference by the federal government because only in homogeneity is there anything of lasting value. The South must defend the ultimate privilege of setting Sambo free. The chronicle of man's immortality is deep within his capacity to suffer and endure and reach out towards the stars. Integration will take time and the white Southerners will have to ask the blacks to exercise more patience until it is achieved. Once a more comprehensive homogeneity exists, then "we would dominate the United States," Gavin believes (p. 156). Gavin leaves the exact nature of this homogeneity unspecified both in the original draft and the setting copy. Likewise, he fails to develop the specific bonds of unity or the values that will be shared by the blacks and the whites in both the North and the South.

The key concept in Gavin's philosophy is his belief in "the divinity of his continuity as Man" (p. 202). The human race must continue to explore its own dynamic and spiritual resources in order to move intelligently into the future. Gavin sees the opposite of what he believes in, when the townsfolk repudiate Crawford Gowrie and deprive him of the full extent of his citizenship in the human race. Gavin is committed to defend Sambo from "the outlanders who will fling him decades back not merely to injustice but into grief and agony and violence too by forcing on us laws based on the idea that man's injustice to man can be abolished overnight by police" (pp.

203-204). The South must expiate the injustice it has caused and this
is something due the blacks whether they want it or not. Gavin in-
structs Chick that there are some things he must always be unable to
bear, such as injustice, outrage, dishonor, and shame. Though Chick
responds to Gavin's instructions by saying that he has not been a
Tenderfoot scout for four years, Gavin remonstrates with a highly
ambiguous, "But just regret it, dont be ashamed" (p. 206).
According to Gavin, the Southerners are in the position like the Ger-
mans after 1933 who were either a Jew or a Nazi or like the Russians
who are either a Communist or dead; like true soldiers they must defend the Lucas-Sambos even if their numbers are small. Just as there
might not be one in a thousand who would grieve for Sambo nor, on
the other hand, be the first to lynch him either, yet all thousand
would stop outside interference. Gavin's view of Sambo is not limited to the South; Sambo exists in Chicago, Detroit, Los Angeles and
is the recipient of many forms of racial prejudice. As is clear, Gavin's
wisdom borders, at times, on impressionistic opacity; yet he is
Chick's mentor and provides a definite personality against which
Chick can appreciate his own nascent philosophical positions.

The novel, however, does not stem from Gavin or his beliefs;
its main concern is the interaction of the characters as they help to
solve Lucas' problem and bring about a viable awareness of justice in
Jefferson. Gavin's philosophy does not save Lucas; it is the courageous act of an old woman and two boys that does this. Alex Sander, as Chick's companion, provides Chick with a friend who shares
with him his childhood experiences. Chick is not entering into a
racial situation totally unprepared; he has eaten at Paralee's house
and is familiar with the Ephraim story which made a deep impression
on him. This story becomes one of the cohesive forces within the
novel. Part of the growth that Chick goes through is to understand
Ephraim's words: "Young folks and womens, they aint cluttered.
They can listen. But a middle-year man like your paw and your
uncle, they cant listen. They aint got time. They're too busy with
facks" (p. 71). While Lucas can be regarded as a symbol of the new
South, Alex Sander is definitely a stereotyped black boy, an interpretation made clear by Clarence Brown in the film of this novel, especially in the gravedigging scene where Alex Sander's eyes pop wide
open with marvelous fear. Yet Alex Sander is credited as being one
of the detectives by Sheriff Hampton and is praised for what he does;
he admits that no one forced him to go though, ironically, he was
not quite sure of the purpose of the mission. Alex Sander's presence,
therefore, makes Chick's action more plausible because Chick not

only has grown up with blacks but he is accompanied by a black friend out to the graveyard.

The two women in the novel, Mrs. Mallison and Miss Habersham, take a more active part in the novel than does Alex Sander. Mrs. Mallison, Faulkner's typical mother, is over-protective and unduly concerned with family routines. While she constantly nags Gavin about his driving abilities and argues with her husband about whether Chick should drink coffee or not at his age, Chick regards her as "a hundred times less noisy than his father and a thousand times more valuable . . ." (p. 208). Chick focuses his attention on his mother at those times when he is tired and near sleep and is particularly sensitive to his mother's touch: "He had had it long enough, even rolling his head but about as much chance to escape that one frail narrow inevictible palm as to roll your forehead out from under a birthmark . . ." (p. 191). When Chick tries to interpret the meaning of the expedition to the graveyard, in terms of his past experience, he thinks both of the time two years before when he went to Mottstown and secretly his mother came to take him home in a hired car after he had hurt his arm, and the time when he jumped Highboy over a concrete water trough. Mrs. Mallison does not lament these past situations nor complain of imaginary ailments like Mrs. Compson in *The Sound and the Fury*; rather she is outspoken in her solicitude for Chick and does not hamper his growth. She supports him in a way that Gavin or Lucas really cannot. Mrs. Mallison is a more competent parent than her husband and is even willing to encounter a certain risk by joining Miss Habersham at the jail.

Miss Habersham, on the other hand, is a far more interesting character because her actions are so atypical of a woman over sixty (Faulkner at various times in the original draft and setting copy placed her age from sixty to eighty). She comes from an old family: Doctor Habersham and two companions came to Jefferson when it was a Chickasaw trading post. Kenneth Richardson believes Miss Habersham has "the insights of a matriarch who is willing to cross mores in order to reveal the truth."[12] Faulkner treats her sympathetically and she reflects something he once said, that he liked to think of a young man as having an aunt or neighbor to listen to because they were often more sensible than men.[13] In her Sears Roebuck catalogue dresses and her expensive New York shoes, Miss Habersham apparently leads a very ordinary life selling chickens and vegetables which she raises and peddles about town in her pickup truck. Faulkner had originally contemplated using a farmer to visit

Gavin on Sunday evening, but he changed to Miss Habersham, perhaps to bring out the ironic contrasts between old/young, black man/
white woman, expected behavior/unusual behavior. Miss Habersham,
the prime instigator in helping Lucas, is more than willing to risk
ostracism by the town even though she does not know fully the
events surrounding Vinson Gowrie's death. Yet she is fully aware
that her age and sex are in her favor and that if the whole enterprise
proves to be a mistake, she would be excused as a dottering old
woman—a situation the sheriff understands when he allows her to
guard the jail.

Miss Habersham's wisdom is not wrapped in abstract thought
or propositions though she can make penetrating distinctions as, for
example, when she tells Chick, "Of course. Naturally he wouldn't tell
your uncle. He's a Negro and your uncle's a man" (p. 89). Chick
knows, too, that it is not the paucity of Miss Habersham's vocabulary
that causes her to say this, but that in her own way she is paraphras-
ing simple truth, something that Lucas and Ephraim, each in his
own way, had realized too. Miss Habersham organizes the trip to the
cemetery with dispatch and once there she has no qualms about
opening up the grave. Her focus is on essentials. When the three
detectives hasten to the sheriff's house to tell him the body-switch,
she reminds the sheriff that they should remember Lucas in everything they do, even though he is not physically present.

She also suggests that they call the district attorney in Harrisburg for permission to exhume Montgomery's body and that they
should do everything quickly, not waiting for daylight. When Chick
envisions Miss Habersham returning home a half-mile from town to
her house, he sees her in motion, as venturing into Crossman, Mott,
and Okatoba counties knowing that the best way to go around an
obstruction is to just go around it, just as she knew that the most
logical way to recover a corpse is to dig up the grave. In his discussion of the oral tradition in Mississippi, Calvin Brown sees this projection of Miss Habersham riding around the country with restless
energy as having the ingredients of a tall tale.[14] Like an insect caught
on a spinning record, Miss Habersham gathers imagined momentum
in her journey until she finally admits to a man in a nightshirt, "*I had
to detour around an arrogant insufferable old nigger who got the
whole county upset trying to pretend he murdered a white man*" (p.
189). In all, Miss Habersham adds a touch of practical gentility, as if
she stepped out of an old English murder mystery that Faulkner had
read. She is effective without being overbearing and perceptive without being pedantic. At the end of the novel Gavin appreciates what

she has done and cajoles a reluctant Lucas into taking flowers to her
to show his gratitude.

The individuals in this novel such as Gavin and Miss Habersham are contrasted with the Gowries, the townsfolk, and the inhabitants of the various beats who have come to witness what happens to Lucas. As a backward, country family, the Gowries are
close-knit, unreflective, and in their own way as much a part of the
mentality of Yoknapatawpha as the McCaslins are. They represent
the clannish, ultra-conservative position in the South and are willing
to convict Lucas without due process of law because their law is
more basic and swifter. The six sons, described in some detail with
the eldest being named after General Nathan Bedford Forrest and the
twins, Bilbo and Vardaman, named after famous Mississippi politicians, just by their numbers show the power they hold in this
story.[15] Yet, Faulkner portrays the twins as moving and looking like
clothing store dummies. Though the Gowries as a unit outnumber
any of the other families mentioned, their presence is summed up in
the person of their father, Nub, who retains sole power and is considered by Faulkner to be a judge in making family decisions.
Though physically impaired, Nub has the independence and strength
one would expect of a descendent of the Scottish highlands. As Elmo
Howell notes, the Gowries represent an ambivalent feeling in Faulkner's attitude towards his county: "He loves it in spite of its faults,
recognizing even in Gowrie's violence an element of character, of
manhood, which seems to be disappearing in mass society. . . ."[16] As
men move into the South and the natives are forced into the outer
reaches of Mississippi, some of the frontier ideal is lost, and the ver-
bose Gavins tend to replace the rugged Nubs.

Nub Gowrie obstinately refuses to permit the exhumation of
his son, but once he is convinced of the plausibility of foul play, he
quickly orders the grave to be reopened. During these moments of
decision, Chick notices that Nub is grieving, as Lucas had done after
Molly died, thus establishing a sympathetic bond between these two
men and their mutual problems. It is at this point, and not necessarily at the end of the novel, that the reader realizes the possibility of
an integrated society based on a common humanity. Later, once
Montgomery's body had been discovered in a shallow grave, Nub
goes berserk and jumps on Vinson's body, now hidden beneath some
quicksand. The moment of truth has come: Lucas did not kill Montgomery because he was in jail at the time of Montgomery's death. A
third party is involved, one who knew both Vinson and Jake Montgomery and who also possesses a gun. Nub Gowrie realizes the fallacy

of continuing to maintain Lucas' guilt and orders his sons to take Vinson's body home.

At this point, the clues begin to mount up: the reader knows that Crawford has an automatic German pistol and that he had been dealing in lumber. Crawford is the only real suspect and before long Gavin has managed to pull together the various threads of the murders mainly with Lucas' help. Jake Montgomery had been buying lumber from Crawford who, with his brother, was under contract to Mr. Sudley. Because Crawford was stealing lumber and there was a possibility Vinson would learn this, Crawford killed Vinson. To indict Crawford, Montgomery dug up Vinson's body with the idea of taking it to the sheriff. But Crawford intervened, killed Jake, put his body in Vinson's grave instead, and finally took Vinson's body down to the quicksand. He is seen in the dark by Miss Habersham and the two boys in the process. Once Chick and his two companions discover Jake's body, Crawford, having also observed the three detectives, digs up Jake's body and places it in a shallow grave. Because he is never really seen, except obscurely at night, Crawford takes on a symbolic identity; he is never developed as a full character. The reader does not dramatically understand the problems he faces nor appreciate his motive for killing two men.

As Miss Habersham instinctively knows, the primary focus of the novel is not on the Gowries but on Lucas, though in the drama of the story he remains relatively passive. Because of this, his character takes on a different perspective; he is in some way a representative of his race and it is more on this symbolic level that the Crawford-Lucas dimension of the story is felt. While Lucas is the catalyst, the focal point is really on the Chick-Lucas relationship and the growth in Chick as he attempts to understand the fulness of this relationship. Viewed this way, the novel can be divided into three segments. Chapters One-Three concern establishing the Chick-Lucas relationship and providing sufficient motivation for Chick to help Lucas; Chapters Four-Eight concern the mystery plot of going out to the cemetery and discovering that Lucas is innocent, at least of killing Montgomery; Chapters Nine-Eleven concern Gavin's philosophical beliefs in the civil rights movement in the South and Chick's further realization of his own commitment to his community and country, especially when he sees the town's reaction to fratricide. The middle five chapters have little stylistic complexity, unlike the flashbacks of the first few chapters and the reveries and philosophical interludes of the last three chapters. It is particularly in the first three and last three chapters that the Lucas-Chick relationship is important.

Because Lucas knows that he is related to the white side of the McCaslin family (his mannerism and speech constantly remind the townsfolk of Jefferson of this), he does not have the identity problems of a Charles Bon or a Joe Christmas because he is proud of his mixed blood. When a townsman in a fit of rage calls, "You goddamn biggity stiffnecked stinking burrheaded Edmonds sonofabitch," Lucas immediately isolates the operative word, "I belongs to the old lot. I'm a McCaslin" (p. 19). As a forthright man, Lucas will not let others stereotype him or lessen his own self-image. Dorothy Greer says in Faulkner's works it is the Negro's attitude, based on many influences, plus the antagonism and prejudices of the white man that make him what he is and give him his ability to withstand circumstances beyond his own making: "The [Negro] race is a Lucas Beauchamp on trial for its life defended by law, and rising with courage and dignity better than the white man in the same situation could muster, calm, stoical, independent."[17] Other blacks do not really associate with Lucas; even Alex Sander does not have that personal relationship that might be expected of a black boy helping a black man. The other blacks remain behind closed doors afraid to venture an opinion or show Lucas some sign of support. Graphically, Lucas, in jail, is surrounded by whites who flow in and out of town; the blacks are there, they are just not visible. Indifferent to the established town customs, Lucas has thus incurred the wrath and hatred of the town; he threatens the very roots of Jefferson's society and though he has not done something like rape a white woman, the townsfolk and inhabitants of Beat Four overact because of their hatred for him.

Though Robert Jacobs maintains that the Lucas-Chick relationship is based on family ties, there is no real evidence for this.[18] Rather Faulkner has been sympathetic to Negroes in his writings as he himself admitted: "He [the Negro] does more with less than anybody else."[19] In 1955 at Nagano, Faulkner said that Lucas was doomed because of his black blood but there was a chance he could be saved: "Anyone can save anyone from injustice if he just will, if he just tries, just raises his voice."[20] With Lucas in the limelight, Faulkner reveals the tensions within this Southern community, not recording in a morbid way its demise, but through references to baptism and crucifixion he dramatizes a story of potential civic regeneration and resurrection, motifs that were definitely on his mind while writing *A Fable:*[21]

Though Joseph Blotner mentions three possible men who

might have served as models, Lucas seems to transcend any biograph-
ical figure because most of the time he is sitting in jail and not interacting with others.[22] He lives on the ten acres of land ("like a postage stamp in the center of an envelope" [p. 8]) he has inherited.[23]
Lucas suggests a figure in a Greek tragedy; his house on the hill resembles the carven ailanthus leaves of the capital of a column. There
is also something essentially primitive and antediluvian about this
domestic scene; the cryptic three-toed prints of the chickens are out
of the age of the great lizards. Thus Lucas is no ordinary person; he
bridges the past and the present and, in terms of the drama of this
story, looks forward to a future age. When Chick sees Lucas, in the
first part of the story, he looks at him as he emerges from the icy
creek and sees Lucas' face manifesting "no pigment at all, not even
the white man's lack of it, not arrogant, not even scornful: just intractable and composed" (p. 7). Chick does not hesitate at first to
follow Lucas to Lucas' house though he feels an impulse to turn into
Edmonds' house. As a gracious host, Lucas offers both food and
warmth by the hearth and when Lucas orders Chick to take off his
clothes in order for them to dry, Chick stands naked in Lucas's
house, enveloped by an "unmistakable odor of Negroes," an odor
which represents in his mind "a condition: an idea: a belief: an
acceptance . . ." (p. 11). Chick accepts the odor as he accepts Lucas'
food—the collard greens, sidemeat fried in flour, biscuits, and butter-
milk. Since this scene is a flashback, Chick tries to analyze its meaning in the present; he thinks, perhaps, it was the food that threw him
off because when he tried to pay Lucas, Lucas merely looked at him
as the coins fell to the floor. Chick violated the unwritten laws of
hospitality. He was condescending. He treated Lucas without thinking of the consequences of his action. Lucas, in return, merely orders
Chick's companions to pick up the coins and return them to him; he
does not lecture or scold because his demeanor conveys how he feels.

Because Chick's relationship with Lucas is unresolved and in
the form of a debt, William Sowder observes that much of *"Intruder
in the Dust* is devoted to the attempt on the part of Lucas and Chick
each to dominate the other: the compositional center of the book is
the account of the ruses each used in an effort to prove the other an
object."[24] While Lucas and Chick do not become intimate companions or confidants, Lucas' situation provides an environment in
which Chick can see the important values in society, in his family,
and in himself. Chick's first encounter with Gavin, not chronologically speaking, but in terms of the drama of the novel, occurs Sunday
noon. The beginning of the first and the end of the third chapters

present the same scene with the intervening material giving background as to why Chick would go to the jail on Sunday in the first place. By using his cyclic imagination, a mode he had previously used in *Absalom, Absalom!*, Faulkner has achieved at the end of the third chapter what the reader could hardly surmise at the beginning of the first chapter.

Initially Chick's attitudes reflect those of his community; his gradual realization is not to proceed in trying to pay off a jejune financial debt, but to respond adequately to the demands made on him by the individuals he knows, as the Corporal did in *A Fable*. His growth is not linear, but zig-zags through the on-going relationship with Lucas, which is confusing to him at first because he has no maps or guidelines to determine the course this relationship will take. As he learns what constitutes the fabric of Lucas' life, he gains an appreciation of Lucas' behavior. Chick would like to clear the debt immediately through gifts—substitute gestures for the complex reactions he feels. Michael Millgate notes the changes in Chick's attitude:

> Charles, it is true, has an acute awareness of Lucas's individuality. But he is aware primarily of Lucas's sheer impenetrability, and certainly it is no commitment to individualism or to the idea of human dignity which first impels him to act on Lucas's behalf. His principal motivation, it appears, is his irritated recollection of an indebtedness to Lucas which his white pride insists that he discharge, but which Lucas's even more stubborn, and more resourceful, pride has consistently frustrated him from discharging. The progress of Charles's initiation is charted very largely in terms of his rejection of his original motive, which derived in large measure from the racial difference between Lucas and himself, in favour of a positive and even passionate awareness of the need to preserve human dignity and avert the shame of mob-violence. . . . This utter atypicality of Lucas, his invincible independence and impenetrability, is what finally undermines any conception of *Intruder in the Dust* as a straightforward moral fable.[25]

Both Chick and Lucas are involved that Sunday noon in a relationship that took four years to establish; the nature of the relationship changed during this time period as Chick recorded it mentally during Lucas' visit to town to pay his taxes. To maintain that Chick comprehended the illusive quality of reality as well as the shifting quality of what appears solid is to overlook the vacillations in his mind as he tried to understand this relationship with Lucas.

The nuances of the Chick-Lucas relationships are complex and can be approached from a number of perspectives. Contrary to Thomas Connolly's views that the factor that enables Chick to grow is the same messianic urge which prompted Ike McCaslin, except in Chick's case, it is politically, not theologically motivated: "The messianic urge, interestingly enough, is a deterministic force over which Chick has very little volitional control."[26] Chick does not allow a boyhood hurt to sway him because he intellectually knows that he must not be part of the "injustice and outrage and dishonor and shame" that would result from Lucas' death at the hands of some intransigent men from the outlying beats. Irving Howe believes "the union of the old and patient Negro with the young and innocent white boy not yet corrupted in the ways of his fathers, Faulkner seems to be saying, will cleanse the land of its bloody and evil heritage."[27] Though the conclusion of the novel points to a hopeful future, it does not mean that Lucas' ownership of land or his gold toothpick bear sufficient testimony that the rehabilitation of the Negro is an economic proposition or that racial identity and social responsibility begin with economic independence. Both Andrew Lytle and Robert Penn Warren see the importance of Chick's growth, and Lytle suggests this is why the story does not end with the murder scene and its solution:

> Instead of leading up to the murder as a final release to the tensions of involvement, by putting it into the past Faulkner uses the act as a compulsive force to catalyze the disparate fragments of appearance into reality, for the story is not about violence at all. It is about a sixteen-year old boy's education in good and evil and his effort to preserve his spiritual integrity.[28]

Edmund Wilson's contention that the book contains a kind of counterblast to the anti-lynching bill and to the civil rights plank in the Democratic platform might have some merit if it could be dramatically shown.[29] Though Chick does not control the events, because the story has a definite communal dimension, nevertheless he consciously modifies his relationship to Lucas, not with the intention of enslaving him, but of providing an expanding freedom for the both of them.

It is after the experience at Lucas' house that Chick feels the import of the community's sentiments: *"We got to make him be a nigger first. He's got to admit he's a nigger. Then maybe we will accept him as he seems to intend to be accepted"* (p. 18). Lucas' house provides Chick with a place for discovery. As a result of that initial encounter, Chick became more and more observant: "He didn't hear it: he learned it . . ." (p. 18). He learns for example, that three years before, Lucas went to the crossroads store in his fine hat, watch-chain, and toothpick and Chick surmises that it was Lucas' mannerisms that caused a ruckus in the store. The half-dollar (actually seventy cents) which Chick had tried to give to Lucas begins to weigh heavy with Chick until it "swelled to its gigantic maximum" (p. 21). Chick even worked for his uncle trying to earn some money with which he could buy gifts for Lucas. Unlike the story of a boy who got into an endless cycle of lifting his calf over the pasture fence and still did it as a grown man, Chick refuses to get into this type of routine. Chick "deserted his calf" (p. 21). Even a present of four cigars, snuff, and a flowered imitation silk dress for Molly could not discharge the weight of his debt, as Lucas constantly thwarts Chick's efforts to gain the upper hand. Soon Chick knows "whatever would or could set him free was beyond not merely his reach but even his ken; he could not wait for it if it came and do without it if it didn't" (p. 23). Life has few clear-cut victories and Faulkner knows that a young man must learn to endure a number of unpleasant moments with grace and resolve.

Gradually Chick begins to widen his vision. He learns that Molly had died and that Lucas' daughter had moved away to Detroit. When encountering Lucas in town (each of the meetings being disturbing as he tried to decipher the tenor of their relationship), Chick reflects, *"You dont have to not be a nigger in order to grieve . . ."* (p. 25). The third time Lucas and Chick meet in town, Lucas looks directly into Chick's eyes, but Chick says Lucas does not recognize him at all: *"He hasn't even bothered to forget me."* (pp. 25-26). After this, Faulkner emphasizes an important theme in this novel: Chick is apparently free because his relationship with Lucas has been terminated. By drifting physically apart from Lucas, Chick thinks he has no obligation towards him and he hopes he can carry "into manhood only the fading legend of that old once-frantic shame and anguish and need not for revenge, vengeance but simply for reequalization, reaffirmation of his masculinity and his white blood" (p. 26). In his own mind he had turned the other cheek: "He was free" (p. 27). After this statement about Chick's illusory, undetermined freedom, Faulkner had originally brought to a conclusion a short story, as indicated on page 26 of the setting copy typescripts. Faulkner

conceived of this part of the novel as a conclusion of Chick's growth;
though Chick has not paid his debt to Lucas. Thus the first twenty-
seven pages of this novel set up a situation in which Chick can grow,
it will take another chapter and a half before Faulkner brings the
story back into the present time at noon on Sunday to give a fuller
indication of the direction that growth will take.

At this point in the novel, Chick still shares the beliefs of the
community as he learns of the events near Fraser's store from those
who were there. Faulkner seems to emphasize constantly Chick's
growth towards freedom as he mentions, at least six times after the
conclusion of the short story mentioned above, that Chick is a free
individual. When Chick visited Gavin's office the Saturday of the
murder, he remembers something very important that subconsciously
bothers him: the one man, Carothers Edmonds, who could help the
situation was in a New Orleans' hospital. After dinner, during which
Gavin implies Lucas is guilty, Chick's thoughts are on Lucas chained
to a bedpost at the constable's house. Chick realizes that he alone is a
key person in this story as Edmonds is out of town. As he returns
home he tells Gavin, "It's all right with me. Lucas didn't have to
work this hard not to be a nigger just on my account" (p. 34). That
evening in bed Chick goes to sleep in "an almost unbearable excrucia-
tion of outrage and fury" as he thinks of what Lucas supposedly did,
though he remembers that Crawford had served time in a federal pen-
itentiary for armed resistance as an army deserter. Chick is aware of
the Gowries and what they represent as they had "translated and
transmogrified that whole region of lonely pine hills dotted meagrely
with small tilted farms and peripatetic sawmills and contraband whis-
key-kettles . . ." (p. 35). Where few outsiders venture to go, Chick
mentally explores what is there.

The murder story is told a number of times in this novel; with
each retelling something is added. Chick considers what the murder
scene was like and the subsequent apprehension of Lucas by Fraser
and his confinement in Skipworth's house, projecting what Sunday
morning would be like devoid of Negroes and filled with outraged
townsfolk. Chick tries to weigh the possibilities that face him: "Lucas was no longer his responsibility, he was no longer Lucas' keeper;
Lucas himself had discharged him" (p. 42). But once Chick sees Lucas in person on Sunday and realizes that Lucas remembers him and
needs his personal help, he begins slowly to change his attitude. Lucas has not changed as he gets out of the car in front of the jail; he is
still "detached, impersonal, almost musing, intractable and composed
. . ." (p. 44). This scene at the end of the third chapter returns the
time scheme of the novel back to the first scene of the first chapter

and forms an *inclusio* with it.

Except for the scene inside the jail cell where Chick again encounters Lucas and is further motivated to assist Lucas because he knows now that Gavin will not help, Chick does not see Lucas during the middle five chapters of the book when he and Miss Habersham and Aleck Sander are trying to solve the murders. Thus Faulkner puts great emphasis on this jail scene, recounting a sympathetic description of the jail itself, the story of the young girl scratching her name onto the glass in 1864, and the views of Will Legate and Mr. Tubbs who reluctantly guard Lucas. The jail is replete with the "smell of creosote and excrement and stale vomit and incorrigibility and defiance and repudiation . . ." (p. 56); a smell far different from that which Chick observed at Lucas' house. Throughout, Gavin dominates the conversation and will not let Lucas tell all that he knows uninterrupted. Lucas' reluctance to trust Gavin is well-founded and he says, with a degree of cautiously hopeful insouciance at the conclusion of their meeting, "I'll try to wait." Their exit from the cell is marked by an echoing sound of extraordinary magnitude: ". . . the last carborundum-grooved door upon their own progenitorless apotheosis behind one clockless lock responsive only to the last stroke of eternity . . ." (p. 65). When Gavin leaves, Chick mentions only the formless "black silhouette" of his uncle, an image he is to use again when he falls asleep (p. 196). At this point, Chick feels that full weight of responsibility. He chokes up with "Me? *Me?*" and as he remembers the Ephraim story of the lost half-dollar (reminiscent of the half-dollar he wanted to give Lucas and also the half-dollar which Lucas shot at in the woods in front of Crawford), he finally achieves a further insight into Lucas: *"He's not only beat me, he never for one second had any doubt about it"* (p. 73). With this, Chick has little doubt that he would help Lucas, especially after Lucas' direct appeal when Chick returned with the tobacco.

The actual story of the exhumation of the bodies is perhaps unduly protracted (as is the screen play of "The Big Sleep" which Faulkner helped to write), though upon reflection Gavin realizes the facts are clear enough. Thus when Nub Gowrie and his sons arrive to meet the sheriff, Gavin, and their crew, the grave is empty, and Lucas' innocence in the murder of Montgomery is definitely established. Faulkner had little trouble composing this section in the original draft and then revising it in the setting copy; the most notable change concerns some additions to Gavin's philosophical statements. Most of the murder story is straightforward and involves the least amount of complication of any of the novel's three parts. Once Vinson Gowrie's body has been discovered at the end of Chapter Eight (an easy chapter for Faulkner to write), Faulkner then started with almost totally new material since he had no original draft to follow as he wrote what was to become Chapter Nine. Since the three detectives had been working Sunday evening and into the early hours of Monday morning, the story continues from 2 P. M. on Monday, keeping at this point an essentially chronological time scheme. When Montgomery's body is brought into the undertaker's, the muder mystery is over and Faulkner merely fills in the details. The emphasis shifts from Chick's awareness of Lucas' situation to his awareness of the town's attitude and how he has changed from agreeing with their position, at least as reflected in Gavin's statements.

Since the town is too large and amorphous to be portrayed by developing individual characters, Faulkner collectively represents them in Chick's mind as being one corporate "Face." To show the fluidity of the crowd's ideas and movements, Faulkner uses two images to try to capture their identity. First, the crowd ebbs and flows, and secondly, it stages the Battle of San Juan Hill with "the faces in invincible profile not amazed not aghast but in a sort of irrevocable repudiation . . ." (p. 185). Chick fuses the experiences of pity, shame, grief, and justice that were part of his experience; dreamily he wants "to leave his mark too on his time in man but only that, no more than that, some mark on his part in earth but humbly, waiting wanting humbly even, not really hoping even, nothing (which of course was everything) except his own one anonymous chance too to perform something passionate and brave and austere not just in but into man's enduring chronicle worthy of a place in it . . . in gratitude for the gift of his time in it . . ." (p. 193), a sequence embodying the heart of Chick's self-realization, the ultimate reaches of the growth that has taken place so far. Faulkner said that he wanted to leave his mark, too, like Kilroy, on this world and perhaps he is sharing some of his desires with Chick. Thus, all history is summed up in the present; the mystery surrounding Lucas is paradigmatic: "Yesterday won't be over until tomorrow and tomorrow began ten thousand years ago" (p. 194). Aiding Lucas is like repeating Pickett's disastrous charge in 1863 or like reliving Columbus' landing in the New World in 1492, because life demands that one commit oneself to new battles and explore new lands whatever the risks or whatever the cost.

Contrasted to Chick's experience of commitment is the experience of avoiding the situation by fleeing. Observing the citizens of Yoknapatawpha, Chick says almost to the point of tedium (at least ten times) that "they ran." These people are not running from Lucas because by now they had forgotten him, they are running from the horrendous act of fratricide committed by Crawford Gowrie. They did not want to have to contemplate the notion of having to lynch Crawford as they had once contemplated lynching Lucas for the exact same crime. Ironically, Lucas will be revered and even become the tyrant over the whole country's white conscience. Chick has gone beyond any of the Boy Scout ranks and entered into adulthood because he is able now to compare his actions with those of his fellow townsmen.

Reflecting to a certain extent the cast of Gavin's mind, Chick, having faced the meaning of death and fratricide, contemplates the meaning of life and birth. It is by the act of eating that man enters the world, perhaps a reflection on the meal at Lucas' house: "By the act of eating and maybe only by that did he [man] actually enter the world . . ." (p. 207). When one is born and reborn through life's experiences, he proclaims his "I-Am into that vast teeming anonymous solidarity of the world from beneath which the ephemeral rock would cool and spin away to dust . . ." (p. 207). Chick has prepared himself to enter into the community he lives with and will hopefully transform it. What is this community like? Faulkner, in a long phrase on page 209, tries to define the essential dynamism of this community by mentioning fifteen times the general word "it"—"that fierce desire that they should be perfect because they were his and he was theirs, that furious intolerance of any one single jot or tittle less than absolute perfection." It has been a long twenty-two hours since Chick and Gavin met the town representative, Mr. Lilley, and learned about the town's values. Chick realizes far more than Gavin that a person who is determined to seek freedom is likewise determined to root this freedom in living with and among other people.

Though the murder mystery has been solved with the help of Lucas, there is the job of catching Crawford and having him face the legal system. To this end, a ploy is devised to take Lucas to Hollymount by way of the Whiteleaf cutoff where Crawford would certainly come to attack Lucas, once Willy Ingrum shared this privileged information with everyone he knew. In all of this, Miss Habersham is not worried because she knows the resourcefulness of Lucas to escape danger. The following Saturday, one week later, the town is back in full swing; it is a busy "Saturday among Saturdays" (p. 236); throughout the novel Faulkner has given a rhythm to the novel by describing the town streets, whether they are empty or full Almost casually, the reader discovers that Crawford had committed suicide in jail with a German Luger and that Lucas is in town wearing a flashy shirt and a pair of zoot pants. With all the bustle in town, Gavin cannot fail to comment on how the automobile has become the American sex symbol:

> So we have to divorce our wife today in order to remove from our mistress the odium of mistress in order to divorce our wife tomorrow in order to remove from our mistress and so on. As a result of which the American woman has become cold and undersexed; she has projected her libido onto the automobile not only because its glitter and gadgets and mobility pander to her vanity and incapacity (because of the dress decreed upon her by the national retailers association) to walk but because it will not maul her and tousle her, get her all sweaty and disarranged. (p. 239)

Gavin appears to be back to normal and making snap judgments, suggesting, perhaps, that the preoccupation of thinking about Lucas is just about over.[30] He can relax a little, talk about other topics, and learn to live with what has happened without being obsessed by it.

When Lucas appears for the final confrontation with Chick and Gavin, he seems, unlike Chick, to have changed little; "the same face which he had seen for the first time when he climbed dripping up out of that icy creek that morning four years ago, unchanged, to which nothing had happened since not even age . . ." (pp. 240-41). Gavin encourages Lucas to take some flowers to Miss Habersham to thank her for her help and insists that Chick not stop making progress in his attempt to do what is right. After Gavin refuses to accept payment, he is finally persuaded and with a bit of fumbling Lucas manages to give him two dollars, a scene that is more complicated in the uncorrected setting copy as Lucas arranges and rearranges his coins. The conclusion though comic, as Cleanth Brooks suggests, does not put Lucas in a demeaning light; rather all the emotions and conflict of the past week are submerged and the three now greet each other in a more relaxed way, because an affectionate joke often expresses "without embarrassing sentimentality, the deepest kind of understanding."[31] Faulkner did not want the novel to end with a heavy-handed moral.

It seems clear that a good deal of Chapter Ten is an effort to tie together the elements of the murder story as expeditiously as possible. Faulkner enjoyed the middle five chapters, but since he had not reached an ultimate conclusion once the two bodies were found, he still had some more explanation to include. Because of the weaknesses in the murder mystery section of the novel (particularly the fact that it takes up about five of the novel's eleven chapters), I think there is room for some psychological reflections on the novel's meaning. In any murder story, whether the actual murder takes place before or during the story, the reader must understand something about the murderer, the victim, and the motive for the murder. Sufficient clues must also exist for the reader to make up his own mind somewhere along the way as to the pattern of the story and the direction it is taking; these clues are often couched in subtleties and the reader must be able to hold in his mind many items until he finds or discovers the discernible pattern. If he is able to enter into the mind of the detective, then the experience becomes all the more enjoyable because he is matching his wits against those of a supposed expert.[32] C. Hugh Holman in his discussion of Faulkner and the detective story says "the detective story is much more concerned with understanding the past through interpretation; it is almost epistemological in its concern."[33] Certainly, Chick in *Intruder* is concerned with understanding the past. The question ultimately is whether the structure of the detective story is sustained and integrated in the overall plot of the novel. Here, *Intruder* is in trouble. Gavin himself has trouble with some primary motivation: "Why did Crawford have to kill Vinson in order to obliterate the witness of his thieving?" (p. 224). Part of Gavin's, and the reader's, inability to answer this is that we do not have a clear picture of the exact nature of the lumber deal that both Vinson and Crawford are engaged in. In addition, the detective story becomes too involved (both Vinson and Jake are exhumed twice); we have no character development of either Vinson or Crawford, nor do we understand fully the reasons for Crawford burying Jake in Vinson's grave. If Vinson's body simply disappeared, then this would cast suspicion on the three detectives rather than throwing the blame on some unspecified third party. Also, the reason for burying Crawford in a shallow grave and not in the quicksand does not make much sense, as it would obviously be easier to find the body in a shallow grave. Finally, why would Lucas put himself in a position where he would be framed and then not really speak out to the proper authorities? These deficiencies in the novel are serious, and while they cannot be excused on one level, perhaps on another level, they can have some significance.

Since a number of the finer points of mystery story writing are missing or underdeveloped in this novel, particularly in the portrayal of the Gowrie family, Faulkner is pointing, as Chick realizes, to some areas of concern within the human conscience. In his own way, Gavin tries to articulate how the Southerner feels about the problem of racial responsibility and civil rights, but as has been indicated, he does not present the most coherent possible picture. If the interlocking relationships among Crawford, Vinson, Chick, and Lucas are seen as being symbolic of some tensions within the Southern mentality, then perhaps the novel makes a bit more sense. Joseph Gold maintains this view:

> The actual digging, the examination of the past reveals the extent to which the present is living in the blind acceptance of falsehood. It turns out that the body in the grave is not that of a murdered man. This discovery leads to the realization that there are two murdered men. Symbolically, it indicates a greater evil in the past than the present wants to admit. The simple judgments and crude prejudices of society turn out to be baseless, and reason and examination lead to an understanding of the underlying complexities of an apparently obvious situation.[34]

Though Faulkner never read any Freud while he was writing *Intruder*, the mystery in this story is part of a far deeper psychological mystery within the Southern psyche.[35] In this view, as developed by Aaron Steinberg, Lucas is seen as an intruder into the white world and also as being a step-child or sibling (the term "boy" has often been used to refer to elderly Negroes) in the unconscious white world.[36] When Lucas is suspected and accused of killing a white man (he is the least likely to prove his innocence), his manner and disposition seem to betray him. Chick breaks a community taboo and defends Lucas because of the guilt feelings he has towards Lucas; by digging up the graves, Chick is probing the white consciousness to find out its secrets. Gavin, as an older member of the white community, tries to delay this process and Chick rejects Gavin's views and acts with the aid of two companions. Gavin's rationalizations are later accepted as being effective for solving the black-white tensions, though this is not really demonstrated in the plot. Basically, "In *Intruder in the Dust*, the unconscious death-wish against the younger child is objectified as Chick, digging up the grave, discovers that the actual murderer was the victim's older brother. In this sense, Chick parallels the psychiatrist in that he probes the unconscious (digs up the grave) to expose the repressed (buried) fratricidal act."[37] The repression of the whites in this murderous act is projected onto Lucas, who stands for the younger brother in society. Once the grave is opened, Faulkner shifts the mystery plot to a presentation of the conscious Southern attitude toward Negroes. Thus Lucas is a device, a catalyst and not really a full character in himself. Steinberg believes "the plot of *Intruder in the Dust* reduces the desperate problem of lynching in the South to the fairy-tale or the comic-strip level," and sees Lucas' request for his receipt as a comic, paternalistic belittling presentation of this black man.[38] Yet the last three chapters do not focus on Lucas, but on Chick's growth to maturity.

One dimension of a psychological appreciation that Steinberg does not develop concerns Chick's dreams which are from a Freudian viewpoint, a reservoir in his unconscious and embody a suppressed renunciation of the concerns of the external world.[39] Just as Gavin finds an expression of the American libido (and perhaps his own?) in the American car, so too, Chick's dreams express wishes which oppose the conscious world (in this case of discrimination) because the mind's censor is relaxed. A dream represents a disguised fulfillment of an unconscious wish and often explains in a fluid way the deeper connections one feels but does not express in everyday conversation. Freud, though opposed by Jung on this, saw phylogenetic references in dreams; that is, they refer not only to the individual's background and desires but to those of the human race as well. As is true with the inhabitants of Yoknapatawpha, they seek free gratification and flee from the realities of the fratricide in order to protect their long-standing beliefs which help them survive. Chick tries to discuss his dreams and discover for himself what they mean: "Besides, it's all right. I dreamed through all that; I dreamed through them too, dreamed them away too; let them stay in bed or milking their cows before dark or chopping wood before dark or by lanterns or not lanterns either. Because they were not the dream; I just passed them to get to the dream—" (p. 205). Chick is probing; what he is trying to express is (somebody or) something about which it is too much to expect for people just sixteen or going on eighty to do. Chick remembers in his dream Gavin's story about English boys his own age who led troops and flew scout airplanes in France in 1918. He identifies very much with these soldiers as he has previously identified with the Civil War soldiers. The deepest recesses of his mind reveal images of conflict (football game) and warfare (Civil War, Battles of San Juan, and World War I) as he attempts to determine subconsciously the nature of his relationship with Lucas.

The vascillation in Chick as revealed in his dreams and reveries is an important part of the perspective of the novel since Faulkner

has chosen to tell the story with Chick as a third-person narrator.[40]
In his state of exhaustion, Chick reveals the connections and relationships he feels linking the past to the present and the present to the
future to give a sense of continuity in his life. Chick's mind encompasses the people around him, especially Lucas, Gavin, Nub Gowrie,
his mother, and the townsfolk, as he perceives what is happening. He
tests the values of others as they enter his subconscious and filter
through this week of crisis. Andrew Lytle sees the novel comprising
narrow physical limits, "but the physical action, while performing at
its own level, releases the flow of reverie and comment which becomes the embodiment of the intrinsic meaning. Since within this
area lies the realm of truth, where all is timeless, the dual consciousness moves through past, present, and even into the future according
to the needs of the particular stage of the story's development."[41]
In this way, Chick interiorizes the experience of his encounter with
Lucas and the murders in Jefferson, achieving for himself an entrance
into the realms of universal truth, which go far beyond being just
another character in a whodunit.

Perhaps Edmund Wilson overreacted to *Intruder* when he
stated that there "has been nothing so exhilarating in its way since
the triumphs of the Communist-led workers in the early Soviet films;
we are thrilled by the same kind of emotion that one got from some
of the better dramatizations of the career of Abraham Lincoln."[42]
And even Everett Carter rhapsodizes when he says *Intruder* is a poem
of superb craftsmanship and total structure using metaphor, character, and plot.[43] While *Intruder* is not one of Faulkner's more highly
rated works, nevertheless it deals with a very important theme: a
young man's growth in his civic responsibilities as perceived over a
period of four years, but culminating in one crucial week; the
emphasis is on action to creatively bring about justice and not a reliance on abstract thoughts and good feelings While Chick has not
reconciled the Jefferson community or offered Lucas a new sense of
security, he has grown with the help of some friends and relatives.
As Faulkner suggests in this novel, the solution for the South's problems will come from a recognition of its problems, an investigation of
the dimensions of the problem and the personalities involved, and a
willingness to do something about the inherent injustices. As he said
in reference to the civil rights problems dramatized in this novel:
"Yes, people have got to do it, not theories. People have got to say:
'No matter how weak I am, I myself, Smith, will not put up with
this.' "[44] Faulkner has shown in *Intruder* that there is hope for the
South.

Notes

*I am grateful to Mrs. Paul D. Summers, Jr., Faulkner's daughter, for allowing me to quote from the typescripts of *Intruder in the Dust* and to the Alderman Library, University of Virginia, for allowing me access to the Faulkner Collection.

[1]Cf. *Lion in the Garden*, eds. James B. Meriwether and Michael Millgate (New York: Random House, 1968), p. 177.

[2]*Lion in the Garden*, p. 202.

[3]James Baldwin, "Faulkner and Desegregation," *Partisan Review*, 23 (Fall 1956), 570.

[4]*Lion in the Garden*, p. 184.

[5]Cf. *Essays, Speeches and Public Letters*, ed. James B. Meriwether (New York: Random House, 1965), p. 88.

[6]*Essays, Speeches and Public Letters*, pp. 102-103.

[7]*Essays, Speeches and Public Letters*, p. 111.

[8]*Essays, Speeches and Public Letters*, p. 186. For a further look at Faulkner's views on civil rights, cf. *Faulkner in the University*, eds. Frederick L. Gwynn and Joseph L. Blotner (New York: Vintage, 1959), pp. 209-227; *Essays, Speeches and Public Letters*, pp. 92-112.

[9]Malcolm Cowley, *The Faulkner-Cowley File* (New York: Viking, 1966), p. 18.

[10]Olga Vickery, *The Novels of William Faulkner* (Baton Rouge: Louisiana State University Press, 1964), p. 142.

[11]William Faulkner, *Intruder in the Dust* (New York: Random House, 1948), p. 48. All future references to this novel will be to this edition.

[12]Kenneth Richardson, *Force and Faith in the Novels of William Faulkner* (The Hague: Mouton Press, 1967), p. 107.

[13]*Lion in the Garden*, pp. 126-127.

[14]Calvin Brown, "Faulkner's Use of the Oral Tradition," *Georgia Review*, 22 (Summer 1968), 163.

[15]Theodore Gilmore Bilbo (1877-1947) was State Senator from 1908-1912, Governor of Mississippi from 1916-1920 and from 1928-1932, and was U. S. Senator elected in 1934, 1940, and 1946, but did not take the oath to serve in the 80th Congress because of sickness. James Kimble Vardaman served in the State House of Representatives from 1890-1896, was Governor of Mississippi from 1904-1908, and served in the U. S. Senate from 1913-1919. Both men were outspoken politicians often involved in lively debates. In May 1911, John Falkner, Jr., William Faulkner's uncle, was President of the Central Vardaman Club of Oxford.

[16]Elmo Howell, "William Faulkner's Caledonia: A Note on *Intruder in the Dust*," *Studies in Scottish Literature*, 3 (April 1966), 252.

[17]Dorothy Greer, "Dilsey and Lucas: Faulkner's Use of the Negroes as Gauge of Moral Character," *Emporia State Research Studies*, 11 (September 1962), 59.

[18]Robert Jacobs, "Faulkner's Tragedy of Isolation," in *Southern Renascence*, eds. Louis D. Rubin, Jr. and Robert Jacobs (Baltimore: Johns Hopkins University Press, 1966), p. 186.

[19]*Lion in the Garden*, p. 79.

[20]*Lion in the Garden*, p. 130.

[21]Irving Malin, *William Faulkner: An Interpretation* (Stanford: Stanford University Press, 1957), p. 89, discusses the event of Chick's falling in the creek as a baptism.

[22]Joseph L. Blotner, *Faulkner: A Biography* (New York: Random House, 1974) II, 1246.

[23]Cf. *Lion in the Garden*, p. 255, for a discussion of the significance in Faulkner's mind of the postage stamp.

[24]William Sowder, "Lucas Beauchamp as Existential Hero," *College English*, 25 (November 1963), 117.

[25]Cf. *The Achievement of William Faulkner*, (New York: Random House, 1966), pp. 219-220.

[26]Thomas Connolly, "Fate and 'the Agony of the Will': Determinism in Some Works of William Faulkner," in *Essays on Determinism in American*

Literature, ed. Sidney Krause (Kent, Ohio: Kent State University Press, 1964), p. 49.

[27]Irving Howe, "The South and Current Literature," *American Mercury*, 67 (October 1948), 497.

[28]Cf. Robert Penn Warren, "Faulkner: The South and the Negro," *Faulkner: A Collection of Critical Essays* (Englewood Cliffs, New Jersey: Prentice Hall, 1966), p. 78. This quote is taken from Andrew Lytle's *The Hero With the Private Parts* (Baton Rouge: Louisiana State University Press, 1966), p. 131.

[29]In 1948, the Republican Party actually had a stronger plank on civil rights than the Democrats. The Republican Party wrote: "Lynching or any other form of mob violence anywhere is a disgrace to any civilized state, and we favor the prompt enactment of legislation to end this infamy. One of the basic principles of this republic is the equality of all individuals to their right to life, liberty, and the pursuit of happiness." They maintained that these rights should not be denied to anyone because of race, religion, color, or country of origin. The Democratic Party wrote: "The Democratic Party commits itself to continuing its efforts to eradicate all racial, religious, and economic discrimination." *National Party Platforms: 1840-1968*, comp, Kirk Porter and Donald Johnson (Urbana: University of Illinois Press, 1970), pp. 452, 453.

[30]Wayne Booth has made a valuable observation about Gavin's intrusion on the meaning of the American automobile: "One's attitude toward the much debated theorizing of Gavin Stevens at the end of Faulkner's *Intruder in the Dust* is not affected markedly by the fact that the ideas are not given directly by Faulkner. The question is whether Gavin's elaborate commentary is essentially related to the nephew's experience of a near-lynching and his consequent growth toward maturity. In any "truth-discovery" novel, and especially in novels which try to lead young people to the hard truths of adulthood, the problem is to make the discovery a convincing outcome of the experience. In *Intruder*, as in many such works, the attitude toward which Faulkner wants his young hero to grow is so complex that neither the boy nor the reader is likely to infer it from the experience itself. They both must therefore be preached at by the wise uncle, sometimes with little direct relevance to the drama. . . . If we choose to join the chorus of protests against these pages, we must be very clear that we are not objecting to authorial commentary but rather to a particular kind of disharmony between idea and dramatized object. Even if Stevens' views could be shown to differ from Faulkner's, the discovery of irony would not save the work; the disharmony would remain. What is more, our objections would not be stronger if these opinions had been given in Faulkner's own name." *The Rhetoric of Fiction* (Chicago: University of Chicago Press, 1970), pp. 181-182.

[31]Cleanth Brooks, *William Faulkner: The Yoknapatawpha Country* (New Haven: Yale University Press, 1963), p. 294.

[32]Cf. William Van O'Connor's *The Tangled Fire of William Faulkner*, pp. 135-145, for a discussion of Faulkner and the detective story. O'Connor looks to the Lucas-white citizens of Jefferson as the center of the story.

[33]C. Hugh Holman, *The Roots of Southern Writing* (Athens: University of Georgia Press, 1972), p. 170.

[34]Joseph Gold, *William Faulkner: A Study in Humanism from Metaphor to Discourse* (Norman: University of Oklahoma Press, 1966), p. 88.

[35]*Lion in the Garden*, p. 251.

[36]For a full and detailed development of this Freudian interpretation, cf. Aaron Steinberg's dissertation, "Faulkner and the Negro" (New York University, 1963), pp. 294-338. Steinberg relies on the psychological views of one of Freud's pupils, Richard Sterba, particularly the material found as Sterba's essay "Some Psychological Factors in Negro Race Hatred and in Anti-Negro Riots," *Psychoanalysis and Social Sciences*, I (1947), 412-415.

[37]Aaron Steinberg, " 'Intruder in the Dust': Faulkner as a Psychologist of the Southern Psyche," *Literature and Psychology*, 15 (Spring 1965), 122.

[38]Aaron Steinberg, "Faulkner and the Negro," p. 331.

[39]A complete analysis of dreams in Faulkner's works has not been done. Important references for such a study might include the following: Ruel Foster, "Dream as Symbolic Act in Faulkner," *Perspective*, 2 (Summer 1949), 179-194. Unfortunately, Professor Foster does not deal with this problem in *Intruder*. Sigmund Freud, *The Interpretation of Dreams*, trans. A. A. Brill (New York: Modern Library, 1913); Frederick Hoffman, *Freudianism and the Literary Mind* (Baton Rouge: Louisiana State University, 1957); Ernest Jones, *The Life and Word of Sigmund Freud*, eds. Lionel Trilling and Steven Marcus (New York: Basic Books, 1961); Carl Jung, *Modern Man in Search of a Soul* (New York: 1934); Ernst Kris, *Psychoanalytic Explorations in Art* (New York: International University Press, 1952); Lionel Trilling, *Freud and the Crisis of our Culture* (Boston: Beacon Press, 1955); Philip Wheelwright, *The Burning Fountain* (Bloomington: Indiana University Press, 1954).

[40]For an extended development of Chick as narrator, cf. John Hart's "That Not Impossible He: Faulkner's Third-Person Narrator," in *Studies in Faulkner*, ed. Neal Woodruff (Pittsburg: Carnegie Institute of Technology, 1961), pp. 29-42.

[41]*The Hero With the Private Parts*, p. 133.

[42]Edmund Wilson, "William Faulkner's Reply to the Civil Rights Program," *New Yorker*, 23 October 1948, p. 234.

[43]Everett Carter, "The Meaning of, and in, Realism," *Antioch Review*, 12 (March 1952), 92.

[44]*Lion in the Garden*, p. 142.

Squaring the Circle in The Sound and the Fury

by

Sanford Pinsker

There is no longer any need to belabor *The Sound and the Fury*'s stature as a Modernist classic. In attitude, in tone, in theme and technique, it stands with the best that was felt and written during the 1920's. And like other thick, Modernist texts, its more complicated sections have been de-coded and its erudite allusions identified. For better or worse, even the dazzling experimentation of *The Sound and the Fury* can begin to look domesticated.

It could hardly be otherwise. In "Ulysses, Order and Myth," T. S. Eliot isolates the central problem for the twentieth century writer as that of discovering a structure capable of pattering chaos. His answer, in a word, was "myth"—as demonstrated in Joyce's *Ulysses* and, by implication, in *The Wasteland*. Granted, "influence" remains a slippery term, but Faulkner's considerable debts to both Eliot and Joyce were clear long before the publication of Joseph Blotner's definitive biography. However, mythic structures are not the only ways of organizing the disparate aspects of modern life, nor is the transfer from, say, Joyce to Faulkner likely to be as obvious as it was in early novels like *Soldiers' Pay* or *Mosquitoes*. That is, myth criticism runs the risk of being insistent about the parallels it discovers, of reducing great literature to the realm of oft-told tales and/or predictable categories.

But that much said, let me suggest some models of the Modernist vision which approach Faulkner's novel from an oblique angle. At one point in *Ulysses* Bloom dreams, first, of a pastoral, suburban house and then imagines he will pay for it by "a solution of the secular problem of the quadrature of the circle, government premium 1,000,000 sterling."[1] Which is to say, Bloom thinks about squaring the circle. Joyce's comic protagonist is a man with a flair for turning abstract ideas to commercial advantage, for technology rather than pure science. Unfortunately, Bloom is also a man who operates on partial, often half-understood information. In short, he is a schlemiel, an inveterate bumbler.

I mention this admittedly small moment in *Ulysses* not to imply that Faulkner read the book with microscopic attention, but, rather, to suggest some larger similarities of vision. At least part of the joke about poor Bloom's scheme to square the circle rests upon its utter impossibility. To be sure, such contests existed in fact and, no doubt, counterparts of Bloom tried their hand at winning the big prize. But as any mathematician will tell you, straight lines are one thing, circles another. That is, linear systems cannot affect a curve. The circle cannot be squared.

And, yet, something very much akin to this impulse occurs regularly in Modernist fiction. For example, a character like Lord Jim finds himself trying desperately to superimpose romantic notions of Herohood onto the resistant fabric of modern life. The result is an impossibility not unlike that of squaring the circle. Jim's problem, of course, is one of discovering "how to be," rather than an exercise in abstract mathematics. That is, his very persistence has the earmarks of tragedy. Or, at least, the *potential* for such a condition.[2] On the other hand, if a mathematician consumed himself with attempts to square the circle, he would be dismissed as a crackpot— and a rather simpleminded one at that. No Marlow would rush to his defense nor would he anguish about how to tell the story. People silly enough to try squaring the circle are simply not "one of us."

All of this is by way of suggesting that the "squared circle" can be a useful metaphor of the modern experience. Or to put it another way: I have no interest in turning mathematicians into the special whipping boys of this article, nor are there elaborate graphs lurking ahead. Rather, I want to focus upon the circle imagery in *The Sound and the Fury*, less as a demonstration of Formalist analysis than as a structuring device for the Modernist imagination. Granted, the sizeable gap between one's ideals and one's actual condition, between the world as we would like it and the uncongenial turf that is, has *always* been with us. Modern life merely exasperated the problem, but in doing so, it dictated the necessity of Modernist forms. Faulkner's *The Sound and the Fury* is an eloquent address to these problems and it is to that book's gritty surfaces I now turn.

The Sound and the Fury is divided into four separate, but unequal, parts. The first quarter—Benjy's section—involves, among

other things, Luster's obsessive search for a missing coin. Not surprisingly, it, too, is a "quarter." But Faulkner's playfulness aside,
quest motifs dominate a wide variety of attempts at forward and/or
linear motion. To be sure, in Luster's case the missing quarter is linked to childish expectations of a circus show. As he puts it:

> "Is you all seen anything of a quarter down here." Luster
> said.
> "What quarter."
> "The one I had here this morning." Luster said. "I lost it
> somewhere. It fell through this here hole in my pocket. If I
> dont find it I cant go to the show tonight."[3]

That the "show" is a circus reenforces the circle/circus imagery
which culminates in Jason's section. Moreover, Luster's search un-
earths teasing reminders that all which glitters is not silver, that frustration can come in a variety of packages:

> "Found it [i.e., a contraceptive] under this here bush."
> Luster said. "I thought for a minute it was that quarter I lost."
> He came and took it.
> "Hush." Luster said. "He going to give it back after he done
> looking at it."
> "Agnes Mabel Becky." he said. He looked toward the house.
> (61)

No single word describes the quotidian experiences in *The
Sound and the Fury* better than "frustration." Each character—with
the possible exception of Dilsey—is a study in dreams which do not
fulfill themselves, in "circles" that remain stubbornly un—squared.
By that I mean, only Dilsey has the comprehensiveness necessary to
have "seed de first en de last" (371). The Compsons have indeed
come full circle and while Dilsey provides a kind of chorus to their
collective decline-and-fall, it is her indomitable spirit which meta-
morphoses mere whining into tragic significance.

In Quentin's section the motifs which Benjy could only feel
and/or bellow become intellectualized. Which is to say, the pains of
Benjy's separation take on the character of Quentin's suicidal brooding. And, yet, their respective streams-of-consciousness reveal as
many deep-seated similarities as they do obvious differences. For
both, Caddy represents a stable condition that has been altered, a
mutability the brothers war against with primal screams on one hand

and sophisticated philosophizing on the other.

Benjy, of course, lives in a world where Time does not exist. Events dovetail into a swirl of sensations roughly divided between those which soothe and those which threaten. That is, Benjy is spared the anguish which, for Quentin, make life-in-Time impossible. But that much said, there are moments when the motifs which transfer from Benjy's section to Quentin's are a matter of degree rather than kind. For example, the quarter Luster searches for so diligently is, in a sense, "found" during the book's second quarter. To be sure, now the speaker is a Hamlet-like Quentin, the quarter an example of Joycean correspondence, if not "metempsychosis" and the "sister" a symbolic shorthand for Caddy, St. Francis's characterization of death as a "little sister" and a very literal Italian waif:

> I found a coin and gave it to the little girl. A quarter. "Goodbye, sister." I said. Then I ran. (165)

The strangely suggestive scene in which Quentin watches three boys trying to catch a fish is even more telling. Granted, the obsessive way in which Quentin describes the water ("I could not see the bottom, but I could see a long way into the motion of the water before the eye gave out, and then I saw a shadow hanging like a fat arrow stemming into the current. . ." [144]) foreshadows his own death by drowning, but observing their quest for the elusive fish also suggests something of the symbolic inflation which turns 25¢ into twenty-fives of larger dimension:

> "They've been trying to catch that trout for twenty-five years. There's a store in Boston offers a twenty-five dollar fishing rod to anybody that can catch him." (145)

In "The Bear," Ike McCaslin will learn those lessons of patience and humility which far outstrip actually killing Old Ben, but Quentin lacks instructors like Sam Fathers or Cass Edmonds. Rather, he inherits a pocketwatch from his grandfather and a flowery brand of post-bellum cynicism from Jason Lycurgus Compson:

> I give you the mausoleum of all hope and desire [i.e., his father's watch]; it's rather excrutiating-ly [sic] apt that you will use it to gain the reducto absurdum of all human experience which can fit your individual needs no better than it fitted his or his father's. (93)

The result turns the motion of Quentin's section into a self—styled quest to obliterate Time. Water imagery blends with that of chiming clocks until the two are fused in a desperate effort to replace an existential flux with an artificial permanence, the linear aspects of forward chronology with the rippling circles of Caddy's lost virginity:

> A quarter hour yet. And then I'll not be. The peacefullest words. Peacefullest words. *Non fui. Sum. Fui. Non sum.* (216)

But there is another aspect of Quentin's section, one which suggests its Janus-like relationship to the novel's overall structure. If the recurrent "quarters" look backwards to Benjy, the wandering (i.e., circling?) aspect of Quentin's flight from Harvard yard foreshadows Jason's frenetic chase a section later. Quentin achieves a semblance of order—in effect, squaring the ragged ends of his personal circle—in the minutiae of suicide. Granted, the obsession with hygiene (Quentin dryspotting the stain on his vest or methodically ticking off items from a mental list) appears somewhat incongruous at first glance, but the very effort to ritualize order—as opposed to the chaos which has run rampant through his interior monologue— suggests that this is a "Hamlet" about to *act*, rather than one ambivalently "thinking":

> ... Then I carried the watch into Shreve's room and put it in his drawer and went to my room and got a fresh handerkerchief and went to the door and put my hand on the light switch. Then I remembered I hadnt brushed my teeth, so I had to open the bag again. I found my toothbrush and got some of Shreve's paste and went out and brushed my teeth. I squeezed the brush as dry as I could and put it back in the bag and shut it, and went to the door again. Before I snapped the light out I looked around to see if there was anything else, then I saw that I had forgotten my hat. I'd have to go by the postoffice and I'd be sure to meet some of them, and they'd think I was a Harvard Square student making like he was a senior. I had forgotten to brush it too, but Shreve had a brush, so I didnt have to open the bag any more. (222)

I have quoted extensively here to convey something of the rhetorical distance between the convoluted snytax which opens Quentin's section and the sparse, almost Hemingwayesque, prose with which it concludes. Indeed, the Quentin Compson who prepares for his suicide via compound, declarative sentences and the Nick Adams who fishes so desperately at the "Big Two-Hearted River" have much in common. The respective breakdowns may have radically different causes—to say nothing of "solution"—but both characters confront the Modernist dilemma of "squaring" that uncongenial circle I described earlier.

Quentin is, then, a Modernist Hero, with all the assets and liabilities the term implies. His predicament suggests a peculiarly Existential *angst*; his persistence teases us into thoughts of a tragic stature. But Quentin not only anguishes *about* Time, the section *per se* is an extended flashback, a way of interjecting the cunning of History into that ongoing flow we call the Compson saga. Jason IV, ironically identified in Faulkner's "Appendix" as "the first sane Compson since before Culloden and (a childless bachelor) hence the last" (420), suggests one possible culmination of those motifs which are both full of "sound and fury" and likely to signify "nothing."

For a man who prides himself on keeping *both* eyes on the main chance, a chart of Jason's erratic motions makes it clear that (a) paranoia is an inefficient way to beat the stock market and (b) that running in circles is an equally inefficient way of moving forward, much less of catching a circus man with a red tie. To be sure, Jason is a monster precisely because his hard-headed "rationality" is so irrational, his "evil" so gratuitous. The scene in which he burns two tickets to the circus before Luster's amazed and disappointed eyes is transference of the baldest sort. Frustrated by conspiracies both real and imagined, Jason strikes back in ways which make him a fit candidate for the Sophoclean revenges awaiting just a few pages later.

But "poetic justices" aside, Jason is a man bent on spoiling his chances for contentment. At bottom, evidences of the nasty and brutish only confirm his world view, one best expressed in no-nonsense maxims like "Once a bitch always a bitch" (223). Sentimentality—which, for Jason, includes everything from human decency and fair play to the Good, the True and the Beautiful—is a fraud. A first-strike capability is the only "sane" way to operate in a world where dogs eat other dogs and races go, inevitably, to the swift. Which is simply to say, Jason *expects* modernity to be fashioned from inhumane stuff. *He* will survive, complete with the chip on his shoulder and a spirit uncluttered by puppy love.

The chaotic energy which drives Jason throughout his section continues in Dilsey's, as the Compson blacks celebrate Easter Sunday and Jason blazes a fume-riddled trail to Mottson. In effect, the image clusters which have dominated the book come full-circle: Caddy's thwarted sexuality is recapitulated in her daughter, Quentin; the much telegraphed "circus" assumes the full weight of its linguistic roots, merging with a tapestry of "circles" that reduce Jason to pure rage.

Significantly enough, the final tableau squares the circle at last, albeit in ways which smack more of irony than reconciliation. *The Sound and the Fury* end, as it must, pointed toward the graveyard. But with Luster at the reins, Queenie moves around the monument in the town square from the "wrong" direction. That is, he drives to the left, rather than the customary right. The disruption fractures Benjy's world: he "roared and roared" (401). Only when square and circle flow predictably does Benjy "hush":

> The broken flower drooped over Ben's fist and his eyes were empty and blue and serene again as cornice and facade flowed smoothly once more from left to right; post and tree, window and doorway, and signboard, each in its ordered place. (401)

At the end of *Ulysses* Bloom drifts off to sleep, dreaming of the circle squared, the prize money won. In one form or another, the vision haunts twentieth century literature, both as a possibility modernity denies and a watershed which Modernist writers cannot cross. Only when the story is "told by an idiot" can it be otherwise.

Notes

[1]James Joyce, *Ulysses* (New York: Modern Library, 1961), p. 718.

[2]Critics differ widely about the character of Jim's "sacrificial" death, with some insisting that it is the stuff of tragic recognition while others emphasize its more "theatrical" (i.e., egotistical) aspects.

[3]William Faulkner, *The Sound and the Fury* (New York: Vintage, 1954), pp. 15-16. Subsequent references are to this edition and will be given parenthetically.

Faulkner's South and the Other South

by

P. P. Sharma

Feeling curious about the unknown region beyond the Ohio, Quentin Compson's roommate at Harvard Shreve McCannon says: "Tell about the South. What's it like there. What do they do there. Why do they live there. Why do they live at all. . . ."[1] Not a few writers have asked themselves these very questions; such has been the intriguing character of the American South. To say that one would have to be born there to understand the South is not right as is proved by the fact that the projections of the native writers themselves are strikingly at variance one with another. One is reminded of what Faulkner said about the truth: "No one individual can look at the truth. It blinds you. You look at it and you see one phase of it. Someone else looks at it and sees a slightly awry phase of it. But taken all together, the truth is in what they saw though nobody saw the truth intact. . . . It was . . . thirteen ways of looking at a black-bird."[2] The South, likewise, is much too baffling and complicated to be reduced to one single image; at best, it is only a generalization.

If we look at the map of the Southeastern section of the United States, we can identify, with C. Hugh Holman, not just one South but three Souths: "a temperate coastal South, variously called the Tidewater and the Low Country, . . . a Piedmont South which extends into and includes the Appalachian and Blue Ridge Mountains, and . . . a Deep South which is largely a semi-tropical Gulf Coast plain."[3] If we further remember that these divisions were settled by particular kinds of immigrants—the Atlantic Coastal plain, for instance, by the British Cavaliers; the hill country by the sturdy and self-willed Scotch-Irish, along with the malcontents and the criminals fleeing the coastal establishment; and the Deep South by adventurers pushing westward and southward to realize their dream of plantation glory—we find enough support in geography and history alike for the demarcation of these three Souths. And although it is possible to demonstrate that Taine's formula of "race, milieu and moment" is at work in the image of the South that Ellen Glasgow, William Faulkner and Thomas Wolfe each offers us, the fact remains that a creative writer's individual response cannot be adequately explained in terms of external and mechanical determinants only. To give just one example: both Faulkner and Eudora Welty are Mississippians; the locale of one is removed from that of the other by no more than three hundred miles. But at times they do not seem to be living in the same universe. The South, therefore, is not what physically exists so much as how one's temperament shapes and fashions it. Obviously, then, it would be futile to enumerate how many Souths there are or can be. That being the case, one has necessarily to be selective. In this paper I consider the South with ideal coloring as we find it in a writer like Thomas Nelson Page and the "Fugitives" of the 1920s; the decaying South as we find it in William Faulkner; and the routine-bound South as we find it in Eudora Welty.

Legend and fact are sometimes at loggerheads. Irrespective of what the historians and social analysts say, the South as it emerges from the writings of some post-bellum authors presents a flattering picture of the plantation civilization. Possibly the agony and the sense of defeat of the Civil War and the humiliation of Reconstruction tended to invest the past with a peculiar glamour. The central character of Stark Young's *The Torches Flare* observes, "It's only natural, of course, that a people who had lost their cause and had a hard time afterward and were so poor and had their pride hurt so, and saw a thing they had been born to dying away from them in a new age, should have created a defense in some sort of beautiful tradition."[4] The tendency on the part of the South, as W. J. Cash says, to "wrap itself in contemptuous superiority"[5] makes the old regime look like a time of idyllic existence, the proverbial Golden Age, in which the imperious kindness of the gentleman-planter is matched by the unswerving loyalty, even obsequiousness, of the Negro. The good and gracious life of the Southern aristocracy and the kindly treatment meted out to the slaves are the main concern of Thomas Nelson Page. He makes a freed slave boast of his old master's wealth and grandeur:

> "Fine old place?" yes, suh, 't is so;
>   An' mighty fine people my white folks war—But you ought ter 'a' seen it years ago,
>   When de Marster an' de Mistis lived up dyah; When de niggers 'd stan' all roun' de do',
>   Like grains o'corn on the cornhouse flo'. "Live' mons'ous high?" Yes, Marster, yes;

D'cut 'n' onroyal 'n' gordly dash; "Eat an' drink till you
could n' res'.
My folks war n' none o' yo' po'-white-trash; Nor, suh, dey
was of high degree—
Dis heah nigger am quality![6]

According to Page the unbridgeable schism was placed between the North and the South only after the Civil War. Earlier, in
spite of their different modes of life, they were moving in the same
direction under the spirit of emancipation. By their interference the
Northern Abolitionists incited the Negroes to rebellion and thus
brought about a permanent rupture: "From this moment dates the
unremittingly hostile attitude of the two sections toward each other.
Before there had been antagonism; now there was open hostility. . . .
The two sections grew to be as absolutely separated as though a sea
rolled between them."[7] Page's South, it appears, leaves little to be
desired either for the blacks or for the whites. The Negro retainer
almost goes into rapture while speaking of his master's splendid mansion "set back far from the road, in proud seclusion, among groves of
oak and hickory" "with the big gate and the carved stone pillars." He
nostalgically recalls, 'Dem was good ole times, marster—de bes' Sam
uver see! Day was, in fac'! Niggers didn' had nothin' 't *all* to do—jes'
had to 'ten to de feedin' an' clannin' de hosses, an' doin' what de
marster tell 'em to do; an' when dey wuz sick, dey had things sent
'em out de house, an 'de same doctor come to see 'em whar' ten' to
de white folks when dey wuz po'ly, an' all. Dyar wan' no trouble nor
nuttin'."[8]

The details that follow furnish enough evidence that "Dyar
wan' no trouble nor nuttin'." When the Negro Ham Fisher, at his
master's bidding, entered and got entrapped in a burning horse stall,
the master flew to Ham's rescue and brought him out in his arms
although the master was maimed and blinded permanently after that.
Similarly, when Sam's young master, to whom Sam was given as a
birthday present and to whom Sam belonged, was in danger of losing
his life in a duel he had undertaken to fight to vindicate his father's
honor, he takes care to set Sam free and to provide enough for him
as well as his wife for as long as they lived. On one occasion when the
old master wanted to chastise Sam for some misdemeanor, his son
"stept right in befo' ole master, an' ketchin' de whup said: 'Stop,
seh! you sha'nt whup 'im; he b'longs to me, an' if you hit 'im
another lick I'll set 'im free."[9] The relations between the two races
are certainly not on the basis of equality, but they are, at any rate,
characterized by compassion and humanity. No wonder, while

reading "Mars Chan," from which I have quoted, Thomas Wentworth Higginson, who had commanded a Negro regiment during the war, actually shed tears.[10]

Although it cannot be denied that Page's South seems much too naive and uncomplex in taking for granted the white's superiority to the black and the latter's ungrudging acquiescence to a basically iniquitous dispensation, there is, nevertheless, some element of truth which finds confirmation even today. Some modern-day Negro writers and leaders, when interviewed, clearly have stated that the values they have subscribed to and the ideals they have followed were more like those of the Southerners than those of the Northerners. Martin Luther King, John Oliver Killens, Whitney Young and Ralph Ellison all have testified to their deeply felt affinity with the South. Ellison, for instance, remarks that "there is an area in Southern experience wherein Negroes and Whites achieve a sort of communication and even social intercourse, which is not always possible in the North. . . . There is an implicably human side to race relationships."[11] It should be recalled that in Harriet Beecher Stowe's *Uncle Tom's Cabin*, written from the point of view of the Northern Abolitionist, the worst tyrannies over the Negro are perpetrated by the Yankees.

The Fugitives' South is akin to Page's as each view is intended to serve as a kind of palliative against a sense of defeat. The Fugitives' South may not be able to prevail against the Leviathan state, but which good cause has not suffered a setback? Were not the Confederate soldiers routed by the Northern raiders? John Crowe Ransom's Captain Carpenter is apparently a gentleman of the old school, but he is beleagured by ruffians. Ransom felt that he was "sentenced from birth to love unusual gods." Donald Davidson affirmed that there is a fundamental difference between the North and the South, partly attributable to the physical surroundings amid which each lives. He cryptically expressed it thus in "Still Rebels, Still Yankees": "If New England [the North] encouraged man to believe in an ordered universe, Georgia [the South] compelled him to remember that there were snakes in Eden."[12] For Davidson, the best thing for the South is to recover its real identity, by rejecting whatever has been imposed on it by sheer brute force in the wake of the Civil War. Through the persona of Lee wandering in the mountains, Davidson was thinking of throwing away this incubus:

Was it for this
That on an April day we stacked our arms

Obedient to a soldier's trust? To lie
Ground by heels of little men,
Forever maimed, defeated, lost, impugned?
And was I then betrayed? Did I betray?
If it were said, as still it might be said—
If it were said, and a word should run like fire,
Like living fire into the roots of grass,
The sunken flag would kindle on wild hills,
The brooding hearts would waken, and the dream
Stir like a crippled phantom under the pines,
And this torn earth would quicken into shouting
Beneath the feet of ragged bands.[13]

This South is essentially the poet's South, built on fantasy rather than on fact. It is, not surprisingly therefore, a romanticized, almost sentimentalized, South, not representing what the South of history might have been but what it should have been. The experiences gained through the First World War and its aftermath coupled with a feeling of being over-ridden rough-shod gave an impetus to the dream of the Old South. This Old South represents a clean break from the prevailing American values of material prosperity through industrialism and the application of more and more advanced technology. It is a return to the existence rooted in agrarian interests, to the good old days when life moved at a leisurely pace, when the landscape was not covered with smokestacks. This South is opposed to chaotic and fragmented life; it would like people to achieve wholeness and integration. Avoiding hurry, finding the still center of things through contemplation and the study of the classics, concentrating on the essential, not being obsessed by economic factors but breathing in a mild, serene air through communion with nature, saving one's individuality from being swamped by a totalitarian state—these are all encompassed within the range of the Agrarians' or the Fugitives' South. Their South, in other words, is more a set of attitudes, a special orientation towards and perspective on a life which they would like to trace back to their own putative antebellum tradition than to any objective reality discoverable in the present-day world.

On pragmatic grounds, however, this South does not seem to be viable. It is still contemplating a white garden. No new insight in regard to racial problems has been forged out of the tumultuous experience of the Civil War. Notwithstanding the opposition to industrialism vehemently voiced by many in *I'll Take My Stand*, it would simply be foolhardy to reject it *in toto*. It is true that a country housewife will not necessarily become a better woman merely by exchanging her old-fashioned ice-box for an electric refrigerator;[14] the old economy is no panacea to all our ills, either. Moreover, to hark back to the age of gleaming white mansions and blooming magnolias or to be lost in the reverie of Ashley Wilkes' "Twelve Oaks": ". . . the white house reared its perfect symmetry . . . , tall of columns, wide of verandas . . . a stately beauty, a mellowing dignity"[15]—is often tantamount to condoning the inequities of the old order.

"Jesus, the South is fine, isn't it?" says the young man from Edmonton, Alberta, as he listens in *Absalom, Absalom!* to the story narrated by Quentin. "It's better than theatre, isn't it. It's better than Ben Hur, isn't it. No wonder you have to come away now and then, isn't it."[16] This comment carries us right into the heart of Faulkner's South. Far from being a lovingly perfect South, this is a sensational South in which arson, rape, murder and other such happenings are taking place.

Faulkner's South is in direct contrast with the South of the romanticists for it courageously reveals some of its own less flattering facets. Gone is the baronial pomp along with a profusion of silk and silver and mahogany and moonlight and champagne. Resources are in such a depleted state that Hubert Beauchamp, Isaac's uncle in *Go Down, Moses*, cannot get around to having a rotted floorboard repaired in his big house on the plantation. Visitors to Sutpen's Hundred are treated to nothing better than a kind of local brew. To Faulkner, the South is ambiguous enough to elicit at least two very distinct responses: the South as it was and the South as it is. Of course, in a writer as full of inconsistencies as Faulkner, such a neat dichotomy is sometimes hard to maintain. There are, in all conscience, dark spots in the past and, conversely, there are redeeming features in the present. However, Faulkner unfolds before us a South which had once possessed, by and large, dignity and honor and heroism; but that South has now become disoriented, trivial and mean-minded. Perhaps that's not well put. One may try any number of variants but the feeling of inadequacy is likely to persist. See what happens to Faulkner himself trying to describe Sutpen in *Absalom, Absalom!* He gets Miss Rosa Coldfield, Mr. Compson, Quentin Compson and Shreve McCannon each to try a hand, and each ends up giving a different version of Sutpen. One can perhaps infer something about Faulkner's attitude towards the South from the following colloquy between Shreve and Quentin, the latter perhaps being the author's surrogate:

"Now I want you to tell me just one thing more. Why do you

hate the South?"
"I don't hate it," Quentin says quickly, at once, immediately;
"I don't hate it," he said. *I don't hate it*, he thought, panting
in the cold air, the iron New England dark; *I don't. I don't!
I don't hate it!* I don't hate it!"[17]

If there are degenerates and perverts in the South today there were
men and women of heroic qualities and noble proportions in the
past. Faulkner's own family provides a paradigm for the South. To
quote Millgate: ". . . Faulkner has had cause to be aware, within his
own family, of the classic Southern experience of a glamorous and
more or less prosperous past contrasted with a relatively controlled
present. . . ."[18] Yoknapatawpha County was at one time inhabited
by the McCaslins, the Compsons, the Sartorises who, in spite of their
evil qualities, were men of great ambition and accomplishment. The
bearers of these stirring names are of decayed fibre and the South is
overrun by a numerous clan of mean and poor whites who are appropriately enough called the Snopeses.

Faulkner has, it appears, incarnated his vision of the South in
Thomas Sutpen. There is some general critical consensus here. For
Vickery, Sutpen is "a mirror image of the South."[19] For O'Connor,
he is "the essence of the history of the South."[20] For Hoffman, he is
"the vision of the South as a whole."[21] Sutpen cannot but strike one
as a truly heroic figure. He is built on a larger-than-life scale. Beginning from scratch he has built for himself a mansion from the like of
which he was in his early days driven away by one of the liveried
slaves. To achieve his spectacular success he had to work with an
astonishing single-mindedness, with a tremendous stamina. But he is
"both the pride and shame of the South."[22] Even while we admire
him for his undaunted courage, for his unflagging energy, for his
ceaseless pursuit of his goal, we also hold him guilty of building his
prosperity upon slavery and of using other human beings—even his
kindred—as mere tools to achieve his aim. He repudiates his Haitian
wife and his son because of his horror of miscegenation. He does not
care for Miss Rosa Coldfield and Milly if they cannot provide him a
male heir to ensure permanence for his "Design." In his scheme of
things, human beings have instrumental, rather than terminal, value.
This is, then—Faulkner seems to be saying in effect—what your so-
called kindly and chivalrous plantation civilization of the South was,
a direct contradiction of what Page and the Agrarians had tried to
make us believe. After filling in the entries both on the credit and
debit side in his ledger one might well describe Sutpen, *mutatis*

mutandis, the South itself, as "the complete statement of . . . ambition, execution and success, guilt, doom and destruction. . . ."[23] It would, however, be a gross oversimplication to regard Sutpen merely as a monster, as Miss Rosa evidently does, for Faulkner had no heart, familiar as he was with the sins committed in the past, to condemn the South outright, for the South was not without some extenuating circumstances. Uncovering the truth relentlessly, he could not help indulging in "a lyric evocation of the Southern past."[24] Sutpen—as well as the South—did make "mistakes" but we should rather pity than condemn them. In a clarificatory, as against creative, mood Faulkner resorted to a more explicit mode of utterance: "To me he [Sutpen] is to be pitied. He was not depraved—he was amoral, he was ruthless, completely self-centered. To me he is to be pitied, as anyone who ignores man is to be pitied, who does not believe that he belongs as a member of a human family, of the human family, is to be pitied."[25]

Faulkner made frequent excursions into the past of the South—that past which he himself created—in order that the South as it exists at present may be properly understood. And there he discovered that all the important families—Howe prefers to call them "clans"[26]—like the Compsons, the Sartorises, the McCaslins, follow more or less the same strategy, dispossessing the Chickasaw Indians of their ancestral land and building their own estate on it through the exploited labor of the Negroes. Nothing scares them so much as the thought of the Negro blood contaminating their "dynasty." In point of fact they all have two families, one white, one black; but their concept of honor, pride, the sanctity of the family and their decencies of life forbid them to admit this. To take one example: Lucius Quintus Carothers McCaslin brings from New Orleans a female slave named Eunice who bears him a daughter, Tomey, and twenty years later he begets a son of her known as Tomey's Turl. Uncle Buddy wins Tennie in a game of poker from Hubert Beauchamp and marries her to Tomey's Turl. The claims of their descendents to the family inheritance are, however, never recognized, although Dorothy Tuck, who has gone into this rather complicated genealogical problem with thoroughness, says that they "were in one sense more legitimate heirs of the first McCaslin than were the white descendants of McCaslin's daughters." To help us further she drives the point home thus: "Because Turl's mother was also the daughter of McCaslin, Turl's descendants were two generations closer to McCaslin. Thus Lucas Beauchamp, who was born in 1874, was McCaslin's grandson while Zack Edmond, who was born in 1873, was McCaslin's great-grandson."[27]

Nobody except Isaac recognized this fact and he thought that renouncing his share of his patrimony was an adequate atonement for
the past sins. Faulkner, however, considered it an all too feeble gesture to offset the great wrong as is apparent from the reply he gave
to Cynthia Grenier's query: "Well, I think a man ought to do more
than just repudiate. He should have been affirmative instead of shun-
ning people."[28] Needless to say, even this amount of fair play is
lacking in others. The defeat of the Civil War and the shame of the
Reconstruction are, therefore, a sort of merited punishment for the
South. The past is imminent in the present, and the sins of the
fathers are, through some kind of nemesis, visited on their sons.

So the South to Faulkner apparently is what it deserves to
be. And when Faulkner described it as he found it, isn't it ironic that
he should have been branded a purveyor of evil, "a salesman of
vice"?[29] It is true that Colonel Sartoris and Thomas Sutpen are
shown to be defending their plantations against the depredations of
the carpetbaggers and also rising equal to the occasion for some time;
they, however, find themselves increasingly helpless against a race of
wily, weasel-like creatures who descend on Yoknapatawpha Country.
They are not altogether foreigners, for Ab Snopes is seen engaged in
the lucrative trade of selling stolen horses and mules to both the sides
in the Civil War. If the Negroes had suffered in the past, so had the
poor white, and in the rise of the Snopeses the wheel appears to have
come full circle. Indeed, neither Faulkner nor we have any sympathy
for the Snopeses, but after we have been convinced that they are a
terrible menace—they have, of course, various gradations—the question that we feel like asking ourselves, and Faulkner would certainly
want us to do so, is this: What kind of South is this into which the
Snopeses find it so easy to infiltrate as though it were their natural
habitat?

This is a South which has been weakened from within. It
does not succumb so much to an outside aggressor as to its own lack
of moral stamina. If the Snopeses swoop down on it like buzzards,
it is because they meet with no resistance at the entry point, as seen
when Ab Snopes applies to Varner's son Jody to rent a farm for the
season. Knowing as he does that Ab had set fire to Major De Spain's
barn some years earlier and that a similar trouble might be in store
for him, Jody however has no courage to say "no" to Ab. Instead, as
a kind of bribe Jody employs Ab's son Flem at his store. From then
on, Flem moves steadily towards more and more success and influence. A large multitude of Flem's cousins pours in. They have the
best of time and they proliferate. Flem, the chief among them, rises

from a mere clerkship to become the owner not only of Varner's store and other effects but also the proud and impotent possessor of Varner's much sought-after and glamourous daughter Eula. Not content with this, he triumphantly moves from Frenchman's Bend into Jefferson, ultimately driving away De Spain and installing himself as the bank president and the owner of his mansion. The Compson property also falls into his hands and he proceeds forthwith to put it to commerical use. The rise of Flem Snopes is a sad commentary on Yoknapatawpha County, and synecdochically on the South. Here in Faulkner's canon is a land from which concern for moral values is fast disappearing. Flem's machinations yield such rich dividends because of the greed and self-seeking in others. But they are no better; only they are no match for him.

One might wonder what has happened in Faulkner's fiction to the great Southern families. The painful fact is that since the beginning of the present century there has been a steep decline in such members as have managed to survive. The old Sartorises had fought with heroism and conviction and a certain amount of grandeur, but their twentieth century descendants have no purpose in life. Mischievous and harebrained, they are content to indulge in acts of daredevilry, ultimately killing themselves. Let us look at some more scions of the once-famous families: Narcissa Benbow, wife of Bayard Sartoris, is pestered with obscene letters by Byron Snopes but she hasn't the resolve to report the matter to the authorities. Regardless of right and wrong, her credo in *Sanctuary* is not to get mixed up with a person people are talking about. Her brother Benbow, too, under her tutelage knuckles under to conventional respectability. Gowan Stevens thinks nothing of leaving a teen-aged girl exposed to great danger. How much liquor he can hold is his criterion of one's manhood. The daughter of a judge, Temple Drake, provokes people into sexually assaulting her. Gavin Stevens of almost ubiquitous presence is too much of an intellectual, too much of a talker, to do anything effective.[30] Some are, through their exclusive preoccupation with the past, ignoring their immediate obligations like Gail Hightower in *Light in August* who keeps conjuring up the scene of the galloping confederate cavalry, while some others are themselves embracing Snopesism like Jason in *The Sound and the Fury*. There is really nobody to hold the fort against the Snopeses.

That the aristocracy in the South, which could presumably act as a bulwark against the inroads of the unscrupulous go-getters, is itself in a putrescent state, is vividly dramatized in *The Sound and the Fury*. The family from which had once come governors and generals is headed by a dipsomaniac, world-weary and cynical, while the mother, afflicted with acute hypochondria, is forever melting in self-pity. The idiot Benjy may well be taken as a syndrome of the entire family. Since there is no center, the family falls apart and Candace and, later, her daughter, take to a promiscuous life. Through the plight of Quentin, Faulkner shows how the old code of honor, far from being a help is a hindrance to a generation which has lost its capacity for action. Instead of avenging his sister's honor, Quentin finds in imagined incest with her a convenient excuse to take his own life: " . . . he loved not the idea of the incest which he could not commit, but some presbyterian concept of its eternal punishment. . . ."[31]

In order to flesh out his apocalyptic vision of the South Faulkner had, no doubt, to accentuate some theatrical elements in it. But life normally is not lived at that heightened plane. Indeed, there are millions of people in the South who share very little in common with the characters that crowd Faulkner's pages. There is, in other words, the South in which people live their unsensational, humdrum, routine-bound prosaic existence. This South, which serves as a foil to Faulkner's, comes to life in Eudora Welty's works, notably in her novel *Delta Wedding*. It is a curious fact that although Shellmound and Magua are not very far from Yoknapatawpha County, yet their inhabitants are so engrossed in day-to-day living as to be scarcely aware of any large issues—somewhat like Hemingway's characters in *The Sun Also Rises*. They spend their days pursuing their business and attending weddings and funerals. Their participation in the life of their community and their sense of belonging in their family, keep them blissfully oblivious of alienation. The pathetic inadequacy of communication torments only those who, like Virginia Rainey in *The Golden Apples*, fail to merge their individual identity with that of the people around them.

Violent happenings are deliberately played down in the Welty universe. This is best illustrated in an episode in *Delta Wedding*. A severe cyclone hits the region, leaving the livestock in great danger. The grandmother Laura Allen, however, insists that first her curtains should be salvaged from the tree tops where they have apparently got entangled before any rescue operations are carried out for the bellowing cattle. And then she proceeds without further ado to mend "what could not help but be torn, so that no one could tell now which curtains they were." The marks of ravages are thus carefully wiped out so that normal life is resumed without any seeming break or interruption.

Family ties are not so tenuous or fragile after all; they still keep people bound to each other whatever the dismal reports of the sociologists might say. Robbie in *Delta Wedding* does eventually come back to be united with George and, like any other Fairchild, participates in the family life at Shellmound. The situation has been well summed by Bryant: " . . . family living is participation moment by moment in whatever comes or happens; and George's unusual capacity for that is the door by which Robbie returns and the window by which Laura comes to see."[32] The solidarity of the family is symbolized by the candle which Aunt Primrose and Jim Allen give to Danby and by a garnet pin which connects Laura not only with Ellen but with her dead mother's whole family.

Here I have presented three versions of the South: the idealized or the romanticized South, the South gripped by a moral chaos, and the South living unconcerned with disturbing issues. Each version has its own strength and validity. Who will deny that the old faith in an uncomplex, even gracious life in harmony with nature, setting great store by individual freedom, looking askance at any semblance of regimentation, is still an enduring and sustaining reality? Also, it is no use pretending that all is right with the South *and* the rest of the world. Are not mechanical and commercial values threatening to overwhelm whatever little of civilization still left over? In case we somehow find ourselves incapable of resolving the crisis, had we not better involve ourselves in day-to-day living in the stability which the framework of the family, battered and ramshackled as it is, still provides to many more people than we imagine? Viewed in this perspective, these three versions made available by the Fugitives, William Faulkner, and Eudora Welty would appear not to be entirely unrelated to each other.

It is, however, William Faulkner's South that has become the South of the thoughtful and the sensitive the world over. Faulkner never allowed his hold on the particulars to be relaxed, but with his rare genius he turned them into universals too. Faulkner's South, while it is firmly anchored to the clearly recognizable reality of Mississippi, is a microcosm of the modern world and a symbol of Man's plight in it. Like the lofty hill "who to the stars uncrowns his majesty, / Planting his steadfast footsteps in the sea. . . ,"[33] Faulkner is both a regionalist and an allegorist *manqué*. But the lesser hills, too, have their uses, not the least among them being to set off the sovereign among them.

Notes

[1]William Faulkner, *Absalom, Absalom!* (New York: Modern Library, 1951), 174.

[2]Frederick L. Gwynn and Joseph L. Blotner (eds.), *Faulkner in the University* (New York: Vintage Books, 1965), 273-274).

[3]C. Hugh Holman, *Three Modes of Modern Southern Fiction, Ellen Glasgow, William Faulkner, Thomas Wolfe* (Athens, University of Georgia Press, 1966), 5.

[4]Quoted by F. G. Davenport, Jr., *The Myth of Southern History* (Nashville: Vanderbilt University Press, 1970), 47.

[5]W. J. Cash, *The Mind of the South* (New York: Doubleday, 1954), 73.

[6]Quoted by Jay B. Hubbell in *The South in American Literature, 1607-1900* (Durham: Duke University Press, 1954), 796.

[7]Page, "From *The Old South*" in Richmond Croom Beatty, et al., *The Literature of the South* (Chicago: Scott, Foresman, 1952), 483.

[8]Ibid., 460-463.

[9]Ibid., 466.

[10]Hubbell, *The South in American Literature*, op. cit., 702.

[11]Robert Penn Warren, *Who Speaks for the Negro?* (New York: Random House, 1965), 344.

[12]Davidson, "Still Rebels, Still Yankees" in Beatty, *The Literature of the South*, 777.

[13]Davidson, "Lee in the Mountains" in Beatty, *The Literature of the South*, 768-769.

[14]Donald Davidson, *Southern Writers in the Modern World* (Athens: University of Georgia Press, 1958), 39.

[15]Margaret Mitchell, *Gone with the Wind* (New York: Macmillan, 1938), 94.

[16]*Absalom, Absalom!*, 217.

[17]Ibid., 378.

[18]Michael Millgate, *William Faulkner* (New York: Barnes & Noble, Inc., 1961), 5.

[19]Olga W. Vickery, *The Novels of William Faulkner* (Baton Rouge: Louisiana State University Press, 1959), 92.

[20]William O'Connor, *The Tangled Fire of William Faulkner* (Minneapolis: University of Minnesota Press, 1954), 94.

[21]Frederick J. Hoffman, *William Faulkner* (New York: Twayne, 1961), 134.

[22]Malvin Backman, "Sutpen and the South: A Study of *Absalom, Absalom!*" *PMLA*, LXXX (December, 1965), 604.

[23]Walter Sullivan, "The Tragic Design of *Absalom, Absalom!*" *Southern Atlantic Quarterly*, L. (October, 1951), 560.

[24]Hyatt H. Waggoner, *William Faulkner: From Jefferson to the World* Lexington: University of Kentucky Press, 1959), 279.

[25]Quoted in *Faulkner in the University*, 80.

[26]Irving Howe, *William Faulkner: A Critical Study* (New York: Random House, 1960), 8.

[27]Dorothy Tuck, *Crowell's Handbook of Faulkner, A Complete Guide to the Works of William Faulkner* (London: Chatto & Windus, 1965), 9-10.

[28]*Accent* (Summer, 1956), 175.

[29]Lewis Leary, Introduction to *Crowell's Handbook of Faulkner*, (London: Chatto & Windus, 1965), xviii.

[30]Although Gavin Stevens develops some redeeming features in *The Town* and *The Mansion*, it is, nevertheless, an exaggeration to call him "a personification of the regenerated South" as does Albert Gerard in "Justice in Yoknapatawpha County . . ." *Faulkner Studies*, II (Winter, 1954), 54.

[31]William Faulkner, *The Sound and the Fury* (New York: The Modern Library, 1946), 9.

[32]J. A. Bryant, Jr., *Eudora Welty* (Minneapolis: University of Minnesota Press, 1968), 25-26.

[33]Matthew Arnold, "Shakespeare," *Victorian & Later English Poets*, ed. James Stephens, *et al.* (New York: 1934), 511.

Chasing Spotted Horses: The Quest for Human Dignity in Faulkner's Snopes Trilogy

by

Elizabeth D. Rankin

In his short critical study, *Faulkner*, Michael Millgate writes that while several episodes of *The Hamlet* appeared previously as separately published short stories, "There is no question . . . of these stories being incorporated in *The Hamlet* simply for their own sakes: they are intimately related to the whole structure and pattern of the novel."[1] Among these stories is the Spotted Horses episode, which covers a substantial portion of the last section of the novel and which Faulkner himself says was the seed of the novel. In a letter to Malcolm Cowley dated August 16, 1945, Faulkner writes: "*The Hamlet* was incepted as a novel. When I began it, it produced Spotted Horses, went no further."[2]

Major Faulkner critics have never had much trouble relating Spotted Horses to the rest of the novel. Says Cleanth Brooks, "The tale of the spotted horses fits perfectly into this story of the rise of Flem Snopes. It is an account of the world of advertising and Madison Avenue, in this instance set down in a little backwater of a community in the far-away days of the dawning twentieth century."[3] Olga Vickery agrees that the episode emphasizes and develops the mercenary character of Flem Snopes: "In the episode of the Texas ponies, Flem Snopes . . . shows that he can not only emulate but surpass Jody Varner in a total indifference to any but economic motives."[4]

Edmond Volpe, however, sees that the episode characterizes not only Flem but the rest of "the hamlet's male population" as well: "The final section of the book continues to highlight Flem's immunity to passion with tales of men caught in the grip of forces as irresistible as love. The hamlet's male population is stripped of its senses by the dream of a horse bargain."[5] Occurring as it does, immediately after his more general remarks on the emotional state of that male population, Volpe's argument clearly implies that the

Spotted Horses episode is intimately connected with the world of the hamlet and its inhabitants.

I would go even further and suggest that the episode is in fact a metaphor for the human condition as Faulkner sees it and portrays it, not only in *The Hamlet* but throughout the Snopes trilogy. Occuring late in the book, the incident sums up and comments on at least four other independent episodes: the Ab Snopes-Pat Stamper tale published separately as "Fool About a Horse," the Labove story which Brooks says "could conceivably stand alone as a short story,"6 the Houston story which he says "obviously could be developed,"7 and the story of Mink Snopes, which is developed in detail in *The Town* and *The Mansion*. In all these episodes, the central characters share a common disillusionment with life and a sense that there is some "conspiracy to frustrate and outrage [their] rights as a man and [their] feelings as a sentient creature." They sense that life is meaningless; that honor, justice and dignity are lost concepts; and that they have been deserted in this meaningless universe by a god who is either indifferent or hostile to their plights. It is the basic existential dilemma, unarticulated and not fully understood here in the backwater hamlet, but still very real and very urgent. Faced with this "existential reality" that they fervently feel, emotionally if not intellectually, Faulkner's men react with desperate blindness, asserting as moral facts the abstractions that they know are meaningless and yet frantically pursue: the "uncatchable horses" that only destroy them.

Ab Snopes is the first example of a character caught in this dilemma, though he is not the best example. We see him first as a barn-burner, a violent, unreasonable, amoral man; and it is not until Ratliff relates his story to Will Varner that we realize that he was not always thus. "He aint naturally mean," says Ratliff. "He's just soured."8 Ratliff proceeds to tell the tale of Ab Snopes and his desire to vindicate "the entire honor and pride of the science and pastime of horse-trading in Yoknapatawpha County" (*Hamlet*, p. 35), and as Brooks notes, "The story of how Stamper outwitted Ab Snopes, as told by Ratliff in the best tall-tale tradition, is the story of a spirited contest for honor."9

Of course Ab loses the contest; he is humiliated; and it is this—among other things, we must assume—which embitters or "sours" him. This is our only chance to see the human, personal side of Ab, and in itself it is too brief to tell us much about him, but in the context of the other stories, it seems to fit into a pattern which they develop more fully.

Labove's case is particularly complex. Amidst the absurdity of the meaningless game that is his livelihood, he nurses grand mythical dreams of love and honor. But his lofty goals rapidly degenerate, first into the "mad" pursuit of an eleven-year-old girl whom he exalts as a goddess, and then into common lust. The ultimate humiliation for Labove is that even his lust is totally ineffectual: it provokes neither reciprocation nor violent retribution from the intended object, Eula, who responds to his "jumble of fragmentary Greek and Latin verse and American-Mississippi obscenity" with mundane schoolgirl annoyance: " 'Stop pawing me,' she said. 'You old headless horseman Ichabod Crane' " (*Hamlet*, p. 122).

Labove's story deserves further attention, but for my purposes here it is enough to say that it adds a further dimension to the theme of disappointed ideals.

Those disappointed ideals are finally linked with the cruelty of the cosmos in the story of Jack Houston. Houston first flees from, but is irresistibly drawn back to, the domesticating force which never has a name but is embodied in the woman he loves. His desperate love of freedom and independence, his own assertive will, forces him first to leave and then to return to her, only to see her killed by the symbol of his sacrificed masculine independence, the stallion. Her death destroys completely his sense of peace and stability and challenges his dormant but still indomitable will and pride which he now directs toward the heavens: " 'I dont understand it,' he would say. 'I dont know why. I wont ever know why. But You cant beat me. I am strong as You are. You cant beat me' " (*Hamlet*, p. 220).

Houston is the first of the *Hamlet* characters to recognize, or at least articulate, the suspicion that is later attributed to Mink: that there is a conspiracy of cosmic forces opposed to man and intent on frustrating and outraging his dignity. In *The Hamlet*, Houston's realization is juxtaposed with his murder. Just as he says, "You cant beat me," the shot rings out, and although the two events do not actually occur simultaneously, they are related simultaneously, with the ironic implication that Houston's defiance is pathetic and doomed.

Unfortunately the story of Houston seems incomplete. As Brooks says, it cries out for development—the kind of development that is given to the stories of Labove and Mink. But perhaps Mink's story itself helps develop Houston's. Mink's is certainly the most extensively treated story in the trilogy, and when we come to understand him as we do at the end of *The Mansion*, we also better understand all those who find themselves in similar dilemmas.

Volpe says that Mink "represents the poor, defeated, exacerbated, earth-bound tenant farmers who populate Frenchman's Bend . . . and his fate is the defeating, degrading, unrewarding struggle of the sharecropper against absolute poverty. In his simple, childish, stupid way, Mink is fighting that primal injustice which ordains some men to an inescapable existence of toil and poverty and others to a life of comparative ease." Citing Mink's "need to assert himself against cosmic injustice," Volpe says that Mink kills Houston "as the agent of a force beyond man which violates basic human rights and dignity."[10] Volpe's description of Mink in *The Hamlet* is a good one, as it points to the irony inherent in Mink's murder of Houston. To Mink, Houston is an agent of cosmic injustice, but we have already seen that Houston is actually just another victim of it, not as pathetic a victim as Mink is, perhaps, but a victim nonetheless.

In *The Mansion*, Mink's desperate and rebellious spirit is expressed in long passages of stream of consciousness. There we see that Mink's desperate attempt to assert order, if not justice, in the face of an indifferent universe, takes the form of a passionate belief in "them—the Them of whom it was promised that not even a sparrow should fall unmarked" (*Mansion*, p. 5). Early in the last novel, Mink is careful to distinguish between a benevolent god, "Old Moster," and the "simple fundamental justice and equity in human affairs" which he calls "Them" (*Mansion*, p. 6). Later he makes an even finer distinction: "*Not justice; I never asked that; just fairness, that's all*. That was all; not to have anything for him: just not to have anything against him" (*Mansion*, p. 106).

Mink's faith in "Them" sets him a little apart from Ab, Labove, and Houston since it seems to posit an abstract value that they have lost faith in. But Mink's faith is actually no more than dogged determination and absolute commitment to himself. It is faith in himself that drives Mink, not faith in anything outside himself.

In the end, Mink's story is the most thoroughly developed and interesting illustration of the human condition *in extremis*. That condition is best summarized by Volpe: "It is as if these people have known and suffered all the blows that outrageous fortune can heap upon them, accepted their fate as inevitable, and accepted a status quo arrangement in which they contain their anger so long as no further injustice is inflicted upon them. Then any occurrence, no matter how minor in comparison to their standard afflictions, is enough to upset the balance and trigger their pent-up fury. Overwhelmed by rage, they move close to madness."[11]

It is in a state close to madness that Volpe finds the men of Frenchman's Bend in the Spotted Horses episode. It is a tale, says Volpe, "of men caught in the grip of forces as irresistible as love." He goes on to explain the situation: "Everyone knows that the horses are wild and that the untrustworthy Flem is engineering the auction. The men make jokes about it; they all expect to be cheated, but they are as helpless as was Labove in the grip of their passion."[12]

The passion that drives the men of the hamlet is their hunger for absolute values: honor, love, human dignity and justice. They know that such values are nothing more than "wild horses," uncatchable dreams, and that the god who oversees their struggles is merely indifferent, if not hostile; and yet they persist in the struggle, helpless and yet determined, injuring themselves and others in the process.

Cleanth Brooks says that "the comedy of the situation and the gusto with which the whole episode is recounted provide the proper undercutting of any argument put too seriously or symbolism set forth too nakedly."[13] But when the naked symbolism suggests the absurdity of the human condition, Brooks's caveat surely does not apply. The comedy of the Spotted Horses episode is black comedy and the gusto is "pent-up fury," and the significance of the episode as metaphor cannot be overlooked.

Thus, Spotted Horses summarizes and symbolizes the basic human dilemma of Ab, Labove, Houston and Mink. It does not, however, suggest the whole range of possible human responses to that dilemma. For one thing, it does not include Flem himself.

At times, especially in the Spotted Horses episode, Flem seems to be identified with the forces of cosmic injustice: he is the "first cause" of the action, but removes himself from the scene, disclaims responsibility, refuses help, and cannot even be proved responsible. In short, he is almost the personification of an existential god.

Later in the trilogy, however, we will find that Flem, too, participates in the human condition. In *The Hamlet* he merely allies himself with the forces of cosmic injustice and takes advantage of them for his own personal gain. For the moment, at least, he is soulless—pure intellect, stripped of the traits that would make him vulnerable to the torments his kinsmen and neighbors suffer.

Diametrically opposed to Flem is Ike Snopes, the idiot. Ike is all vulnerability, all soul. Devoid of intellect, he is the ultimate victim, and as such elicits the sympathy of Ratliff. Though Ratliff himself is not directly involved in the Spotted Horses episode, this is not to say that he chases no spotted ponies of his own. Ratliff is obsessed with the abstract threat of "Snopeses," and although his attitude is essentially quite different from that of the other horse chasers, he is involved in the chase nonetheless. The metaphor for Ratliff's involvement, though, is the buried treasure episode, wherein Ratliff unknowingly aids in the ruin of Henry Armstid and discovers that all men are both victims and victimizers.

Before this episode, Ratliff was willing to protect Ike from "Snopeses" but declined to aid "the folks that cant wait to bare their backsides to them" (*Hamlet*, p. 326). In the buried treasure affair, however, Ratliff finds himself caught with his own pants down and learns to make a more positive commitment to all his fellow men.

These, then, are the four major types of human beings who inhabit *The Hamlet*: the innocent victim (Ike), the rebel (Mink, *et al.*), the victimizer (Flem), and the victim-philosopher (Ratliff). The last three will become even more familiar in *The Town* and *The Mansion*, where they will be joined by two new species of being: the poet and the woman.

The poet is a self-deluded creature, an anachronism of sorts, who simply refuses to believe in a meaningless universe. Personified by Gavin Stevens in *The Town* and *The Mansion*, the poet is in one sense foreshadowed in *The Hamlet* by the behavior of Jody Varner. While Jody is by no means the romantic that Gavin is, his chivalric ideal of female chastity reflects the same refusal to deal with the facts of human experience that characterizes Stevens. There is a little bit of Stevens also in Labove, who mythicizes mundane reality into a "poet's dream."

The woman as a character type is epitomized by Eula Varner

Snopes in *The Town*, but implied also by her presence in *The Hamlet*. In addition, the womanly ideal is represented in the first novel of the trilogy by the quiet, unobtrusive set of female characters who serve as foils to the more violent men. One remembers Ab Snopes's wife calmly and methodically running her bucket of milk over and over through her hard-won separator. Juxtaposed with Labove is young Eula herself, passionless, listless, passive and totally indifferent to his lust. In Houston's background is the quiet, patient, yet determined girl who literally puts him through school and finally marries him before she is killed. Mink's woman is the nymphomaniac he finds in the lumber camp—the woman who marries him, bears his children and sells her body to pay for his defense. And then, of course, there is Ike's cow—the ultimate embodiment of the bovine simplicity that characterizes most of the women of *The Hamlet*. But bovine is too pejorative a term; the women of *The Hamlet* are bovine only in their calm, instinctive, unruffled acceptance of life. The philosophical implications of such an attitude are developed only later—in *The Town*.

So the two new species of human beings introduced in *The Town* are not completely new. Both Gavin Stevens, the poet, and Eula Varner Snopes, the woman, are to some extent implicit in the earlier novel.

Gavin himself is a kind of undisillusioned Labove, an early Quentin Compson. He exists in a world of "poets' dreams," which he desperately adheres to in spite of all evidence to the contrary. At the end of *The Mansion*, when the fact of Linda Snopes's involvement in Flem's murder is pressed upon him by Ratliff, Gavin resists vociferously: " 'I wont believe it!' Stevens said. 'I wont! I cant believe it,' he said. 'Dont you see I cannot' " (*Mansion*, p. 431).

Gavin cannot believe in Linda's moral corruption because she has been for him the last embodiment of a moral ideal—an ideal that must exist in human form if it is to exist at all. As the trilogy ends, we find Gavin being born into the realization that Mink Snopes has lived with forever. The Heidelberg Ph.D. learns a vital lesson from the uneducated poor white trash: that we are all "poor sons of bitches that have to cause all the grief and anguish they have to cause" (*Mansion*, p. 430).

Whether Gavin will ever admit the full truth of this statement and apply it to Linda and himself as well as to Flem and Mink, is a

question left unanswered. But the juxtaposition of Gavin's realization with Mink's death implies that the former is the beginning of a
long, painful process, while the latter is the end. The situation is
similar to the end of *Absalom, Absalom!* when Quentin fervently
denies to Shreve that he hates the South. In that episode we see the
seed of self-realization that will result in Quentin's suicide in *The
Sound and the Fury*. Stevens's end is left only implied.

Throughout *The Town*, however, and for most of *The Mansion*, Gavin remains obsessed with what Eula calls "poets' dreams,"
i.e., high ideals—truth in its most abstract and intimidating sense.
Characteristically, he makes a telling point about himself without
knowing it when he says: "poets are almost always wrong about
facts. That's because they are not really interested in facts: only in
truth" (*Town*, p. 88). Gavin, of course, is consistently wrong about
facts in the novels, but he is passionately concerned with "truth."

At the other end of the spectrum from Gavin is Eula Varner
Snopes, the archetypal woman. Eula is representative of a certain
class of Faulkner's women that Olga Vickery calls "embodiments of
nature," women whose "concern with feelings and emotions and . . .
reliance on the immediate intuitive response to experience" make
them threats to the very existence of the "masculine hierarchy."[14]
While many of the women in *The Hamlet* and *The Town* share certain aspects of Eula's personality, she herself is the purest example of
the category of individuals she refers to inclusively as "women."

" 'Women,' " Eula says, " 'aren't interested in poets' dreams.
They are interested in facts. It doesn't even matter whether the facts
are true or not, as long as they match the other facts without leaving
a rough seam' " (*Town*, p. 226). Women cherish no illusions that the
universe is a meaningful one, but neither are they in rebellion, conscious or unconscious, against that universe. " 'You just are, and you
need, and you must, and so you do,' " says Eula (*Town*, p. 94). Later
she makes a further distinction between men and women (men who
are not-poets, that is). " 'Women dont care whether they are facts or
not, just so they fit,' " she tells Gavin, " ' and men dont care whether
they fit or not just so they are facts' " (*Town*, p. 330).

This statement is not easy to understand, but it is clarified by
the example Eula gives, the example of Manfred de Spain: " 'You
cant just stand meekly with your head bowed and no blood and all
your teeth too while somebody takes your pocketbook because even

though you might face the friends who love you afterwards you never can face the strangers that never heard of you before. . . . He'll have to fight. He may go down fighting and wreck everything and everybody else, but he'll have to fight. Because he's a man" (*Town*, p. 331).

These words could as easily refer to Ab Snopes, Labove, Houston, or Mink as Manfred de Spain—as Gavin's later paraphrase of Eula's remarks reveals. Gavin's statement that men " 'dont give a damn whether they fit or not, who is hurt, how many are hurt, just so they are hurt bad enough" (*Town*, p. 358) bears a striking resemblance to a passage describing Labove's agony in the earlier novel: "Then he thought that was exactly what he wanted: for somebody to get hurt, and then he asked himself quietly, Who? and answered himself: I dont know. I dont care" (*Hamlet*, p. 123). To be concerned with facts, then, as men are concerned with facts in Eula's terms, is to rebel, to assert the *fact* of personal dignity, to flaunt it in the face of cosmic injustice, indifference, meaninglessness.

Women, says Eula, are concerned with an entirely different kind of fact—not moral fact or metaphysical fact, but common, everyday fact, "the immutable facts necessary to the living of life while you are in it" (*Town*, p. 293). Women don't care whether moral values are facts, i.e., meaningful concepts at all, as long as they fit, as long as they offer an acceptable explanation without raising questions.

It is the women involved in the Spotted Horses episode who seek restitution for damages in the courts. They, like their husbands who chase uncatchable horses, seek justice, but for them justice is not an abstract term; it is a cash amount. Mrs. Armstid's pathetic suit for the five dollars Flem has cheated her of is denied on the basis of falsely sworn evidence that Snopes did not keep the money, but she is neither surprised nor outraged. "Dont expect," says Eula, and Mrs. Armstid has expected nothing.

Mrs. Tull, however, is no Mrs. Armstid. She is outraged. She is violent. And she responds to her husband's calm acceptance of his injury with "man-like" fury: " 'Dont you say hush to me! You'll let Eck Snopes or Flem Snopes or that whole Varner tribe snatch you out of the wagon and beat you half to death against a wooden bridge. But when it comes to suing them for your just rights and a punishment, oh no. Because that wouldn't be neighborly.' " In her assertation of the moral facts of rights and punishment, Mrs. Tull resembles Ab and Labove and Houston and Mink—she "expects." But in her implicit belief that rights may be pursued within the law and paid for in hard cash she reveals that she is a "woman" after all. Justice as an abstract concept has no meaning for Mrs. Tull; justice is the product of a system of law which "fits" the everyday facts of life together, whether they are moral facts or not, and leaves no seams.

Until now, apparently, the law has fit things together to Mrs. Tull's satisfaction. But now the seams begin to show. The cash, which Eck Snopes is even willing to pay, is denied the Tulls on a technicality. What we see in Mrs. Tull's outraged reaction to the judicial decision is either a "woman" becoming a "man" or a "woman" rejecting a piece of the puzzle that she now realizes doesn't fit. The latter explanation is most likely because her last words suggest that she is now trying to fit a new piece into the puzzle: " 'Dont hush me! Get on to that wagon, fool that would sit there behind a pair of young mules with the reins tied around his wrist! Get on to that wagon, all of you!' " (*Hamlet*, p. 338). Instead of directing her anger toward the cosmic forces of injustice, or toward society, the law, or her antagonists as instruments of that injustice, she blames her husband, the original victim. If law does not explain, make sense of facts, match action and result without leaving rough seams, then something else must. It must have been the victim's fault all along.

In this regard, the women of *The Town* are less equivocal than Mrs. Tull. Eula herself, Maggie Mallison, and the young Linda Snopes are all women for whom moral truth is a meaningless term. Says Maggie, " 'Women aren't interested in morals. They aren't even interested in unmorals' " (*Town*, p. 48). This is not because they are cynics or simpletons or innocents, but because they "learn at about two or three years old . . . the knowledge about their-selves that a man stumbles on by accident forty-odd years later . . ." (*Town*, p. 101). While these are Ratliff's words, later to be echoed by Gavin Stevens, and while they are doubtlessly completely un*true*, they "fit" in the context of the novel. For one thing, they explain what is otherwise unexplainable: the unfathomable, other-worldly, mythic character of Eula Varner Snopes.

In a way, Eula is not a character at all. She is a product of the male imagination. In *The Hamlet*, this is especially true. Viewed through the eyes of the country people, her brother Jody, Labove, her hungry suitors, Ratliff, and the anonymous but by no means unobtrusive narrator, Eula is the archetype and epitome of womanhood. "Her entire appearance," the narrator tells us, "suggested some symbology out of the old Dionysic times" (*Hamlet*, p. 95). Through-out the first half of *The Hamlet* until the time she leaves French-man's Bend to marry Flem Snopes, Eula remains primarily a symbol. At that point in the novel, however, she becomes a "calm, beautiful mask," a face. No longer "the nucleus, the center, the centrice," she is now seen in profile, and when Ratliff sees her returning to French-man's Bend, she is described as such: "The beautiful face did not even turn as the surrey drew abreast of the store. It passed in profile, calm, oblivious, incurious. It was not a tragic face: it was just doom-ed" (*Hamlet*, p. 270).

Of course we know nothing more about Eula Varner Snopes here, at the end of the novel, than we knew at the beginning. Both the Dionysic symbol and the beautiful mask clash sharply with the Eula whose rare direct speeches, never more than a line or two, re-veal her rude country manner. But the mask, the face, is somehow more individualized than the "mammalian female meat" (p. 100), "the body, which seemed always to be on the ouside of its garments" (*Hamlet*, p. 122). It is physically nearer the brain, if nothing else. So there is at least a hint in *The Hamlet* of the Eula Varner who will emerge as a near-real, though still mysterious, human being in *The Town*.

In *The Town*, our vision of Eula is still filtered through the eyes and minds of the three narrators, but through her conversa-tions with Gavin Stevens and her actions, especially her suicide, we learn more about her. Gavin's first private encounter with Eula is in his office the night after he has presented his suit against Manfred de Spain in the power-plant brass scandal. When Eula arranges to meet Gavin in his office to offer her body to appease him, her reasons are simple ones. She does not come to "save" de Spain or to "save" Flem, as Gavin thinks she does. If she is concerned with saving any-one, it is Gavin Stevens; and it is neither his reputation nor his honor she is concerned with, only his happiness. " 'What do you want here?' " he asks, and she replies, " 'Because you are unhappy . . . . I dont like unhappy people. They're a nuisance' " (*Town*, p. 93).

But of course Gavin cannot accept such a simple explanation. He insists on interpreting her actions for her, until she finally says, " 'You spend too much time expecting. . . . Dont expect. You just are, and you need, and you must, and so you do. That's all. Dont waste time expecting' " (*Town*, p. 94). This is Eula's philosophy, and it is consonant with her actions (or inactions) in *The Hamlet* and in

The Town. It also explains her suicide.

The suicide itself tells us something about Eula: that the calm beautiful mask is a woman capable of dramatic action. In this regard, the suicide is foreshadowed by the incident in *The Hamlet* when Eula is reported to have aided her lover, McCarron, by beating off their ambushers with the blunt end of a buggy whip. Both events are seemingly uncharacteristic of Eula, and, at first, quite puzzling. Of the suicide, Gavin Stevens asks Ratliff: " 'So maybe you can tell me because for the life of me I cant figure it out. Why did she do it? Why? Because as a rule women dont really care about facts just so they fit; its just men that dont give a damn whether they fit or not, who is hurt, how many are hurt, just so they are hurt bad enough" (*Town*, p. 358).

Of course the "rule" that Gavin invokes here is Eula Varner's own rule. The irony is that it applies very well here, but he does not see it. Enveloped in his own "hurt," in his own romantic world in which Eula is a mythic quantity not to be "wasted," Stevens cannot see that Eula's suicide is the only piece that will "fit" and complete the puzzle of her life.[15] Eula cares very much who is hurt, but she sees that either of the alternatives available to her alive would hurt more people than would her death. Eula's daughter, Linda, is her first concern, and, as Gavin says to Eula, " 'Either way she [Linda] is lost. Either to go with you, if that were possible, while you desert her father for another man; or stay here in all the stink without you to protect her from it and learn at last that he is not her father at all and so she has nobody, nobody' " (*Town*, p. 330).

As a woman with an intuitive sense of herself, born with the awareness that life is not intrinsically meaningful, and that "you just are, and you need, and you must, and so you do," Eula sees that the only way to save her daughter is to sacrifice herself. Of course Eula does not mean to save Linda in the sense that Gavin wants to save her—from being a Snopes; Eula simply wants to provide Linda with a set of facts that will fit together without leaving a seam.

In *The Mansion* we will see that Eula's suicide has not, in fact, preserved the puzzle intact for Linda. The workable fact that Linda has accepted at the end of *The Town*—that Flem is truly her father—is exploded when she leaves Jefferson and goes to live in Greenwich Village. It is in the "man's world" that Linda enters with her husband, Barton Kohl, that she loses her naive "woman's" idea that "it doesn't matter if they are facts or not as long as they fit" and starts to become desperately concerned with those "facts." Away from the bucolic, protective atmosphere of the isolated Southern town, Linda stops being merely a woman and starts to become a human being.

Even her physical appearance denies her womanhood. "She was tall for a woman," says Ratliff, "so tall she didn't have much shape (I mean, the kind that folks whistle at)" (*Town*, p. 174). Chick Mallison, who first meets her on her return to Jefferson after the war, says that "when she shook hands she really had driven that ambulance and apparently changed the tires on it too, speaking not loud but in that dry harsh quacking voice that deaf people learn to use" (*Town*, p. 199). Linda's physical appearance has not really changed (she was never the archetypal woman her mother was); but the mannish aspects of her appearance have become accentuated.

Linda is a new kind of woman—the Eve, in a sense, to Eula's Lilith. As Lilith, Eula is not really human; she is pre-human. This is why her suicide is not tragic in the way Quentin Compson's is tragic. Eula exists not as a human alternative to the pursuers of spotted horses, but as a foil to them. As Gavin Stevens muses when she leaves him for the last time, she is "not *not been* but rather no more *is*, since *was* remains always and forever, unexplicable and immune, which is its grief" (*Town*, p. 334). Eula as Lilith is separate and distinct from man; she can draw distinctions between the sexes which, based on her experience, seem perfectly valid. But Linda participates in the nature of man; she is formed from the rib of Adam and falls with Adam (but not—and here is where the Biblical parallel breaks down—necessarily *before* him).

So Linda, too, is a chaser of spotted horses. Her complicity with Mink in the murder of Flem Snopes reveals her obsession. In fact, Linda seems more perverse than Mink himself, because we have seen her ideal potential as a daughter of Eula destroyed, whereas that potential in Mink remains only negatively implied.

But Linda is really no different from the other "poor sons of bitches that have to cause all the grief and anguish they have to cause." Each of the "poor sons of bitches" has his own individual wild horse to pursue, but all share a common sense of frustration and despair—all except Ratliff and Flem.

Ratliff feels the frustration but not the despair. He is obsessed with "Snopeses" as a plague spreading through hamlet and town and has assumed the responsibility for trying to curb it. Neither his successes (the goat-buying episode) nor his failures (the buried treasure fiasco) are heroic, but he takes seriously his commitment to protect the innocent, encourage the good, and frustrate the corrupt.

If any incident can characterize the "bland, shrewd, inscrutable" Ratliff, it is a short segment of his conversation with Bookwright in *The Hamlet* as the two watch the idiot, Ike Snopes, dragging his toy in the road:

> "And yet they tell us we was all made in His image," Ratliff said.
> "From some of the things I see here and there, maybe we was," Bookwright said.
> "I dont know as I would believe that, even if I knowed it was true," Ratliff said.

The paradoxical, yet quietly affirmative statement sums up Ratliff's metaphysics and his psychology. Ratliff simply refuses to believe in an absurd, meaningless, indifferent universe, although he knows it is the only universe there is. In existential terms, Ratliff, has made that difficult "leap of faith," not necessarily toward God but toward the innate dignity of his fellow man.

In refusing to believe what he knows is true, Ratliff at first might seem to resemble all the others who run from the truth, blindly and desperately, stumbling as they go. But Ratliff does not run from the truth out of fear, as Gavin Stevens does; he simply turns toward a positive vision in hope. He is not perfect; he makes mistakes and errors of judgment, even hurts people inadvertently (the Armstids, for instance); but he is beyond doubt the most positively portrayed character in the trilogy.

One mistake Ratliff makes is that he never fully understands Flem Snopes. He comes close; but his proximity to Flem, while it makes him aware of the danger, does not allow him to see the pathos of this extraordinary ordinary little man. The passage in the trilogy that best explains Flem is, ironically, one that is meant to describe, of all people, Wallstreet Panic Snopes, Eck's boy. And of course only Gavin Stevens could be blind enough and fool enough to confuse these polar opposites. The passage occurs early in *The Town* when Stevens, half listening to Ratliff relate the story of the spotted ponies, speculates on the un-Snopesian nature of Eck Snopes and his children:

> And then suppose, just suppose; suppose and tremble: one gen-
> eration more removed from Eck Snopes and his innocence;
> one generation more until that innocent and outrageous belief
> that courage and honor are practical has had time to fade and
> cool so that merely the habit of courage and honor remain; add
> to that then that generation's natural heritage of cold rapacity
> as instinctive as breathing, and tremble at that prospect: the
> habit of courage and honor compounded by rapacity or rapacity
> raised to the absolute *nth* by courage and honor: . . . Genghis
> Kahn or Tamerlane or Attila in the defenseless midst of in-
> defensible Jefferson. (*Town*, p. 35)

Stevens here comes very close to defining the genesis and character
of Flem Snopes, born after father Ab's sense of "honor and pride"
has "soured" and left only that habit of honor and pride which manifested itself in burning barns. The "cold rapacity" that Stevens calls
the natural heritage of the next generation is the greedy, predatory
nature not of the coming generation, but of the first generation to
find itself alone in an amoral universe.

Of course Flem does not consciously discover himself in such
a position. As I have said before, he simply allies himself with universal forces he sees at work around him. And the empty habit of courage and honor he has inherited from Ab becomes perverted into outright audacity and the desire for false respectability. So the parallel
is perhaps not an obvious one. Still, there is irony in the fact that the
monster Gavin foresees and fears in Eck Snopes's innocent son, Wallstreet, is already ravishing the town though he doesn't realize it.

Ratliff might recognize the appropriateness of Gavin's interior monologue as a description of Flem Snopes, but he might not.
Because Ratliff is content to ascribe Flem's reckless and ruthless ambition to the search for respectability, not to honor and pride. For
Ratliff, even as early as *The Hamlet*, Flem is a man who has simply
sold his soul for money and has found out only too late that money
is not enough: " 'That's right,' Ratliff said. 'When it's jest money and
power a man wants, there is usually some place where he will
stop; . . . But when it's respectability he finds out he wants . . . there
aint nothing he will stop at, aint nobody or nothing within his scope
and reach that may not anguish and grieve and suffer' " (*Town*, p.
259).

Ratliff wisely sees the danger of Flem's new ambition, but he does not see its full significance. Until now, Flem has had nothing to do with the wild horses of human dignity and freedom. Now he joins the chase. But respectability is not the name of the spotted pony; respectability is just the spots. The horse itself, what Flem must have, is human dignity, meaning, significance. Like the others, he has begun to seek moral value in an amoral world. Of course he does not realize that respectability is a moral term or even the rough facade of a moral quality. The fact is irrelevant to him, and to Ratliff; but it is not irrelevant to us, for it allows us to see Flem not as an inscrutable, inhuman force but as a man who is very much like other men.

Flem's new-found desire for respectability is his downfall, his tragedy, if we want to call it that. Flem is the classic over-reacher, successful as long as he confines himself to sheer rapacity, but doomed as soon as he begins to desire loftier goals. His is the tragedy of all men; it is what makes them human—that desperate need to assert moral fact in the face of an indifferent and amoral universe.

If Flem Snopes is not ultimately a true tragic figure, it is because he does not realize—or at least we do not see him realize—the futility of his quest until it is over. He has been spared the revelation that comes early to Labove, Houston and Mink. He has been spared their anguish, their suffering, their rage. But he is also denied the nobility, the human quality that makes us, ironically, *respect* them.

So the trilogy ends not with Flem's death but with Mink's. And, again ironically, it asserts in Mink's death a principle that it has denied and ridiculed and undercut throughout: that there is a realm of "the beautiful, the splendid, the proud and the brave, right on up to the very top itself among the shining phantoms and dreams which are the milestones of the long human recording—Helen and the bishops, the kings and the unhomed angels, the scornful and graceless seraphim" (*Mansion*, p. 436).

Notes

[1]Michael Millgate, *Faulkner* (New York: Capricorn Books, 1971), p. 85.

[2]Malcolm Cowley, *The Faulkner-Cowley File* (New York: Viking Press, 1966), p. 25.

[3]Cleanth Brooks, *William Faulkner: The Yoknapatawpha Country* (New Haven: Yale University Press, 1966), p. 185.

[4]Olga Vickery, *The Novels of William Faulkner* (Baton Rouge: Louisiana State University Press, 1964), p. 173.

[5]Edmond L. Volpe, *A Reader's Guide to William Faulkner* (New York: Farrar, Straus and Giroux, 1964), p. 314.

[6]Brooks, p. 177.

[7]Brooks, p. 179.

[8]William Faulkner, *The Hamlet* (New York: Random House, 1940), p. 29. All textual references to the Snopes trilogy will refer to the Vintage editions of *The Hamlet* (1940), *The Town* (1961), and *The Mansion* (1965).

[9]Brooks, p. 182.

[10]Volpe, p. 313.

[11]Volpe, p. 314.

[12]Volpe, p. 314.

[13]Brooks, p. 188.

[14]Vickery, p. 288.

[15]Significantly, Stevens also reconstructs the buggy incident to suit his own romantic vision of life. He refers to McCarron as the one "that fought off the five or six men who tried to ambush you in the buggy that night, fought

them off with the buggy whip and one hand because he had to use the other to shield you with, whipped them all off even with one arm broken" (*Town*, pp. 94-95). Stevens claims to have heard this story from Ratliff, but Ratliff knows the true story of the buggy incident, as he reveals only five pages later. The mature Gavin Stevens, recalling his adolescence later, will admit: "I can even believe Ratliff when it suits me" (*Town*, p. 135).

*Continuity and Change: The Horse, the Automobile,
and the Airplane in Faulkner's Fiction*

by

Richard A. Milum

Undoubtedly some of the most useful and widely appreciated materials in the workshop of William Faulkner's literary imagination have been those related to the world of horses and horsemanship. A natural part of Faulkner's life from boyhood days in his father's livery stable until the final stages of his outdoor life in Virginia, horses were important to the man himself, and understandably constitute a continuing and significant part of his fictional world. Most critical attention to the subject has focused on the delightful horse-swapping and horse-stealing episodes such as the Ab Snopes-Pat Stamper confrontation and the "Spotted Horses" episodes of *The Hamlet* (1940)[1]; the highjinx surrounding the "Notes on a Horse-thief" section of *A Fable* (1954)[2], and Ned McCaslin's antics in *The Reivers* (1962). These particular instances, of course, place Faulkner clearly within the "tall tale" tradition of the American frontier, and their primary associations (especially for the American reader) lie there. Notwithstanding the special attention they have received, however, these few episodes constitute but a fraction of the total presence of the horse in Faulkner's work, and when that presence is evaluated in terms of the author's overall treatment, we find that Faulkner's equestrian inclinations are actually informed less by the American frontier than by the heroic tradition with which the horse was originally associated. The observation, moreover, is not particularly unusual when we consider that it effectively applies to much of the literature of the American West. Delineated most explicitly, perhaps, by Owen Wister in an essay on the American cowboy (1895), the notion has permeated our national fiction. Wister contends emphatically that

> in skill as to the horse, the knight and the cowboy are nothing
> but the same Saxon of different environments, the nobleman

in London and the nobleman in Texas; and no hoof in Sir
Thomas Mallory shakes the crumbling plains with quadruped
sound more valiant than the galloping that has echoed from
the Rio Grande to the Big Horn Mountains.[3]

To Faulkner, of course, such heroic associations fall within the
compass of a comprehensive life style which reflects his participation
in the Southern cavalier legend.[4] Beyond its physical significance and
its function as the etymological base of the very term *cavalier*, the
importance of the horse to that tradition throughout literature is
manifested in its symbolic contributions to the image of its owner.
Sir Walter Scott, who has been credited with (or accused of) more
than a nominal influence in perpetuating the cavalier tradition in the
American South, explains in his "Essay on Chivalry" that it was the
horse's importance to military nations in the age of chivalry which
gave special distinction to its owner, and for that reason it quickly
became the symbol of his personal value.[5] This historical circumstance, enriched by modern psychological associations, renders the
horse particularly useful to Faulkner in portraying characters who, in
one way or another, must measure up to, or be measured by, ideals
of masculinity which have been derived from the chivalric code.

As a part of its function as a measure of character, moreover,
the horse becomes for Faulkner a symbol of decadent European
aristocracy in much the same terms as the aristocratic relics brought
back from pre-revolutionary France by Issetibbeha, or the colonial
mansions of plantation owners such as Louis Grenier and Thomas
Sutpen, who likewise emulated cavalier models. The horses of Yoknapatawpha County, in fact, function almost exculsively in support
of the Southern aristocratic life style. For the most part they figure
either as valuable cavalry mounts, such as Colonel John Sartoris's
roan stallion Jupiter, and Drusilla Hawk's Bobolink, or as special
racing breeds such as Jason Compson I's two-furlong mare, or Ned
McCaslin's (Mr. Van Tosch's) sardine-eating Lightning of *The Reivers*. And falling into the same category are the finely matched team
which pulls Louis Grenier's imported English carriage, or the two
riding horses which Charles Bon maintains on the University of
Mississippi campus.

Far more than a material status symbol, however, the spirited
horse in Faulkner's work—or its metaphorical extension to the automobile and the airplane of later episodes—evolves, quite in line with
Scott's historical observation, as one of the most significant expres-
sions of individual merit or family pride. Several of Yoknapatawpha
County's oldest families, in fact, boast of daring and reckless cavalry

escapades performed by their forbears during the Civil War, and preserve the tales from generation to generation as testimonials of a proud cavalier heritage. The genre, perhaps, is best represented in *Sartoris* (1929) by the famous "anchovy" raid on General Pope's mess tent which results in the death of young Bayard Sartoris I, and which stands at the front of the novel as an introduction to the determined Sartoris impulse for self-destruction. The story is related by Miss Virginia Du Pre, whose voice in the telling "rings proud and still as banners in the dust."[6] What is more, we learn that

> ... as she grew older the tale itself grew richer and richer, taking on a mellow splendor like wine; until what had been a hare-brained prank of two heedless and reckless boys wild with their own youth had become a gallant and finely tragical focal point to which the history of the race had been raised from out the old miasmic swamps of spiritual sloth by two angels valiantly fallen and strayed, altering the course of human events and purging the souls of man. (*Sartoris*, p. 9)

In *The Reivers*, another daring, if not fatal, incident takes on significance. There, young Lucius Priest speaks of the Gayoso Hotel in Memphis

> to which all us McCaslins-Edmondses-Priests devoted our allegiance as to a family shrine because our remote uncle and cousin, Theophilus McCaslin, Cousin Ike's father, had been a member of the party of horsemen which legend said (that is, legend to some people maybe. To us it was historical fact) General Forrest led at a gallop into the lobby itself and almost captured a Yankee General.[7]

In the same novel Faulkner uses the device to achieve quite a different, although consistent, effect in the case of Dan Grinnup, a habitual drunkard and part-time driver for the Priest livery stable. Lucius tells us that the man's name "was not Grinnup at all but Grenier: one of the oldest names in the county until the family went to seed" (*The Reivers*, p. 8), and that "at times at some cold and scornful pitch of drink, he would say that once Greniers led Yoknapatawpha society; now Grinnups drove it" (*The Reivers*, p. 8).

In terms of individual characterization, one of the more subtly effective applications of the device occurs in the final episode of *The Unvanquished* (1938), "An Odor of Verbena." There young Bayard

Sartoris is called to the ritual of revenge in response to the death of his father at the hand of J. B. Redmond, his one-time business partner turned political rival. Bayard receives news of the slaying from Professor Wilkins at the college where he is studying law. In response to the professor's offer of assistance, Bayard requests a fresh mount for Ringo, who has carried the fateful news from Jefferson. Professor Wilkins impulsively offers his own horse, "a short-legged deep-barrelled mare who looked exactly like a spinster music teacher, which Mrs. Wilkins drove to a basket phaeton." The prospect is woefully inappropriate, however, and Bayard's reaction is significant; "we both realized that was funny . . . which was good for me, like being doused with a pail of cold water."[8] Having introduced a comic element at this solemn moment, the professor has provided Bayard with an emotional release from the impending ritual of revenge and reminded him, however unintentionally, that it must be rejected. Ringo, who was Bayard's accomplice in the revenge of Rosa Millard's death earlier in the novel, understands instinctively the solemn ritual which must prevail and arrives at the college with fresh mounts from the local livery stable. Both men can return to Jefferson with the required dignity. And the following day, although Bayard rides to town to put an end to the revenge cycle, he does so on his father's roan stallion, Jupiter, a horse well-known throughout the battlefields of the South, from Mississippi to Virginia.

Faulkner's horses, then, are clearly and customarily an important ingredient of the heroic pose, and it eventually becomes apparent that a character's relationship with them, or his affinity for them can provide a reliable measure of his relationship to the cavalier tradition in general. Those who find horses an irresistible attraction, or who are otherwise closely identified with them, display a dedication to the tradition which ranges, according to the degree of their involvement, all the way from a foolish self-indulgence to a sometimes fatal obsession. A dispassionate regard, a lack of skill in handling, or a deliberate antipathy toward horses, on the other hand, indicates the degree to which a character is immune to the temptations of the past, as well as his measure of success in adjusting to the present. The principle is implied by Cleanth Brooks in his analysis of the Reverend Gail Hightower of *Light in August* (1932). Brooks labels Hightower's obsession with the absurdly romantic image of his grandfather riding wildly into Jefferson on a Confederate cavalry mount with his sabre waving and being shot from the saddle as indicative of his dehumanizing allegiance to a dead tradition.[9] The same perspective applies throughout *The Unvanquished* to the image of Drusilla Hawk, who is regarded by young Bayard Sartoris as probably "the best woman rider in the country" (*The Unvanquished*, p. 101), and who actually defies an entire Yankee patrol in order to save Bobolink, the gift of her fiancee who was killed at Shiloh, by threatening to shoot the horse rather than surrender it. Bayard's first brief glance of his fatally romantic cousin occurs as "Bobolink came up the road out of the trees and went across the railroad and into the trees again like a bird, with Cousin Drusilla riding astride like a man and sitting straight and light as a willow branch in the wind" (*The Unvanquished*, pp. 100-01), The introduction is fitting for a young woman who will shortly reject her femininity to ride off to war as a member of Colonel John Sartoris's cavalry unit and eventually become the high priestess of the revenge code which the novel itself ultimately rejects.

The affinity for horses is particularly useful to Faulkner as an element of character contrast. In *Sartoris*, for instance, young Bayard demonstrates destructively romantic Sartoris tendencies by nearly getting himself killed in a wild ride through the streets of Jefferson on an unbroken stallion, while Horace Benbow exhibits characteristic Benbow "serenity" by his total lack of interest in horses (except for the delicate products of his glass blowing) and an inability even to drive an automobile, a skill which in the chronology of Faulkner's work eventually becomes a symbolic extension of horsemanship. A similar contrast is developed ironically in *Absalom, Absalom!* (1936), in which Thomas Sutpen's daughter, rather than his son, exhibits the spirit of the cavalier, continually urging the coachmen to race the coach on the way to church while her brother Henry timidly endures the ordeal. Much of the same kind of irony is inherent, of course, in the fact that Charles Bon, the son Sutpen cannot recognize, is in every conceivable way the cavalier spirit incarnate.

The principles involved in using the horse as a measure of character, moreover, apply not only to Faulkner's aristocrats, but throughout the entire range of the Yoknapatawpha social structure. Nothing is unusual, of course, in finding the serfs of society engrossed—admiringly, although sometimes humorously and often resentfully—with the ideals, rituals and symbols of the aristocracy. The principle certainly applies in Faulkner's work to the whole range of associations involving the cavalier tradition, and the horse, as a central symbol of that tradition, is no exception. Brooks, once again, in his discussion of *As I Lay Dying* (1930), pretty clearly identifies the "poor white" Jewel Bundren as an inheritor—in spirit at least—of the cavalier tradition, especially with regard to his love of horses. Working both day and night in order to buy a horse, Jewel becomes pre-occupied with the animal to the point where his brother Darl, whom Brooks refers to as "the anti-heroic intelligence" of the novel, "is bitter and even cruel in taunting Jewel for having a horse for a mother."[10] Darl's mental association of the man and the beast, in fact, is so complete that it underlies his total reference to Jewel. In the scene where the barn catches fire, Darl describes his brother rushing into the blaze to save his mother's coffin. From Darl's perspective, Jewel is actually "riding on it, clinging to it until it crashes down and flings him forward and clear" (*As I Lay Dying*, p. 212). Although Darl's view is extreme, to think of Jewel is necessarily to think of a man and his horse; and finally, it is Jewel's sacrifice of his horse which enables Anse to buy the rig in which the family finally reaches Jefferson, a gesture which Brooks says is "in many ways the most heroic thing he [Jewel] does."[11]

The extension of heroic values to non-aristocratic levels of Yoknapatawpha society, then, suggests that the equestrian "tall tales" of the Faulkner canon should also be re-examined from the cavalier perspective. In spite of his great admiration for the yarn, Faulkner most often invests it with a significance which transcends the genre of frontier humor. The ambush by Bayard and Ringo of an entire Yankee cavalry unit in the opening scenes of *The Unvanquished*, the pursuit of Tommey's Turl in *Go Down, Moses*, (1942), and the "Spotted Horses" episode of *The Hamlet* stand as cases in point. With specific reference to "Spotted Horses," for instance, John Lewis Longley speaks of Flem Snope's "instinctive grasp of the kind of folly and foolishness that men were capable of and the predictibility of profit to be gained from the manipulation of these impulses to folly."[12] James Gray Watson further points out that throughout *The Hamlet* "horses and horse trading are associated with the principle of masculinity," and that the " 'peasants' are no less susceptible to the lure of horses" than the aristocrats.[13] The weakness and the motivation pointed out by Longley and Watson are consistent with the cavalier bequest, and Flem Snopes, the central anti-traditional force of the canon, simply takes advantage of them.

The effect of merging the two traditions is evidence of a quality in Faulkner's work which Longley identifies as a "sense of extension; the ability to raise a private and local fiction to the level of a timeless and universal myth."[14] An indigenous element of the American frontier, the horse, with its combined literary, historical and psychological associations, becomes symbolic as well of a decadent European culture which represents a point of weakness, a potential source of corruption, and a dangerous risk to those individuals in Faulkner's work (regardless of birthright) who find themselves variously caught up in the cavalier ethic.

The Horseless Carriage

As an agent of the cavalier tradition, the horse receives an inevitable challenge from the automobile in stories set chronologically after the turn of the century. To transfer completely the richly allusive value of the horse to a machine would be impossible, and, to be sure, the transition is not achieved without some resistance on the part of those dedicated to the tradition. Reactions vary, but among the older generation they range from a stubborn refusal to acknowledge the very existence of the challenge to outright and active hostility. Aunt Sally Wyatt of *Sartoris*, for example, is said to have "lived much in the past. For her time had gone out drawn by horses, and into her stubborn and placid vacuum the squealing of auto brakes had never penetrated" (*Sartoris*, p. 175). Demonstrating active hostility, as might almost be expected, is Colonel John Sartoris, who needs but one encounter with the automobile to justify his writing into the city ordinance an edict "against the operation of any mechanically propelled vehicle inside the corporation limits" (*The Reivers*, p. 28). And old Simon Strother, servant to the Sartoris family in *Sartoris*, is typical of Faulkner's Negroes, whom Faulkner consistently portrays as some of the most dedicated adherents to the cavalier tradition as a whole. His scorn for young Bayard's new automobile is revealed in one of the routine "conversations" he holds with John Sartoris, even though the Colonel has been dead for over forty years:

> Gent'mun equipage, . . . Ridin' in dat thing, wid a gent'mun's proper equipage goin' ter rack en ruin in de barn . . . Yo' own son, yo' own twin grandson, ridin' right up in you' face in a contraption like dat . . . and you lettin' 'um do it. You bad ez dey is. You jes' got ter lay down de law ter 'um, Marse John . . . . (*Sartoris*, pp. 113-114)

Such characters, in their instinctive refusal to acknowledge or accept the new machine, display simply one more instance of an unwillingness to accept the inevitability of change—a notion which more than one observer has pointed to as a major cause for the failure of the old aristocratic order.

With some of the old guard, however, opposition to the automobile is mitigated either by the force of circumstance or a lack of resolve. Boss Priest of *The Reivers*, for instance, firmly believes that "the motor vehicle [is] an insolvent phenomenon like last night's toadstool, and, like the fungus, would vanish with tomorrow's sun" (*The Reivers*, p. 25). Yet the old banker is forced by John Sartoris's presumptuous edict to buy a car of his own rather than appear to be dictated to by the president of Jefferson's junior bank. The irony of his situation is pointed out by his grandson, Lucius:

> it was as though, despite his lifelong ramrod-still and unyield-
> ing opposition to, refusal even to acknowledge, the machine
> age, Grandfather had been vouchsafed somewhere in the begin-
> ning a sort of—to him—nightmare vision of our nation's vast
> and boundless future in which the basic unit of its economy
> and prosperity would be a small mass-produced cubicle contain-
> ing four wheels and an engine. (*The Reivers*, p. 28)

As an unwilling harbinger of our country's future, however, Boss Priest must be convinced by Boon Hogganbeck that, like a good horse, the automobile must be exercised daily in order to keep it in good running condition and to maintain its financial value. Gradually, however, the old man's resistance softens as he allows the family outings to escalate from a weekly to a daily schedule, and even takes it upon himself eventually to prepare his Yoknapatawpha neighbors for more of the same. "We must get them used to it," he tells his wife. "Who knows? There may be another automobile in Jefferson in the next ten or fifteen years" (*The Reivers*, p. 39). From this rather cautious concession Boss Priest eventually arrives at a point where he visualizes the effects the machine will have on his sons's livery stable. "He will still be in the livery business," he tells his daughter-in-law. "He will just have a new name for it. Priest's Garage maybe, or the Priest Motor Company. People will pay any price for motion. They will even work for it. Look at bicycles. Look at Boon. We don't know why" (*The Reivers*, p. 41). Having envisioned the limitless possibilities of his automobile, coupled, perhaps, with an extreme example of the unreliability of horses, Boss Priest can no longer deny the machine a place in his gentleman's world.

Ned McCaslin, Boss Priest's Negro coachman, likewise recognizes the automobile's capacity, at least for mischief, but his attitude contains an ambiguity of which he seems basically unaware. Originally, his feelings are consistent with those expressed by old Simon

Strothers in *Sartoris*. He thinks that Boss Priest could have more profitably invested his money in a horse, and subsequently demonstrates the courage of his conviction by actually trading the Winton Flyer for a horse, thereby precipitating the major action of the novel. His scorn for the contraption is so much a foregone conclusion, in fact, that Boss Priest will not insult him by asking him to wash it. Unlike Simon, however, Ned is instinctively eager for a ride in the car, and his claim is based on the fact that his veins contain more of cavalier blood than anyone else involved. He is, according to accepted family legend, a grandson to Lucius Quintus Carothers McCaslin, and in his view the "moiling Edmondses and Priests . . . were mere diminishing connections and hangers on" (*The Reivers*, p. 31). By regarding his seat in the automobile as a right of inheritance, Ned shows himself to be instinctively aware of the machine's kinship to the cavalier tradition.

Such kinship is exemplified most clearly, perhaps, by Aunt Jenny of *Sartoris*. Although she is unequivocally and tortuously possessed by the cavalier spirit, the old woman is not rigidly opposed to the automobile. In fact, her first twenty-minute ride with young Bayard III elicits a decidedly game response: "I wish I smoked cigarettes," she said, and then: "is that as fast as it'll go?" (*Sartoris*, p. 78). To her the automobile is not so much a threat to the old order as it is simply another means by which the Sartoris males can risk their necks and thereby worry their women-folks.

Her treatment of Old Bayard is illustrative of this attitude. Despite his professed aversion to the machine, the old banker begins riding about the countryside with his reckless grandson, Bayard III, allegedly to slow the car down at least while he is in it. Aunt Jenny, however, accuses the old man of feeling a grudging attraction to the car in spite of himself. "I believe anyway," she says, "that you like to ride in that car, only you won't admit it, and you just don't want him to ride in it when you can't go too" (*Sartoris*, p. 85). In her eyes his gesture simply reflects the old Sartoris penchant for recklessness in disguise, and, interpreted as such, the manner of old Bayard's death becomes a sad fulfillment of his destiny rather than the defeat of an aging cavalier by a hostile, mechanized environment.[15]

So once the initially hostile responses are modified, the automobile offers the same opportunities for wild, reckless daring as did the horse. Faulkner himself is reasonably clear about the symbolic relationship of the two. In his essay on the Kentucky Derby, for instance, Faulkner contends that the horse fulfills for man "something deep and profound in his emotional nature and need"; it provides

> a sublimation, a transference; man, with his admiration for speed and strength, physical power far beyond what he himself is capable of, projects his own desire for physical supremacy, victory, onto the agent.[16]

And in *Pylon* (1935) he speaks in quite similar terms, only this time of the automobile, calling it

> a machine expensive, complex, delicate, intrinsically useless, created for some obscure psychic need of the species if not the race, from the virgin resources of a continent, to be the individual muscles, bones and flesh of a new and legless kind.[17]

Faulkner clearly thinks of the two as providing pretty much the same function and embodying the same psychological truths about the nature of man.

The actual historical transition of our way of life from the horse to the machine, in fact, involves many cases in which the characteristics of the horse, at least for a time, were attributed to the invention by which it was supplanted. The locomotive, of course, was initially labeled an "iron horse," and even today freight cars are referred to as "rolling stock." The automobile was not only a "horseless carriage," but for years much of its basic design (driver on the left, engine in front) was dictated by our previous experience with the horse. That tyranny of custom at the end of one era and the beginning of another is captured most memorably, perhaps, in Bill Mauldin's famous cartoon depicting the grizzly old cavalry sergeant facing the agony of having to shoot the trusty Jeep which has just sustained a flat tire.[18]

Once we understand that like Mauldin's cavalry sergeant, Faulkner's characters also associate the automobile with the cavalier tradition, we can expect an individual's responses to it to provide the same measure of his relationship to the tradition. Young Bayard Sartoris, for instance, having failed to kill himself by riding the wild stallion, turns naturally to the automobile. Once, having failed to negotiate a curve at a bridge crossing, he is by chance discovered almost immediately and dragged free of the wreckage. Besides having narrowly escaped drowning, he is seriously injured and must spend several weeks in bed. Almost immediately after his recovery, however, Bayard returns to the near-fatal scene and repeats the dangerous maneuver, this time successfully; and typically, he offers no better explanation than an awkward "I just wanted to see if I could do it" (*Sartoris*, p. 263). So whether the *modus operandi* for his exploits is a horse, an automobile, or (as we shall see later) an airplane, Bayard's inclination for self-destruction remains the same.

Rafe MacCallum represents the opposite tendency, and his relationship to the tradition is succinctly implied by his initial reaction to Bayard's new car. Meeting Bayard in Jefferson, Rafe declines Bayard's offer to "show you what she'll do," with a firm but courteous "No, much obliged" (*Sartoris*, p. 121). A natural horseman and a shrewd horse trader, Rafe shares, along with the whole MacCallum family, many of the positive qualities of the old cavalier order—strength, courage, loyalty to family and friends; but he happily lacks the fatal attraction to danger so strong in Bayard, and the automobile represents for him no cause for irresistible attraction or unreasoning aversion.

By and large, however, the younger members of the old aristocratic families, the direct inheritors of the long-corrupt cavalier tradtion, make the transition easily and willingly—especially those who are in some way a sacrifice to or victims of the tradition. Their affinity for the automobile becomes symbolic of their corruption and decay. Most notable of the group, at least to the rest of the Jefferson community, is Manfred de Spain, who embodies all the more flamboyant aspects of the cavalier stance, but whose decadence leaves him vulnerable and ultimately defeated by the unscrupulous Flem Snopes. Lucius Priest reveals to us in *The Reviers* that Manfred's "red E.M.F. racer" is of a vintage with Boss Priest's Winton Flyer and Mr. Buffaloe's homemade machine, but that he regards it as incidental to his history of the automobile in Jefferson because

> Although De Spain [sic] owned it and drove it daily through Jefferson streets for several years, it had no more place in the decorous uxorious pattern of a community than Manfred himself did, both of them being incorrigible and bachelor, not in the town but on it and up to no good like one prolonged unbroken Saturday night even while Manfred was actually mayor, its very scarlet color being not even a scornful defiance of the town but rather a kind of almost inattentive disavowal.
> (*The Reivers*, p. 25)

Manfred's red racer with its muffler cut-out provides, moreover, the mocking sound which taunts Gavin Stevens during his mismatched rivalry with Manfred for the affections of Eula Snopes.

In *The Sound and the Fury* (1929), the unfortunate pass to which the Compson family has come can likewise be measured by their associations with the automobile. Caddy, for instance, after her disgrace, leaves Jefferson in the first automobile some of the country people around the town have ever seen,[19] and in the last glimpse we have of her she stands "doomed" in a magazine photograph along with a German staff general, beside "an open powerful expensive chromiumtrimmed sports car" (*Sound and Fury*, p. 12). The promiscuity of her daughter Quentin is likewise linked with an automobile as she regularly misses school in the afternoons to go for rides with her boyfriends. And Jason, who tries futilely to rein in his rebellious young niece, stands characteristically, halfway between the old and the new in his attitude toward horses and automobiles. He is contemptuous of the former and unable to adjust to the latter. He resents having to keep the horse and buggy, but cannot succeed in using the automobile to his advantage. He seldom rides in his own car without getting a headache, and on one occasion is soundly humiliated while attempting to thwart the amorous escapades of Quentin and her young man with the red tie. They simply lure Jason away from his car, let the air out of the tires, leave him stranded in the country without a spare tire or an air pump, and drive off taunting him from their Ford. And to complete the family protrait, it is the idiot Benjy, totally committed to the status quo and violently opposed to even the most insignificant of changes for whom they must keep the horse and buggy, because he won't ride in Jason's car.

The Flying Horse

So the automobile, far from delivering a death blow to the cavalier tradition, whose central image it threatens with obsolescence, ironically provides a means for Faulkner's cavalier to effect a transition to the modern world. And the vitality of that transition is further enhanced by the advent of another war (the cavalier's customary preoccupation), and the invention of another machine, the airplane. Once again, as with the automobile, Faulkner develops clear associations between the airplane, the horse and their appeal to men. In *The Reivers*, for instance, Lucius Priest describes the excitement of the crucial heat between Lightning and Acheron as having a "dreamlike and unhurried quality probably quite familiar to people who fly aeroplanes in close formation" (*The Reivers*, p. 297). And in *Pylon*, a poster in a riding shop window shows the contestants of the air-race leaning on their machines "as if the aeroplanes were a species of esoteric and fatal animals not trained or tamed but for an instant inert, above the neat brief legend of name and accomplishment or perhaps just hope" (*Pylon*, p. 7). In fact, Jiggs, the companion and mechanic for the unorthodox "family" of pilots, is at least in spirit, an ex-horse trainer who has worn out his boots. Accordingly, his main concern throughout the novel is for a new pair which he contemplates in the shop window (in the opening sentence) as they sit "upon their wooden pedestal in unblemished and inviolate implication of horse and spur" (*Pylon*, p. 7). The relationship between the machine and the animal is most explicitly expressed, however, by the unnamed reporter who explains that Laverne's son "was born on an unrolled parachute in a hangar," and that "he got dropped already running like a colt or calf from the fuselage of an airplane" (*Pylon*, p. 31).

Yoknapatawpha society, having been acclimated, perhaps, by its experience with the automobile, offers only token resistance to the airplane, and predictably that comes once again from Aunt Jenny Du Pre of *Sartoris* who scorns the machine simply because it is superfluous.

> Do you reckon that when my Bayard came back from The War that he made a nuisance of himself to everybody that had to live with him? But he was a gentleman, he raised the devil like a gentleman ... look what he did with a horse ... He didn't need any flying machine. (*Sartoris*, p. 230)

But in telling and retelling the story of "her Bayard's" death prior to the second battle of Manassas, however, she elevates the incident to the point that Bayard and Jeb Stuart have become "two angels valiantly fallen and strayed" (*Sartoris*, p. 9). Her choice of words, moreover, underlines the continuity of experience between the cavalryman and the combat pilot, because young Bayard III's feverish conversation about "his" war likewise contains images "of a life peopled by young men like angels, and of a meteoric violence like that of fallen angels, beyond heaven or hell and partaking of both" (*Sartoris*, p. 126). As fallen angels, then, the Sartoris kinsmen achieve a poetic dimension affirmed later in the novel by Horace Benbow. While waiting to play tennis at Belle Mitchell's, Horace finds himself in a conversation with a young lady about poets and aviators.

The association brings the young woman to mention the Sartoris boys, and Horace asks: "Were they poets? . . . I mean, the one that got back? I know the other one, the dead one was" (*Sartoris*, p. 186). Horace, who loves Milton and Keats as well as the classics, obviously understands the poetry of experience, and perhaps also detects a connection between Johnny Sartoris and Pegasus, the flying horse, symbol of poetic inspiration.

Without the benefit of a literary education, however, Cecily Saunders of *Soldiers' Pay* (1926) also regards air combat within the cavalier frame of reference. Her letters to Donald Mahon, we are told, contain "all the old bunk about knights of the air and the romance of battle."[20] Any cavalier, in fact, would have thrived as a pilot in World War I, for as Faulkner himself points out, that was a time before fliers carried parachutes, and before flying was depersonalized by mechanical devices.[21] Johnny Sartoris, for instance, was slain by no blind shot fired by an unknown and unknowing assailant. " 'It was Ploeckner,' [Bayard] added, and for the moment his voice was still and untroubled with vindicated pride. 'He was one of the best they had. Pupil of Richthofen's' " (*Sartoris*, p. 46). Recalling Cecily Saunders' "knights of the air," in fact, the whole encounter resembles a medieval tournament replete with names, insignias, heroic effort, and romantic gestures. Bayard describes Johnny's death:

> The Hun stopped shooting then, and all of us sort of just sat there for a while. I couldn't tell what John was up to until I saw him swing his feet out. Then he thumbed his nose at me like he was always doing and flipped his hand at the Hun and kicked his machine out of the way and jumped. He jumped feet first. You can't fall far feet first, you know, and pretty soon he sprawled out flat. There was a bunch of cloud right under us and he smacked on it right on his belly, like what we used to call gut-bursters in swimming. But I never could pick him up below the cloud. (*Sartoris*, p. 252)

The story will no doubt be re-told again and again until Johnny and his R.F.C. squadron assume an equity in Sartoris family legend with Bayard I and Jeb Stuart's cavalry troop.

Fate, however, is not so generous to Bayard III. As a combat pilot he was a member of the fighting elite—a group of men, fearless, reckless, proud—a fraternity from which the uninitiated were forever and disdainfully excluded. Back in Jefferson after the Armistice, he is condescending and insulting to a veteran of the British infantry, insensitive to the servants, irresponsible to his family and friends. The wartime experience, the romantic encounter, has left him unsuitable for fruitful participation in a peaceful society, and his sole preoccupation is to fulfill the wish for death which eluded him during the war. Accordingly the airplane becomes the vehicle of that fulfillment, as it was for his brother, and as were an automobile for his grandfather and a horse for the first Bayard.

In *Pylon* flying emerges as symbolic of the general disillusionment and restlessness of youth in the post-war world. The barnstormers and the race pilots "ain't human," says the reporter. "No ties" (*Pylon*, p. 30). Their experience admittedly involves courage, but a courage which must go largely unappreciated because it has no apparent utility in the practical, earth-bound world. Consequently the juxtaposition of the two worlds provides an ironic comment on the status of this new cavalier. His manhood will be tested at Feinman Airport, just outside a city appropriately named New Valois, Franciana, but which is dedicated simultaneously to "The Aviators of America and Colonel H. I. Feinman, Chairman Sewage Board." And we are further informed that the airport, the tournament site, was literally "Raised up and Created out of the Waste Land" (*Pylon*, p. 11). In spite of the setting, however, Roger Shumann, who has damaged his own plane, enters the race in a plane he knows to be defective, and in a valiant but reckless effort to win a large purse for his family, loses his life when the plane breaks up and crashes. Nor does his moment of truth lack the customary heroic gesture.

> They said later about the apron that he used the last of his control before the fuselage broke to zoom out of the path of the two aeroplanes behind while he looked down at the close-peopled land and the empty lake, and made a choice before the tailgroup came completely free. (*Pylon*, p. 141)

And following Shumann's death, Jiggs, in a sacrifice reminiscent of that made by Jewel in *As I Lay Dying*, pawns his highly prized riding boots in order to buy presents for Shumann's widow and her son. Such gestures, however honorable, have no discernable relevance in a modern wasteland. In the context of *Pylon* they represent the code of ethics surrounding the game of air-racing. In another context, however, similar gestures represent the "game of Sartoris"; and although we know that game to be "outmoded and played with pawns shaped too late and to an old dead pattern," (*Sartoris*, p. 380) we know also that it contains a sense of order and beauty sadly lacking in much of the modern world.

This basic dichotomy, moreover, permeates the Faulkner canon. In terms of order, beauty, and the overall quality of life, the Southern cavalier past is far superior to the Snopes-dominated present. Faulkner, however, was detached enough from his materials to recognize that the exotic beauty of the Southern past was the beauty of a decadent tradition, that the grand gestures had long since lost their meaning, and that a failure to recognize that condition would render the individual obsolete, and the artist irrelevant. Like it or not, Snopesism, through all its self-aggrandizing ways, contains an awesome vitality. Faulkner's belief in the "old verities . . . love and honor and pity and pride and compassion and sacrifice" is well known; but his art demonstrates, in addition, that he believes man is eternal in his weaknesses as well as his strengths. One of the consistent "problems of the human heart in conflict with itself," in fact, involves the seductions of decadent beauty. Another is man's irresistible inclination, and always in terms of that "old dead pattern," to make the grand gesture—a gesture which traditionally precedes his fall. And by establishing the horse as the central image of that grand but futile gesture, and extending its qualities to the automobile and the airplane, Faulkner has found, in the midst of change, yet another means of stressing the continuity of human experience.

Notes

[1]The Snopes-Stamper episode first appeared as "Fool About a Horse" in *Scribner's Magazine*, August, 1936; "Spotted Horses," in *Scribner's Magazine*, June, 1931. Both were slightly revised for inclusion in *The Hamlet*.

[2]Previously published as *Notes on a Horsethief*, Greenville, Mississippi: Levee Press, 1950.

[3]Owen Wister, "The Evolution of a Cow-Puncher." *Harper's New Monthly Magazine*, 91 (September, 1895), 602-17. Consider also Harold McCracken. *The American Cowboy* (Garden City, New York: Doubleday, 1973), p. 11. "He [the American cowboy] is recognized as the last of a long line of cavaliers, although he is probably better known today than the knights of King Arthur's Round Table, or the Spanish *conquistadors*, who brought to

America the cowboy's horse and the cattle on which the economy of our western empire was built."

[4]For a complete description of the legend and its use in Southern fiction see: Wilbur J. Cash, *The Mind of the South*, 1941; F. Garvin Davenport, Jr., *The Myth of Southern History: Historical Consciousness in Twentieth-Century Southern Literature*, 1967; and William R. Taylor, *Cavalier and Yankee: The Old South and American National Character*, 1961.

[5]Walter Scott, *The Miscellaneous Prose Works of Sir Walter Scott* (Boston: Wills and Lilly, 1829), 6, p. 4.

[6]William Faulkner, *Sartoris* (New York: Random House, 1929), p. 19.

[7]Faulkner, *The Reivers* (New York: Random House, 1962), p. 96.

[8]Faulkner, *The Unvanquished* (New York: Random House, 1934), p. 245.

[9]Cleanth Brooks, *William Faulkner: The Yoknapatawpha Country* (New Haven: Yale University Press, 1963), p. 56.

[10]Brooks, p. 158.

[11]Brooks, p. 162.

[12]John Lewis Longley, *The Tragic Mask: A Study of Faulkner's Heroes* (Chapel Hill: University of North Carolina Press, 1957), p. 154.

[13]James Gray Watson, *The Snopes Dilemma: Faulkner's Trilogy* (Coral Gables: University of Miami Press, 1970), p. 70.

[14]Longley, p. 159.

[15]For a differing viewpoint see Glenn O. Carey. "William Faulkner on the Automobile as Socio-Sexual Symbol," *The CEA Critic* 36 (January 1974), 15-17. From a point of basic agreement, i.e., that the automobile in Faulkner's work does indeed function as a "socio-sexual symbol," Professor Carey, taking his lead from Gavin Stevens, associates that machine with the sexual sterility and spiritual deterioration of modern times. From such a perspective, Old Bayard's death certainly represents a defeat of the old order. Both perspectives, in fact, regard the automobile as a threat to Old Bayard; Professor Carey's note lays the blame on modern society; here Bayard, the old Cavalier, finally succumbs to the "old dead pattern" of his Sartoris ancestors.

[16]Faulkner, "Kentucky: May: Saturday," *Sports Illustrated*, May 1955, pp. 57-58.

[17]Faulkner, *Pylon* (New York: Random House, 1935), p. 87.

[18]Bill Mauldin, *Up Front* (New York: Henry Holt and Company, 1944), p. 114.

[19]Faulkner, *The Sound and the Fury* (New York, Random House, 1935), p. 87.

[20]Faulkner, *Soldiers' Pay* (1926, rpt. London: Chatto and Windus, 1930), p. 35.

[21]Faulkner, *Lion in the Garden: Interviews with William Faulkner*, 1926-1962, eds. James B. Meriwether and Michael Millgate (New York: Random House, 1968), pp. 138-139.

Faulkner: Meteor, Earthquake, and Sword

by

Jerry A. Herndon

Cleanth Brooks tells us that we cannot take the Sutpen story as a literary analogue of antebellum Southern history.[1] At least, if we do, we must take account of Sutpen's very un-Southern attempt to seize the reality of the concepts of aristocracy and tradition in the realm of abstraction. Professor Brooks writes:

> ... Sutpen's manners indicate his abstract approach to the whole matter of living. Sutpen would seize upon "the traditional" as a pure abstraction—which, of course, is to deny its very meaning. For him the tradition is not a way of life "handed down" or "transmitted" from the community, past and present, to the individual nurtured by it. It is an assortment of things to be possessed, not a manner of living that embodies certain values and determines men's conduct.[2]

Brooks asserts further that Sutpen only attains "a kind of acceptance," and that "Sutpen does remain outside the community. . . ."[3] He says,

> We must be prepared to take such traits [as Sutpen's cold rationalism] into account if we attempt to read the story of Sutpen's fall as a myth of the fall of the Old South. Unless we are content with some rather rough and ready analogies, the story of the fall of the house of Sutpen may prove less than parallel.[4]

Miss Rosa Coldfield would apparently agree with Brooks. To Quentin Compson she described in outrage the founding of Sutpen's Hundred:

...in the long unamaze Quentin seemed to watch them overrun suddenly the hundred square miles of tranquil and aston-
ished earth and drag house and formal gardens violently out
of the soundless Nothing and clap them down like cards upon
a table beneath the up-palm immobile and pontific, creating
the Sutpen's Hundred . . . .[5]

Miss Coldfield said caustically,

He wasn't a gentleman. He wasn't even a gentleman. He
came here with a horse and two pistols and a name which
nobody ever heard before . . . a man who rode into town out
of nowhere with a horse and two pistols and a herd of wild
beasts that he had hunted down singlehanded because he
was stronger . . . than even they were . . . who . . . concealed
himself behind respectability, behind that hundred miles of
land which he took from a tribe of ignorant Indians . . . and a
house the size of a courthouse . . . and . . . called it Sutpen's
Hundred as if it had been a king's grant in unbroken perpetuity
from his great grandfather . . . . (AA, pp. 14, 16)

No, said she, Sutpen did not fit the pattern: "he was no
younger son sent out from some old quiet country like Virginia or
Carolina with the surplus negroes to take up new land . . ." (AA, p.
17).

But surely a case can be made for the existence of a closer
parallel between Sutpen's story and the story of the fall of the Old
South than is suggested by either Professor Brooks or the initial remarks of Miss Rosa Coldfield. Such a case can be based not only on
the text of *Absalom, Absalom!* but also on symbols and allusions
which tie the Sutpen story to the histories of the Compsons, the
McCaslins, and the Sartorises.

I

That Faulkner intended the Sutpen story as an analogue of

antebellum Southern history seems clear. The outlines of the Sutpen story were already known to Quentin:

> It was part of his twenty years' heritage . . . a part of the town's
> —Jefferson's—eighty years' heritage . . . . Quentin had grown
> up with that; the mere names were interchangeable and almost
> myriad. His childhood was full of them; his very body was an
> empty hall echoing with sonorous defeated names; he was not
> a being, an entity, he was a commonwealth, (AA, pp. 11-12)

Miss Coldfield admitted Sutpen's bravery, then confessed his identity with other planter/soldiers when she lamented:

> . . . that our cause, our very life and future hopes and past
> pride, should have been thrown into the balance with men
> like that to buttress it—men with valor and strength but without
> pity or honor. (AA, p. 20)

Listening to her, Quentin felt as if he were viewing a mighty drama, one obviously charged with significance for him:

> . . . the long-dead object of her impotent yet indomitable
> frustration would appear, as though by outraged recapitula-
> tion evoked . . . .
> . . . the ghost mused with shadowy docility as if it were
> the voice which he haunted . . . . Out of quiet thunderclap
> he would abrupt (man-horse-demon) upon a scene peaceful
> and decorous as a schoolprize water color, faint sulphur-reek
> still in hair clothes and beard, with grouped behind him his
> band of wild niggers like beasts half tamed . . . . in attitudes
> wild and reposed, and manacled among them the French arch-
> itect . . . . Immobile, bearded and hand palm-lifted the horse-
> man sat . . . . Then . . . Quentin seemed to watch them over-
> run suddenly the hundred square miles of tranquil and aston-
> ished earth and drag house and formal gardens violently out of
> the soundless Nothing . . . . (AA, pp. 7-8)

Mr. Compson told Quentin that Sutpen "was not liked . . . but feared . . . . But he was accepted [by 1860] . . ." (AA, p. 72). And Sutpen like other planters had, in using but not acknowledging the black, sown "dragon's teeth" (AA, p. 62). Mr. Compson said,

> . . . I have always liked to believe that he intended to name
> Clytie, Cassandra, prompted by some pure dramatic economy
> not only to beget but to designate the presiding augur of his
> own disaster . . . . (AA, p. 62)

His face, mused Mr. Compson, must have seemed to Miss Rosa in
1866

> that ogre-face of her childhood seen once and then repeated
> at intervals and on occasions which she could neither count
> nor recall, like the mask in Greek tragedy, interchangeable not
> only from scene to scene, but from actor to actor and behind
> which the events and occasions took place without chronology
> or sequence . . . . (AA, p. 62)

Sutpen, said Mr. Compson,

> was acting his role . . . [but] while he was still playing the
> scene to the audience, behind him Fate, destiny, retribution,
> irony—the stage manager, call him what you will—was already
> striking the set and dragging on the synthetic and spurious
> shadows and shapes of the next one. (AA, p. 72)

He said that the war scattered "the black foundation on which . . .
[Sutpen's Hundred] had been erected . . ." (AA, p. 78). His comment suggested the flaw in the South's, and Sutpen's, "design"; as
he put it ironically (in another context) "there was a nigger in the
woodpile . . ." (AA, p. 72). Further, he said that 1860 brought "the
destiny of Sutpen's family [to] the gorge which would be the land's
catastrophe too . . ." (AA, p. 74).

Miss Coldfield herself spoke of Sutpen's attachment to the
Coldfields as sign of "a fatality and curse on our family . . . . Yes,
fatality and curse on the South and on our family . . ." (AA, p. 21).

Clytie, said Miss Rosa,

> . . . in the very pigmentation of her flesh represented that
> debacle which had brought Judith and me to what we were
> . . . [and] she . . . remained to represent to us the threatful
> portent of the old (AA, pp. 156-157)

Nothing could be more symbolic than Bon's funeral, as reported by Miss Coldfield. She admitted she never saw the body and could not even tell if the coffin bore a body's weight; she called him "the abstraction which we had nailed into a box . . ." (AA, p. 153). She told of the funeral "service": Theophilus McCaslin cried, "I can pray for any Confedrit soldier," then raised the Rebel yell over the grave: "Yaaaay, Forrest! Yaaaay, John Sartoris! Yaaaaaay!" (AA, p. 152). Henry's shot, said Miss Coldfield, made a sound which "was . . . the sharp and final clap-to of a door between us and all that was, all that might have been . . ." (AA, p. 158).

Sutpen's attempt to restructure his design by using the poor white, Wash Jones, was symbolic. He showed the same flaw—the willingness to use others without acknowledging their humanity—which had cursed the land with slavery and brought tragedy. At first Jones could not see Sutpen's ruthlessness. Though a poor man, he felt closer to Sutpen, because both were white, than he did to the poverty-stricken blacks:

> . . . Father said how for that moment [before the War] Wash's heart would be quiet and proud both and that maybe it would seem to him that this world where niggers, that the Bible said had been created and cursed by God to be brute and vassal to all men of white skin, were better found and housed and even clothed than he and his granddaughter—that this world where he walked always in mocking and jeering echoes of nigger laughter, was just a dream and an illusion and that the actual world was the one where his own lonely apotheosis . . . galloped on the black thoroughbred, thinking maybe, Father said, how the Book said that all men were created in the image of God and so all men were the same in God's eyes anyway, looked the same to God at least, and so he would look at Sutpen and think *A fine proud man. If God Himself was to come down and ride the natural earth, that's what He would aim to look like.* (AA, p. 282)

He expected honor and compassion from Sutpen. Perhaps, said Mr. Compson, when Sutpen rode out to see his child:

> . . . there broke free and plain in midgallop against the yellow sky of dawn the fine proud image of the man on the fine

proud image of the stallion and . . . the fumbling and the
groping [in Jones's mind] broke clear and free too, not in
justification or explanation or extenuation or excuse, Father
said, but as the apotheosis lonely, explicable, beyond all human
fouling . . . . (AA, p. 287)

But Sutpen failed him. And Jones cut him down with the
scythe. Surely the scythe symbolized time itself. Jones, significantly, thought of Sutpen as typical of his class. In his disillusionment, while waiting for Sutpen's neighbors to come after him, he
must have mused, said Mr. Compson, of those

> . . . who had galloped also in the old days arrogant and proud
> on the fine horses about the fine plantations—symbol also of
> admiration and hope, instruments too of despair and grief; these
> it was whom he was expected to run from and it seeming to
> him probably that he had no less to run from than he had to
> run to; that if he ran he would be fleeing merely one set of
> bragging and evil shadows for another . . . Father said that
> maybe for the first time in his life he began to comprehend how
> it had been possible for Yankees or any other army to have
> whipped them—the gallant, the proud, the brave; the acknow-
> ledged and chosen best among them all to bear the courage
> and honor and pride. (AA, pp. 289-290)

Perhaps his final assessment, said Mr. Compson, was in these
terms: " 'Brave! Better if narra one of them had ever rid back in '65
. . .' " (AA, p. 290). When Major De Spain and the other planters
attempted to seize him, Jones grasped the scythe and charged: "he
was running toward them all . . ." (AA, p. 292).

Sutpen's tragic flaw, his lack of compassion, was aptly pointed
out by Miss Coldfield: He was a man " . . . with valor and strength
but without pity or honor" (AA, p. 20). Faulkner wrote: "They did
not think of love in connection with Sutpen. They thought of ruthlessness rather than justice and of fear rather than respect, but not of
pity or love . . ." (AA, p. 43). Miss Coldfield emphasized his lack of
"pity and gentleness and love and all the soft virtues . . ." (AA, p.
154). He had the hard virtues, but not the soft ones, and to this
extent he failed to measure up to Faulkner's conception of the gentleman. And so he failed in his grand design. Colonel John Sartoris,
one recalls, also allowed his hard virtues to blot out his soft ones.

Eventually his ruthless arrogance helped cost him his life. John Sartoris's son Bayard had earlier followed his father's code of vengeance, but by the time of his father's assassination he had achieved sufficient self-mastery to follow the gentler virtues taught him by his grandmother, Mrs. Rosa Millard. He forebore vengeance.[7]

Miss Coldfield's perceptiveness in Sutpen's case did not extend to her own weakness. She prided herself on being a lady, and felt this status was emphasized by her refusal of Sutpen's brazen overture. She justified her own existence by denying the validity of his: She denied that he was a gentleman and gloated over the tragic downfall of his family and design (AA, pp. 14-21, 177). She so misconstrued Judith's character as to have a cynical inscription placed on her niece's tombstone (AA, pp. 210-211). But when she discovered that Henry's murder of Bon was motivated by love, not hatred, that he still loved his family—he came home to die—and that Clytie received and protected him—she was shattered. She discovered that one can be neither a lady nor a gentleman simply by negative action, by refusing to participate in life or to love anyone. She was a character as empty as Laura in Katharine Porter's "Flowering Judas." Miss Coldfield's talisman also was the word "no."[8] She refused to participate in life, and she founded her existence on hatred—hatred of her father, hatred of the Confederate soldiers whose exploits she poetized, hatred, above all, of Sutpen (AA, passim, esp. pp. 68, 83, 167-171, 177). When she discovered Henry's presence in the old Sutpen house—when she realized that neither it nor the Sutpen tradition was empty—she realized her own emptiness. This was what Quentin saw in her face (AA, pp. 370-371). The book poses the question: Can a flawed tradition produce greatness? The answer is yes. A refusal to participate in life at all produces nothing. Miss Coldfield, had she accepted Sutpen's gambit, might have helped him build something; as it was, she did nothing at all. She was very much like her sister Ellen who bore Sutpen's children but retreated from life,

> . . . a woman, who, if she had had the fortitude to bear sorrow and trouble, might have risen to actual stardom in the role of the matriarch, arbitrating from the fireside corner of a crone the pride and destiny of her family . . . (AA, p. 69)

Quentin, having heard the Sutpen story and Miss Rosa's negative interpretation, knew what their discovery at the Sutpen place meant. He finally ceased to correct Shreve McCannon when he referred to Miss Rosa as "Aunt Rosa" (AA, pp. 174, 176, 362, 376);

Quentin knew she did not deserve the distinction. She was not a lady. Perhaps the final blow struck Miss Coldfield's consciousness
when she saw the house ablaze (AA, p. 376); perhaps she saw an
analogy between Clytie's protective slaying of Henry and Henry's
shooting of Bon (AA, pp. 370-376). At any rate, as McCannon said,
she had waited three months to go after Henry because she had
found that " . . . hating is like drink or drugs and she had used it so
long that she did not dare risk cutting off the supply, destroying the
source, the very poppy's root and seed" (AA, pp. 373-374). Her
heart was as cold as her name.[9]

Rosa Coldfield did not long survive her final journey to Sutpen's old place. She died on a cold day in January, and the frozen
earth had to be broken up with picks in order to dig her grave (AA,
pp. 173, 377). She had, as Quentin observed, been dead a long time:
She was "an old lady that died young of outrage in 1866 one summer . . ." (AA, p. 174).

The Sutpen story intensified Quentin's suicidal depression by
reminding him of his own family's tragic history. Henry's act—a
heart-rending, courageous act—he could not face until forced to because he himself was incapable of such courage and love (AA, p.
172). As Faulkner wrote of him in the Compson Genealogy, he was
"incapable of love . . . ."[10] He was haunted by his inability to measure up to the heroic past, and the Sutpen story confirmed his desperate gloom. Henry's mere presence in that house, perhaps, told him all
he needed to know: At last he had the key to the motivation of some
of the central characters in this tragic drama. He discovered the truth
of an observation his father had made:

> Have you noticed how so often when we try to reconstruct the
> causes which lead up to the actions of men and women, how
> with a sort of astonishment we find ourselves now and then re-
> duced to the belief, the only possible belief, that they stemmed
> from some of the old virtues? (AA, p. 121)

One example he gave was "the murderer who kills . . . out of . . .
pity . . ." (AA, p. 121). This Henry did; Bon forced his hand because
of his need for recognition as Sutpen's son; both Judith and Clytie,
despite their personal wrongs, gave to their family the last full measure of devotion. Their lives therefore were charged with the significance so lacking in the lives of Rosa Coldfield and Quentin Compson.

Echoes of Poe's "The Fall of the House of Usher" cluster in

this story.[11] Sutpen's mansion was established "in a shadowy miasmic region something like the bitter purlieus of Styx . . ." (AA, p. 69). Later, the setting was described as "a miasmic and spirit-ridden forest" (AA, p. 93), and the suggestion was made that the house possessed

> . . . a sentience, a personality and character acquired, not so much from the people who breathe or have breathed in . . . [it] inherent in the wood and brick [but] . . . in this house an incontrovertible affirmation for emptiness, desertion; an insurmountable resistance to occupancy save when sanctioned and protected by the ruthless and the strong. (AA, p. 85)

And Quentin's thoughts near the close of the novel echoed the nihilistic mood of "The Raven":[12] "Nevermore of peace. Nevermore of peace. Nevermore Nevermore Nevermore" (AA, p. 373).

II

Thomas Sutpen rode into Jefferson "in 1833" (AA, pp. 11, 31). This fact links his story with that of the McCaslins.[13] Ike McCaslin discovered through entries in the plantation ledgers that his forefather had brutally practiced both miscegenation and incest, then refused to acknowledge his slave children. He pieced together the implications of the entries recording the bequest to Thucydus, Tomasina's death "in child bed" as she gave birth to Turl, and her mother's suicide on "Cristmas Day 1832." Tomy died, said the entry, in "June 1833 . . . Yr stars fell." The entry recording Turl's birth also commented: "yr stars fell" (GDM, pp. 266-267, 269).

It is obvious that Faulkner intended to present the McCaslin story as an analogy of antebellum Southern history. Ike portrayed the New World as man's second chance defiled. The old crime of pride manifested itself anew in the enslavement of human beings (GDM, pp. 254-300). The ledgers recording this family's relationship with its slaves and ex-slaves was a "chronicle which was a whole land in miniature, which multiplied and compounded was the entire South . . ." (GDM, p. 298). Ike called this relationship, which had become the sharecropping system in his lifetime, an "edifice intricate and complex and founded upon injustice and erected by ruthless rapacity and carried on even yet with at times downright savagery . . ." (GDM, p. 298).

Both Old Carothers McCaslin and Thomas Sutpen bought huge tracts from the Chickasaws (GDM, pp. 254-255; AA, pp. 16, 34). Both practiced miscegenation, then denied their get any personal, human acknowledgement. They are bound together by Faulkner's references to 1833, "the year the stars fell." He used these references as omens foreboding evil. This was consistent with folk attitudes in the neighboring state of Alabama, according to Carl Carmer, who published his study, *Stars Fell on Alabama*, in 1934. This was two years before Faulkner published *Absalom, Absalom!*, and eight years before he published *Go Down, Moses*. And it was twelve years before he published the "Appendix: Compson: 1699-1945." Carmer wrote:

> Alabama felt a magic descending, spreading, long ago. Since then it has been a land with a spell on it—not a good spell, always. Moons, red with the dust of barren hills, thin pine trunks barring horizons, festering swamps, restless yellow rivers, are all part of a feeling—a strange certainty that above and around them hovers enchantment—an emanation of malevolence that threatens to destroy men through dark ways of its own . . . .
>
> What the strange influence is or when it began is a matter for debate. . . .
>
> But those who really know, the black conjure women in their weathered cabins along the Tombigbee, . . . say that on the memories of the oldest slaves their fathers knew there was one indelible imprint of an awful event—a shower of stars over Alabama. Many an Alabamian to this day reckons dates from "the year the stars fell"—though he and his neighbor frequently disagree as to what year of our Lord may be so designated.[14]

Faulkner said the year was 1833. He was correct. On November 13th of that year an incredibly brilliant shower of meteors, popularly known as "shooting stars," appeared over America. They were visible across the continent. People recorded their observations of them in such places as Connecticut, Alabama, Mississippi, Missouri, Dakota Territory, and northern Mexico (present-day New Mexico). In Missouri, Mormons driven from their Jackson County homes by mobs saw the stellar display as a sign of their coming deliverance and of the impending punishment of their enemies.[15] Josiah Gregg, however, saw the display as one which ministered to superstition.[16] Prince Maximilian of Wied, sojourning at Fort Clark on the Missouri (in what is now North Dakota), recorded Indian impressions of the event:

> On the 13th of November, early in the morning, several Indians arrived, who related, with much gravity, that in the preceding night they had observed an extraordinary number of falling stars, all moving in a westerly direction, which they said was a sign of war, or of a great mortality . . . . Many other Indians visited us, of whom several were in mourning, that is, rubbed over with white clay, and all of them spoke of the ominous phenomenon.[17]

At this time, whooping cough raged in the Indian villages along the upper Missouri; and cholera had broken out in St. Louis. The latter disease had also reached some of the lower Missouri trading-posts.[18] The Sioux, by the way, recorded this astronomical display on their famous pictographic calendar, the "winter count"kept by Lone Dog. It is on display today at the South Dakota State Historical Society at Pierre.[19]

An astronomer, Charles P. Olivier, wrote that

> . . . we may truly say that meteoric astronomy was born on Nov. 13, 1833, when the great Leonid shower appeared over America.
>
> This shower is estimated to have furnished 200,000 meteors for a given station between midnight and dawn, numbers of them brilliant, and many leaving trains. The terror excited among the masses of the population was great, the superstitious fully expecting the end of the world was about to come. . . . There were enough trained men who saw the phenomenon for several to detect that the meteors really had a radiant in the constellation Leo [hence the name], that is, a point in the sky from which they seemed to shoot away as spokes from the hub of a wheel. . . .
>
> Professor Denison Olmstead of Yale University, New Haven, was the man who, at the time, made excellent observations on the Leonids and then concluded that what had occurred was due to the earth's encounter with a swarm of particles moving around the sun.[20]

In 1946, Faulkner wrote an "Appendix" for *The Portable Faulkner*, an appendix giving a history of the Compsons. It began with a comment on Ikkemotubbe, "a dispossessed American king" who traded to Jason Lycurgus Compson "a solid square mile of virgin North Mississippi dirt" for a fast quarter-mile horse. Faulkner said Compson's tract was "forested then because these were the old days before 1833 when the stars fell . . ." (SF, p. 3).

III

Cleanth Brooks writes that "the fall of the house of Compson . . . is . . . sometimes regarded as a kind of exemplum of the fall of the old aristocratic order in the South . . . ." He then admits: "perhaps in some sense it is."[21]

Faulkner suggested a parallel between the Compson and the Sutpen stories by having the founders of each ill-starred dynasty appear in Yoknapatawpha County in a year marked by a natural phenomenon portending doom. Significantly, both men purchased land from the Chickasaws, a tribe presided over by a chief called "Doom" (SF, p. 3).[22] Sutpen, as indicated, arrived in 1833, the year the stars fell. Jason Lycurgus Compson "rode up the Natchez Trace one day in 1811 . . ." (SF, p. 6), the year of the great New Madrid, Missouri, earthquake which terrified residents of the Mississippi and Ohio River Valleys. The first shock, which occurred well before dawn on December 16th, formed Reelfoot Lake in northwest Tennessee. The initial quake was followed, according to some authorities, by at least one tremor per day for an entire year. Forests were levelled, flatboats on the Mississippi disappeared forever in holes which suddenly engulfed them then closed again; at one point parts of the Mississippi River flowed backward to the north, and observers saw hills heaving like waves of the sea. Thunderous noise, like the crack of doom, as well as a sulphurous stench and obscurity and gloom, accompanied the shocks. At night, fiery blasts like lightning bolts sometimes seemed to erupt from the earth. People grew faint and seasick on the dry, trembling land while the thunderous rumblings struck terror into their hearts.[23] And this great series of earthquakes was preceded by a brilliant comet.

Robert Penn Warren's verse tale of a heinous murder committed by Thomas Jefferson's nephews, *Brother to Dragons*, portrays this savage crime as occuring on the night of the great New Madrid earthquake.[24] Warren called 1811 "the *annus mirabilis*," a year of ominous signs and portents.[25] His note said that "the passage on the Annus Mirabilis is drawn from" a letter published by C. J. Latrobe in 1835 as part of his *The Rambler in North America*, volume one. The passage cited from Latrobe in Warren's note:

> Many things conspired to make the year 1811 the *annus mirabilis* of the West. During the earlier months, the waters of many of the great rivers overflowed their banks to a vast extent, and the whole country was in many parts covered from bluff to bluff. Unprecedented sickness followed. A spirit of change and recklessness seemed to pervade the very inhabitants of the forest. A countless multitude of squirrels, obeying some great and universal impulse, which none can know but the Spirit that gave them being, left their reckless and gambolling life and their ancient places of retreat in the North, and were seen pressing forward by tens of thousands in a deep and solid phalanx to the South. No obstacles seemed to check their extraordinary and concerted movement. The word had been given them to go forth, and they obeyed it, though multitudes perished in the broad Ohio, which lay in their path. *The splendid comet of that year long continued to shed its twilight over the forests, and as autumn drew to a close, the whole valley of the Mississippi, from the Missouri to the Gulf, was shaken to its centre by continued earthquakes.*[26] (Italics mine)

Again, an artist used the date of this natural occurrence to reflect the derangement of man's world.

The year 1811 also saw the triumphant entry into the Mississippi Valley of the white man's genius via technology: For the first time, a steamboat plied the Ohio and Mississippi, voyaging from Pittsburg to New Orleans. Thereafter steamboats navigated these rivers in both directions. When the *New Orleans* reached Natchez on this historic trip, "an old negro," presumably a slave, was heard to remark: " 'By golly, ole Mississip done got her massa dis time.' "[27] A similar sentiment could no doubt be attributed to Jason Compson,

Carothers McCaslin, John Sartoris, and Thomas Sutpen when each man arrived in Mississippi.

There was another striking and instructive parallel between the appearance in Mississippi of Jason Lycurgus Compson and the arrival of Thomas Sutpen. Each man arrived with only his horse, the clothes on his back, a small saddlebag, and two pistols (SF, p. 6; AA, pp. 14-16, 33). Perhaps that explains why the second Jason Lycurgus (later General) Compson became the "demon's" (AA, p. 9) friend: He knew his own grandfather had started out the same way Sutpen had (AA, p. 12).

IV

By 1833, the passage of twenty-two years, a generation, had softened the town's memory of Compson beginnings, and the family was an accepted part of the local aristocracy. By 1860, time had softened the memory of Sutpen's impact on the community, and "he was accepted . . ." (AA, p. 72). He was sufficiently one of the local people to be voted into command of the Yoknapatawpha County regiment, displacing John Sartoris (AA, pp. 80, 126). Apparently by that time his neighbors with "Virginia or Carolina" origins didn't make an issue of his past—or the lack of it.

Since Sutpen was eventually accepted by the community, why did it react so violently to him at first? It may be conjectured that Sutpen's brutal founding of his "tradition" gave his neighbors a fore-shortened view of their own history, a microcosmic image of themselves. And they tried to repudiate it. But time softened the harsh outlines of his achievement as it moderated the conduct of his feral slaves, and the community absorbed him. Like the rest, he could, he thought, look forward to

> . . . a thousand days or maybe even years of monotony and rich peace, and he, even after he would become dead, still there, still watching the fine grandsons and great-grandsons springing as far as eye could reach . . . . (AA, p. 271)

As Cleanth Brooks observes,[28] Sutpen's fighting with his slaves was eventually accepted by his neighbors as a novel if somewhat barbaric spectacle. But it was more than that. It demonstrated the iron reality underlying the relationships of even those masters and slaves made accustomed to the usages of the peculiar institution in its most benevolent phases, usages smoothed and polished by the hands, hearts, and tongues of generations. What was the real basis of slavery? Why, *at bottom*, did the thoroughly domesticated slave wait so agreeably and solicitously upon his master, handing him his mint julep with a flourish and a smile? *Because he had to*. Sutpen demonstrated by hand-to-hand combat, no holds barred, the ruthless reality of slavery, and for that matter, of all earthly political and social systems.

For example, consider the conflict in which Sutpen participated. Had the South conquered and subjugated the North, would not the South have ruled? And what would have established political legitimacy in this case? The same thing that established the legitimacy of Northern rule over the South (though the relationship was modified by conciliatory attitudes later adopted): military force.

At this point, since there are important similarities between the Sutpens and the Compsons, it is instructive to look at a symbol utilized by Faulkner in portraying the origins of the Compson dynasty. This is the claymore referred to repeatedly in the Appendix Faulkner provided to *The Sound and the Fury* in 1946. Quentin Maclachan Compson "fled to Carolina from Culloden Moor" with this weapon, a Scottish broadsword (SF, p. 4). England's military forces established her supremacy over the troops led by Prince Charles Edward Stuart in this battle; had the Scottish forces won, would not the claim of "Bonnie Prince Charlie" to the British throne have been legitimized—by force of arms? As it was, the house of Hanover continued to reign. Charles Stuart Compson fought for the British in the American Revolution, serving in Georgia under Tarleton. "He still had the claymore . . ." (SF, p. 4). Had England won this war, would not the legitimacy of her rulership have been established by force? Was not American independence established by the same means?

Charles Stuart Compson still carried the claymore when he joined the Burr-Wilkinson conspiracy "to secede the whole Mississippi Valley from the United States and join it to Spain" (SF, pp. 4-5). Had these plotters possessed the military might to bring off their planned coup, would not the world have perforce recognized the result as a legitimate political entity? But the plot failed, and the United States continued to rule the Southwest, primarily through the military genius and devotion of Andrew Jackson, who also appeared in Faulkner's Appendix. Faulkner described Jackson as

> a Great White Father with a sword. (An old duelist, a brawling lean fierce mangy durable imperishable old lion who set the wellbeing of the nation above the White House and the health of his new political party above either and above them all set . . . the principle that honor must be defended whether it was or not because defended it was whether or not.) (SF, pp. 3-4)

It was Jackson's policy of Indian removal which "dispossessed" old Ikkemotubbe, his fellow Chickasaws, and the other Indians of the Southeast. And what legitimized the dispossession? The same thing which would have allowed the Five Civilized Tribes to remain in the Southeast had they been strong enough: *force.* The same thing which brought Doom's own accession to the Chickasaw kingship (GDM, pp. 165-166). The message of both *Absalom, Absalom!* and the Appendix to *The Sound and the Fury* is crystal clear. One simple reality underlies and creates the legitimacy of all human political and social institutions: the sword.

Notes

[1]Cleanth Brooks, *William Faulkner: The Yoknapatawpha Country* (New Haven: Yale Univ. Press, 1963), pp. 296-307.

[2]Ibid., p. 298.

[3]Ibid., p. 297.

[4]Ibid., p. 306.

[5]William Faulkner, *Absalom, Absalom!*, Modern Library edition (New York: Random House, 1951), p. 8. All references to *Absalom, Absalom!* are to this edition; all subsequent citations will occur in the text of this paper and will consist of the letters *AA* and appropriate page numbers.

6The wild ride and the tumbling into the ditch of Sutpen's elegantly uniformed body, "regimentals . . . saber plumes and all" (AA, p. 186), is also heavily symbolic.

7William Faulkner, *The Unvanquished* (New York: Random House, 1938). There was miscegenation in the Sartoris family too. Faulkner wrote in "There Was a Queen" that "old Bayard" Sartoris was "half-brother" to Elnora, the family's black servant, "though possibly but not probably neither of them knew it, including Bayard's father . . . ." *Collected Stories of William Faulkner* (New York: Random House, 1950), p. 727.

8*The Collected Stories of Katharine Anne Porter* (New York: Harcourt, Brace & World, 1965), pp. 90-102, esp. pp. 97, 102.

9Her supposedly "heroic poetry" (AA, p. 68) Miss Coldfield herself described ironically as "embalming . . . the War and its heritage of suffering and injustice and sorrow . . . blotting from the breathable air the poisonous secret effluvium of lusting and hating and killing . . ." (AA, p. 169).

10Prepared for *The Portable Faulkner*, ed. Malcolm Cowley (New York: The Viking Press, 1946); also printed as "Appendix: Compson: 1699-1945" in the Modern Library edition of *The Sound and the Fury and As I Lay Dying* (New York: Random House, 1946), pp. 3-22. The citation is to the latter text, p. 10; all subsequent references to this appendix will be to this edition and will be identified by the citation *SF* plus appropriate pagination.

11Edgar Allan Poe, *Tales and the Raven and Other Poems*, introduction by Jay B. Hubbell (Columbus: Charles E. Merrill, 1969), pp. 64-82; see esp. pp. 64-67, 74-75, 78, 82.

12*The Poems of Edgar Allan Poe*, ed. Floyd Stovall (Charlottesville: Univ. Press of Virginia, 1965), pp. 95-99.

13All references to *Go Down, Moses* are to the Modern Library edition (New York: Random House, 1955); citations will be identified by the letters *GDM* plus pagination.

14Carl Carmer, *Stars Fell on Alabama* (New York: The Literary Guild, 1934), pp. xiii-xiv.

15B. H. Roberts, *The Missouri Persecutions* (Salt Lake City: Bookcraft, 1965), pp. 108-109.

16Josiah Gregg, *Commerce of the Prairies*, ed. Max L. Moorhead (Norman: Univ. of Oklahoma Press, 1954), p. 220.

17Maximilian, Prince of Wied, *Travels in the Interior of North America, 1832-1834*, in *Early Western Travels, 1748-1846*, ed. Reuben Gold Thwaites

(New York: AMS Press, 1966), XXIV, p. 15.

[18]Ibid., pp. 14-15.

[19]Joseph H. Cash, *The Sioux People* (Phoenix: Indian Tribal Series, 1971), pp. 99-106.

[20]Charles P. Olivier, "Meteor," *The Encyclopedia Americana* (New York: The Americana Corp., 1971), XVIII, p. 713. Walt Whitman recorded his memory of this spectacular shower of meteors, which occurred when he was 14 years old: See Gay Wilson Allen, *The Solitary Singer: A Critical Biography of Walt Whitman* (New York: Macmillan, 1955), p. 548 note 77.

[21]*William Faulkner . . .* , p. 306.

[22]Old Carothers McCaslin bought his land from this chief too (GDM, p. 166).

[23]John Haywood, *The Natural and Aboriginal History of Tenessee . . .* ed. Mary U. Rothrock (Jackson, Tenn.: McCowat-Mercer Press, 1959), pp. 28-31.

[24]Robert Penn Warren, *Brother to Dragons: A Tale in Verse and Voices* (New York: Random House, 1953), p. ix. He wrote that Jefferson's nephews perpetrated their crime "on the night of December 15, 1811—the night when the New Madrid earthquake first struck the Mississippi Valley . . . ." Most authorities cited the date as December 16th.

[25]Ibid., pp. 99-101; note, pp. 218-219.

[26]Haywood's account said the quakes began about the time of the comet's disappearance (p. 29). Edmund Flagg's *The Far West; or, A Tour Beyond the Mountains* (1838) gave an account, apparently based on Latrobe, which mentioned "the magnificent comet of the year . . . [which seemed] , indeed, to verify the terrors of superstition. . . . All that summer [it] was beheld blazing along the midnight sky, and shedding its lurid twilight over forest and stream . . . ." This account is reprinted in *Early Western Travels . . .*, XXVI, p. 63. Flagg also mentioned the epidemics which had followed the extensive spring flooding. A very circumstantial account of the great earthquake was given by a Scottish botanist, John Bradbury, in his *Travels in the Interior of America in the Years 1809, 1810, and 1811 . . .* (1817); this account is reprinted in *Early Western Travels . . .* , V; see pp. 198-212, especially pp. 204-210. Bradbury was in charge of a boat with a cargo of lead, en route to New Orleans; when the quake occurred he was on the Mississippi, moored for the night. He was probably about sixty miles or so south of New Madrid. He and his crew felt fortunate to escape destruction. His descriptions of the quakes are quite graphic; he recorded forty-five shocks between December 16th and December 21st. He also mentioned the comet of that year. The thunderous violence of the quakes, he

wrote, " . . . produced an idea that all nature was in a state of dissolution" (p. 208).

27Henry E. Chambers, *Mississippi Valley Beginnings: An Outline of the Early History of the Earlier West* (New York: G. P. Putnam's Sons, 1922), pp. 306-307. Flagg also alluded to the opening of steam navigation on these rivers; see *Early Western Travels . . .* , XXVI, pp. 62-63.

28*William Faulkner . . .* , pp. 299-300.

Flem Snopes: A Crazed Mirror

by

Woodrow Stroble

No attentive reader finishes William Faulkner's Snopes trilogy without sensing a radical shift of emphasis from *The Hamlet* to the next two novels. Indeed, critics invariably direct attention to this, and more often than not criticize the adjustment as a dwindling of artistic power or purpose which they imagine is the natural result of the twenty-six years that passed between the appearance of *The Hamlet* and *The Town*. But the difference objected to is more than a matter of the action moving from Frenchman's Bend to Jefferson, or of major new characters being introduced in the second novel, or even of events recapitulated in slightly variant forms. The difference is more fundamental, and by critical consensus generally has been accounted a change in tone, with usually only passing notice given Faulkner's demurral of carelessness which introduces *The Mansion*. But the notice should be more cautious, for Faulkner's explanation of the "discrepancies and contradictions" is couched in a vague metaphor.

He speaks of having learned more "about the human heart and its dilemma than he knew thirty-four years ago." Sadly, too many readers have passed off this remark as the author's feeble attempt to account for factual inconsistencies in the last two novels. But if *The Town* and *The Mansion* are read with Faulkner's remark in mind, the reader is alerted not only to a change in tone after *The Hamlet* but, more importantly, to a change of vision. Faulkner's tone shifts to accomodate a vision enlarged after *The Hamlet*—a vision consummately dramatized in the enigmatic death of the novel's principal "antagonist" (it is difficult to know how to label Flem Snopes), which more than anything else embodies what Faulkner learned about the dilemma of the human heart.

A comparative look at the respective treatments of issues and events in the first novel, and the next two, best illustrates the

essential change in tone after *The Hamlet*. In the first novel, right
and wrong are clearly defined values: Mink Snopes is wrong to murder Jack Houston, but V. K. Ratliff is right to prevent Ike Snopes'
unnatural—or rather, immoral—"love affair" with a cow; Flem
Snopes is wrong to exploit the poor whites of Frenchman's Bend,
but Hoak McCarron is right to exercise his manhood with Eula Varner. Then, in the next two novels, right and wrong shade into less
well-defined hues; ambiguity, doubt, and paradox govern events, particularly in the last novel, *The Mansion*, in which even the "only out-
and-out mean Snopes" (as Ratliff describes Mink) assumes unex-
pected degrees of dignity and integrity. It is, in fact,the sense of expectations disappointed which offends so many readers who lay
down *The Hamlet* and take up *The Town*—a feeling that the perspectives they have been afforded in *The Hamlet* (and the values implicit
in those perspectives) have been arbitrarily or unreasonably under-
mined. But what does a close reading reveal about the sources of
certainty in *The Hamlet*?

Ostensibly an undramatized narrator manipulates the reader's
responses to events in *The Hamlet*, since the novel throughout is
within his omniscient control. But the reader cannot escape the feeling that it is Ratliff's sensibility which pervades the world of Frenchman's Bend and influences his perception of events. The narrator so
often yields his story-telling privilege to Ratliff, that it is easy to forget who is speaking. Ratliff narrates the story of the horse trade between Ab Snopes and Pat Stamper, as well as the barn-burning history behind Ab Snopes. And when he is not relating past events, he
is usually interpreting present events to one or another of the inhabitants of Frenchman's Bend, or even to himself, as in the notable
Flem-in-Hell scene that he imagines. And the sense of Ratliff's consciousness pervading the events of *The Hamlet* is augmented by the
essentially identical sympathies of the Frenchman's Bend population.
Only the Snopeses—with the possible exception of Eck—are dis-
tanced from the "fellow-feeling" of Ratliff and the farmers who discuss local lore and exchange gossip. The indisputable effect of this
social identity is to lend Ratliff even more impressive credentials as
spokesman for Frenchman's Bend. And, because of his humane
superiority to even the farmers—as witnessed by his assisting Mink's
family while Mink awaits trial, and his cancelling Flem's note for
Ike's ten dollar inheritance—he assumes a position of moral elevation
from which his perspective on the events of *The Hamlet* would seem
to be yet more privileged and authoritative.

Ratliff's consciousness, then, is a looming presence in

The Hamlet, and the simplicity of the issues and conflicts of the novel is actually due to the reader's unconscious identification with Ratliff's perceptions and interpretations of events. Good and evil, right and wrong, are polarities clearly defined in Ratliff's mind, and the conflicts between them either easily resolved, or their proper resolutions seldom in doubt. On only two occasions does Ratliff's self-confidence waver: once during his discussion with Mrs. Little-john concerning his "right" to interfere in Ike's love affair—which isn't really a doubtful moral issue for Ratliff—and again during his emotional outburst before Bookwright regarding the depredations of the Snopeses in Frenchman's Bend—particularly the victimization by Flem of Mrs. Henry Armstid: "I could do more, but I won't. I won't, I tell you!" [1] But even this is an ambiguous response, and that it can be claimed as an instance of Ratliff's self-doubt is questionable. Rather, it would seem to suggest not a doubt on his part of his *right* but of his *obligation* to interfere.

That readers have generally accepted Ratliff's "ethical" position with regard to the events of *The Hamlet* is best instanced by the critical reaction to the novel's ending, in which Ratliff is finally victimized by Flem, as has been nearly everybody else in French-man's Bend. Generally, the feeling is that Faulkner should not have allowed Ratliff to fall to Flem's scheme to sell the worthless Old Frenchman's place, that such a breach of faith between author and character is a deplorable conclusion to the novel. The objection is just another instance of the misunderstanding of Faulkner's vision and is closely related to the misdirected criticism of the change in tone after *The Hamlet*, for both objections can be traced to the same source: V. K. Ratliff.

It is easy to speculate that Faulkner, toward the end of *The Hamlet*, recognized the inordinate authority he had allowed one of his characters, who, by contrast with the other pre-eminently human—and therefore flawed—personalities in Frenchman's Bend, stood among them a titan of moral excellence. Thus, by defeating all the major characters except Flem Snopes—and possibly Eula Varner Snopes—Faulkner concludes the rural phase of his trilogy by ironi-cally both underwriting and compromising the ethical and emotional principles represented by the poor whites of Frenchman's Bend. He underwrites these values by involving even their foremost champion—Ratliff—in their community of human weakness; and he compro-mises these values by finally defeating that same champion. So the novel concludes on a note of triumph in the midst of apparent defeat, a triumph of "good" paradoxically accomplished in its defeat by the force of "evil." Ratliff, through his baptism in defeat, emerges even more prominently as the moral arbiter of *The Hamlet*.

But it is easy to understand why so many readers are disappointed, even shocked, by the reduced stature of Ratliff in *The Town* and depressed by the atmosphere of moral ambiguity that permeates the second and third novels. In *The Town* there is no undramatized narrator, and Ratliff shares his narrative duties with two other narrator-participants. This narrative reduction not only diminishes Ratliff's role, but also subjects his reliability to closer scrutiny. In *The Town* Ratliff reveals, for the first time, that he is an imaginative man who relates his experiences on a very selective basis. For example, in the Spotted Horses episode of *The Hamlet* someone leaves the corral gate open and the ponies escape. In *The Town*, Ratliff "remembers" the event and designates Henry Armstid as the unwitting culprit. In view of Armstid's particular suffering as a result of the open gate, it is easy to imagine that it suits Ratliff's ironic sensibility to assume that Henry caused his own suffering. And Gavin Stevens, at one point in *The Town*, testifies to Ratliff's ironic penchant when he thinks of Ratliff having told him Eula's child, Linda, was already walking when her parents returned with her from Texas: "Ratliff would have invented the walking, being Ratliff. In fact, if there had been no child at all yet, Ratliff would have invented one, invented one already walking for the simple sake of his own paradox and humor, secured as he was from checkable fact, by this much miles and time between Frenchman's Bend and Jefferson two years later."[2] And when he reviews the seduction of Eula Varner, Ratliff frankly admits his revisionist predilection: ". . . and her [Eula] likely having to help hold him [McCarron] up too off of that broke arm; not jest her first time but the time she got that baby. Which ain't likely to happen jest the first time but between what did happen and what ought to happened, I don't never have trouble picking ought" (100).

Finally, Ratliff's reliability is compromised by virtue of the competing viewpoints of his fellow narrators, Charles Mallison and Gavin Stevens. Ratliff's reconstruction and foreseeing of events are impressive feats, but the reader is constantly reminded—by the shifting of narrative perspectives—that human testimony is inherently fallible. This examination of Ratliff's credibility as narrator after *The Hamlet* is not to discredit his humanity, for he is truly a remarkable character among all Faulknerian characters; but it is an attempt to suggest the crucial effect Faulkner achieves by reducing Ratliff's presence.

To ignore this effect is to miss the basis of the tonal shift after *The Hamlet* and allows too many readers to leave the trilogy with the conviction that Flem Snopes is pure, unadulterated evil, and that his death signals Faulkner's essentially ethical vision. But only in *The Hamlet* is Flem Snopes an unequivocal figure whose essence is unremitting evil practiced with unreflecting callousness. In *The Town*, with the undramatized narrator gone, and his narrative duties assumed by three of Faulkner's characters, of whom Ratliff is only one, the reader discovers himself subtly transformed from a passive observer to active participant in unfolding the significance of events. By virtue of "Chick's" limited public version of Flem Snopes' history in Jefferson, Gavin's blatant idealism, and Ratliff's severly reduced role as commentator,[3] the reader is not simply invited, but actually coerced, to account for witnessed and unwitnessed events. Indeed, Ratliff's penchant for prophecy—as witnessed by his obscure insistence in *The Town* that Gaviŋ "missed it" and in *The Mansion*, to Chick, that "It will be worse than that"—maneuvers the reader into the peculiar position of one confronting a "detective" novel.

The reader might question the peculiar reticence exercised by Ratliff regarding Flem Snopes' pursuit of respectability in *The Town*. He treats it as a secret of such import that it cannot be immediately revealed to Gavin Stevens. His laconic observations, twice iterated in chapters reserved exclusively for the bare statement, that "he [Gavin] missed it" (153) and the remark "And still I couldn't tell him," (177) suggest an inordinate concern for concealment of a seemingly innocuous insight to Flem's motivation. But like the removal of Montgomery Ward from his "atelier," so Ratliff's secret is to assume deeper significance by virtue of subsequent disclosures. For example, the anti-Snopes forces assume Flem has Montgomery Ward sent to Parchman simply to secure himself respectability, but in *The Mansion* the reader learns Flem's motive is to secure twenty additional years of imprisonment for Mink, and safety for himself. And the alert reader, always testing the relationships that exist among Faulkner's characters irrespective of their personal testimonies, recognizes the sensitive rapport between Gavin and Ratliff, and Ratliff's concern for the fragile nature of Gavin's idealism. When he infers Flem's drive toward respectability, Ratliff is able to project the consequences of it, and foresee that Eula will be the price Flem will pay for it. Of course, Ratliff cannot know in advance the particulars of coming events, but he knows that Eula will somehow have to suffer, for he has already warned Gavin—whose prognostics by contrast are seldom borne out by eventualities—that Eula is "that-ere twenty-dollar gold piece." Both Ratliff's quiet, but insightful meditations and the hastily conceived mistake regarding Montgomery Ward's eviction from Jefferson, caution the reader to carefully consider the "raw" data of the novel, exclusive of the emotional colorings added by the narrators.

One consequence of independently examining Faulkner's trilogy is puzzlement regarding Flem Snopes. Once the reader recognizes that his initial assessment of Flem has been influenced in large part by a witness who is blatantly lacking in disinterestedness, he returns to the events of *The Hamlet* to review what he knows are relatively indisputable facts.

The Hamlet opens with Ab Snopes' advent to Frenchman's Bend, where Jody Varner learns his nefarious history and thinks he can use his information to cheat Ab and his family of the meager wages a year's share-cropping will earn. The initial event of the novel, then, reveals an aggressive exploitation of a Snopes family, one member of which is young Flem. This cannot be emphasized too much, for Faulkner's strategy with regard to the character of Flem Snopes— even if formulated after *The Hamlet* appeared in print—can be traced to this event. Faulkner, even as early as *The Hamlet*, must have recognized that Flem could not be a self-made man. It is no coincidence that Flem's model of business conduct is old Will Varner, as is symbolized by his emulating Will's black bowtie. Nor should the reader forget Will Varner's own forms of rapacity, particularly with respect to his neighbors' wives.[4] Flem differs from old man Varner only in having perfected his principles of economic exploitation. Of particular note, in this connection, is Flem's impotence, which explains both his failure to follow in Varner's concupiscent footsteps and his success as a businessman. Flem's single-minded drive toward financial success is clearly a compensation reaction to his physical disability.[5] Ratliff's imagined scene between Flem and a Negro woman coupling on the floor behind the store counter is more revealing of Ratliff's fallibility as narrator than of Flem's pathetically compulsive greed.

At the end of *The Town*, Ratliff is to ascribe to Byron Snopes' half-Indian offspring "The last and final end of Snopes out-and-out unvarnished behavior in Jefferson, if that's what I'm trying to say" (370). But seldom is Snopesian conduct "unvarnished" by Ratliff in *The Hamlet*, and if the reader remembers that it is Flem who is the intended victim at the novel's outset, he cannot but approve Flem's initial success against the Varners, whose record in Frenchman's Bend is already of dubious virtue. By novel's end, Flem is to parlay his initially modest success against the Varners into a total triumph over all of Frenchman's Bend, over even V. K. Ratliff. And despite Ratliff's inveterate dislike for Flem, Flem's management of Will Varner's store is above reproach, for he never overcharges—a scruple not shared by Jody Varner—and even insists that Will Varner pay for his tobacco. The rapidity with which Flem rises in Will Varner's financial world also testifies to his competence, and the authority Will gives him testifies to his honesty.

Flem is, of course, not a principled man in the ordinary sense of the word, and any attempt to whitewash him would be to misread Faulkner. But Flem's reprehensible conduct, like Popeye's in *Sanctuary*, is considerably ameliorated by the recognition of its psychological and social background. Also, readers are too ready to condemn Flem for orchestrating his marriage to Eula and exploiting Henry Armstid's wife. But in the first case, neither Eula's pregnancy nor her family's hypocritical reaction to it is Flem's doing. And in the second, Mrs. Armstid suffers much more from her husband's insensitivity and coiled rope than Flem's indifference. In both circumstances, Flem is seen to benefit from the moral corruption of his victims. He does not corrupt the people around him; rather, he waits passively for their habitual cupidity to drive them to him. In each instance, Flem is the intended victim: first, as a purchaser of "soiled goods" when he marries Eula, and second, as a horse trader to be "beat" in a deal. Ratliff comments significantly after the debacle of the spotted horses, "I never made them Snopeses and I never made the folks that can't wait to bare their backsides to them" (321). Certainly Flem is guilty of unscrupulous exploitation of his victims, but his victims are not always spotless lambs. In some cases, they are fellow wolves.

As noted above, many critics detect a change in Faulkner's attitude toward Flem after *The Hamlet*, and regret it as an artistic flaw. But this response is no doubt due in large part to the unchallenged evaluation of Flem by Ratliff in the first novel. The readers' expectations regarding Flem are so conditioned by the narrowness of Ratliff's vision that they cannot adjust to the broader, and more comprehensive, vision of the next two novels, in which villains are made more nearly humane, and humanists made more nearly villains.

Edmond Volpe explains Flem's defeat of Ratliff as a kind of humanization by Faulkner of the character who most nearly represents his views.[6] But Volpe does not see the profitable application of the same argument to Flem's defeat at the opening of *The Town*. Clearly Faulkner is interested, from the very beginning of the second novel, in dramatizing the expanded vision thiry-two years have afforded him. The significance of Flem's defeat by Mr. Harker, Tom Tom and Tomey's Turl is the same as the effect of Ratliff's defeat. Both men are humanized, although each retains a measure of his previously idealized stature, Ratliff in the moral dimension and Flem in the pragmatic.

In a sense, each man fails through abandoning the one principle which has consistently protected him. Ratliff forgets to practice the ethical reserve he usually exercises when confronted by Flem's enormities, and tries to out-maneuver Flem in the purchase of the Old Frenchman's place. In the emotional outburst before Bookwright noted above Ratliff swears he will not interfere with Flem on Mrs. Armstid's behalf. But his vow is separated from the final section of the novel—in which he is outsmarted by Flem—only by the hearing concerning the legal liabilities of Eck and Flem for the damages done by the Texas ponies. Presumably, the two events are related and one may see in the latter Ratliff's attempt, despite his vow, to finally put a stop to Flem's successfully "grazing up" Frenchman's Bend. To Ratliff the venture is a moral obligation, success in which would represent a victory for the whole community, with himself the local champion leading the campaign against Snopesism. However self-righteous may be Ratliff's motive, it is nevertheless honorable.

Flem, on the other hand, succeeds in Frenchman's Bend by remaining rigidly fair in his dealings in the technical sense, no matter how usurious they are. But once in Jefferson, he abandons the trader's peculiar sense of fair play—first manifested in the confrontation between Ab Snopes and Pat Stamper—and steals the power plant brass. Afterward, an unspecified number of years pass, during which Flem apparently returns to legally and socially endorsed forms of business. And it is not until he has become vice-president of Colonel Sartoris' bank that he returns to manipulating situations to suit his acquisitive ends.

But the change from passive to active exploitation is now sanctioned by even the most respectable members of the community, for the commodity he now desires is outside the concern of civil law and of paramount importance to social law—Flem is actively (in the lexical and Ratliffian senses of the word) pursuing social respectability. Consequently, Flem is able to coerce even civil law to abet his plan to "railroad" Montogmery Ward into Parchman prison, for Hub Hampton refuses to scandalize the community by making public the true nature of Montgomery Ward's crime. Even Gavin Stevens approves the maneuver! And again the law is warped, with Gavin's consent, when Flem removes I. O. Snopes from Jefferson by equally adroit machinations. For the scrupulous reader who persists in tearing away the webbing spun about events by Chick, Ratliff, and Gavin, the lesson Flem learns from Jefferson is easily inferred—thievery is an unacceptable road to respectability, but hypocrisy is not.

Cleanth Brooks, however, faults Flem's pursuit of respectability because it reduces him from the sheer abstraction of "an elemental force."[7] Hence, he complains, Flem becomes more human and therefore more vulnerable. But the reader must recognize Brooks' objection as a case of the critic preferring form to vision. He must also remember the demurral of carelessness with which Faulkner introduces *The Mansion*. Michael Millgate recalls Faulkner's remarks to James B. Meriwether who questioned this adjustment in Flem's character. Faulkner explained that, in Millgate's words, "he had simply changed his mind about some incidents and characters, and that it was now *The Hamlet* which needed to be rewritten in order to bring it into line with *The Town* and *The Mansion*."[8] It is ironic that so many of Faulkner's readers have reversed his argument, and "preferred"—a Ratliffian inclination—that Faulkner have retained the mythic mode of *The Hamlet* in the subsequent novels of the trilogy.

Clearly Faulkner realized that the idealization of the mythic mode is a kind of de-humanization of character, and that his expanded conception of humankind could not permit a simple dismissal of any man or woman—Flem or Eula—by reduction to type. Paradoxically, Brooks admires Faulkner's refusal to condescend to his characters, manifested in his unwillingness "to set any limits to what they will do in terms of trickery, mad folly, or even heroism: the human being is obviously capable of almost anything. This conviction springs not from a weary cynicism but from a profound conviction of the powerful mystery that resides in human nature."[9] Yet Brooks would have Faulkner deny Flem—and Eula— their right to the human capacity for doing anything, and therefore would have Faulkner deny them their part in the "powerful mystery that resides in human nature."

Perhaps the cirtical jaundice against Flem Snopes has as its source the desire to excuse the many moral failures of the non-

Snopeses of Yoknapatawpha County. Too many of Faulkner's readers have identified with the non-Snopesian characters, ignoring what
Brooks remarks above, that Faulkner refuses to pity his characters in
a condescending way. As a consequence, abandoning a critical perspective, they ascribe to Flem and his fellow clansmen the most
heinous crimes, discovering in Snopesism the source of all evil in
Frenchman's Bend and Jefferson. But Edmond Volpe intelligently
points out that Snopesism is really a "red herring,' that leads too
many readers away from Faulkner's vision. He notes that whenever
Faulkner draws near to one of the Snopeses, that Snopes "becomes
detached from the tribe."[10] The younger Ab Snopes, Eck, Wallstreet Panic, eventually Mink, and even Montgomery Ward are
notable instances of Volpe's point. Volpe concludes that what
actually persists in the novels isn't Snopesism, but "Flemism."[11]
His point is well taken, for it discovers that Flem is in large part a
"strawman" created by a self-righteous society. First in Frenchman's
Bend and then Jefferson, the in-group Flem attempts to infiltrate
uses him to justify its own forms of aberration and rapacity. Clearly,
Flem could not survive, let alone prosper, in a moral society.

      One last comment about the events of *The Town* is appropri-
ate here. Perhaps the most damning accusation leveled at Flem is that
he "killed" Eula by using her in his gambit to gain the presidency of
the bank. But Gavin Stevens, to whom most readers respond with at
least compassion, if not always admiration, is as much responsible for
Eula's suicide as Flem. Had Gavin consented to marry Linda, as Eula
asked, he would have given Eula the chance to elope with DeSpain.
But, because of his moral code, Gavin's agreement is so qualified as
to be essentially a refusal, which eliminates for Eula the option of
elopement, and condemns her to suicide to protect her daughter. It
cannot persuasively be argued that Flem knew in advance Eula would
resort to suicide when he used her to gain the bank presidency. In
fact, Eula's suicide is her supreme renunciation of Flem, with whom
she would otherwise have had to go on living once DeSpain was removed from the bank. It is likely that Flem expected her to either
leave town with DeSpain or to continue living with him—however un-
happily—in Jefferson. Her ultimate rejection of him by suicide must
have been a surprise even to Flem.

      In *The Town*, essentially two plot lines are developed: the love
relationship between Eula and DeSpain as contained in the larger
perspective of Gavin's "love" for Eula, and Flem's rise to power and
respectability. Eula's suicide concludes both lines. Little more can be

said about Flem's development as a character because, as always, it is submerged beneath the consciousness of the three narrators. But the reader must speculate about the effect upon Flem of his wife's infidelity. It would seem that his latent hostility and resentment—suggested or suspected nowhere in the novel—rises almost to the surface when he chooses the inscription to be cut into Eula's gravestone. Although it does not explicitly declare Flem's meditations, it does represent, as Newton's statue did to Wordsworth, "The marble index of a mind for ever/Voyaging through strange seas of Thought, alone."

The *Mansion* finally undermines, if it does not precisely repudiate, the conception of Flem as inhuman monster, and his enemies as humanely compassionate. But again Brooks objects to Flem assuming a depth of character that renders him less a type of evil and more a man with his share of human complexity. When Eula, in *The Town*, who has lived with, if not slept with, Flem for eighteen years, warns Gavin Stevens not to get to know Flem because one will "have to pity him" (331), Brooks complains that "this tantalizing hint of a human soul within the monster has to be put down as a failure of tone."[12] But Brooks badly misrepresents the figure of Flem Snopes by making him a mere symbol, for in so doing he needn't question his origin as a human being, or account for the formative influences upon his character. Consequently, he cannot see that Flem is not solely responsible for his evil, but that his society shares the blame. For Flem is not an alien from outside the human species: he is its creation born within its collective womb and nurtured by its hypocrisy.

And as this "fallacy of typology" misrepresents Flem, so it misrepresents Linda Snopes. Just as Brooks views her part in Flem's murder as morally supportable because it strikes directly at "the brain-center of Snopesism," so Olga Vickery defends Linda. By "contributing to the destruction not of a specific Snopes, but of Snopesism itself—the destroyer of life, love, human values, and human dreams," Linda achieves a "transcendent humanity"[13] and is thereby licensed to murder with moral impunity. To support her view as more than a personal reading, Vickery claims Gavin Stevens as her witness. After she allows that Linda, as dispenser of justice, "seems capricious if not incomprehensible by ordinary standards, insofar as she not only uses Mink but makes Gavin her agent and her accomplice," Vickery borrows one of Gavin's meditations to justify Linda's act: "With a final kiss for Gavin, at once chaste and passionate, she withdraws from the human world, away from 'the ceaseless gabble with which man has surrounded himself, enclosed himself, insulated himself from the penalties of his own follies' " (236). The implication of Vickery's sentence is that Linda rises above man's verbal rationalizations and thereby assumes a special dispensation through which murder is a moral act. But the original context of that part of her sentence taken from one of Gavin's observations suggests something entirely different from what Vickery would have us infer. I cite Gavin's internal monologue in its entirety to make my point: "But again I don't know. Maybe it didn't take even three years of freedom, immunity from it[hearing] to learn that perhaps the entire dilemma of man's condition is because of the ceaseless gabble with which he has surrounded himself, enclosed himself, insulated himself from the penalties of his own folly, which otherwise—the penalties, the simple red ink—might have enabled him by now to have made his condition solvent, workable, successful." Plainly, the original sense of Gavin's thought is that Linda has learned, through deafness, to face her own fallibility as a human being rather than drown it in a flood of rationalization, an example of which might be Vickery's talk of a "transcendent humanity."

Finally, James Grey Watson, jumping on the Brooks bandwagon, not only defends Linda's agency in Flem's death, but Mink's too: "Given scope by Linda's transcendent humanistic love and depth by Mink's intensely personal determination to assert his individual human identity, their murder of Flem is a strictly moral act. . . ."[14] Watson argues—with dubious logic—that Gavin's "reaffirmation of their love after he discovers Linda's involvement in Flem's death exonerates her of cruelty or inhumanity."[15] One assumes, by logical projection, that Mink, too, benefits in like manner from Gavin's kindness to him after the murder. But again, to make Gavin a guage of the trilogy's moral vision is a serious critical error.

These rhetorical excesses all stem from an uncompromising insistence upon Flem's monolithic consciousness, and frequently lead to allegations against him that are preposterous. Watson, for instance, claims, "In the events of the Cotillion Ball, though, the rapacity of Flem's motives and the ruthlessness of his methods are both revealed."[16] But what does Flem do? Of all the people who attend the ball, Flem is the *least* responsible for the disgraceful events that occur. Warren Beck, in his enthusiastic dislike of Flem, so loses his critical perspective that he lays blame on Flem for the undistinguished political career of his kinsman, Clarence Snopes.[17] apparently forgetting it was Will Varner who manipulated Clarence into office.

So, too, when critics are not blaming Flem for every ill in the three novels, they are extolling other characters for very questionable conduct, or extending them sympathetic absolution in a way that reflects their personal persuasions rather than Faulkner's broader, more tolerant vision. Olga Vickery so admires Eula that she says of her, "Yet hers is also a victory since she could not be defeated, only destroyed."[18] Maybe Gavin Stevens would subscribe to this rationalization, but one seriously doubts that it speaks for Faulkner. About Mink, Vickery argues, "His response is, of course, demonic, yet is nevertheless firmly grounded in his recognition of the value of the individual man. Accordingly he can wait for almost forty years, confident that he will be given his chance since there must be 'a simple fundamental justice and equity in human affairs, or else a man might just as well quit.' By accomplishing his vengeance Mink affirms the significance of his life though, ironically, at the cost of losing twenty years of it." [19] "Ironically," indeed! Even with an awarencess of the critical assumption that the "ethical" dimension of a novel exists independent of the reader's world, one must ask if Mink's successful quest for vengeance validates the "rightness" of Flem's murder and exonerates those who participated in it; and more importantly, one must ask if Mink's faith in a "simple fundamental justice and equity in human affairs" is supported by Faulkner's vision. Looking only at the seemingly insurmountable obstacles that Mink overcomes in the thirty-eight years between his vow to kill Flem and its fulfillment, one might assume the moral world of the trilogy underwrites Mink's faith. But finally, the one character who seems least able to affect Mink's ethical conviction overturns it. When Flem Snopes passively awaits his execution and calmly sits watching Mink *twice* pull the trigger of the instrument of his destruction, it is not Mink's moral world that is being upheld: it is the endorsement of something far more horrific. Mink's success is finally not achieved by a kind of ultimate justice, but is *provided him* by his victim.

Critics' explanations of Flem's calm acceptance of death reflect their discomfort concerning the ending of the trilogy. James Gray Watson is content to write off Flem by simply ignoring him as a man capable of volition: "Their [Mink's and Linda's] revenges, motivated by a deep personal injury and justified by transcendent moral injunctions, clearly project the self-destructive element inherent in the Snopesian principle of unremitting inhumanity. It is entirely consistent with this principle that Flem's tolerance of Linda's presence in his mansion and his failure to take steps against Mink's release

from Parchman result finally in his passive acceptance of death."[20]
But why "unremitting inhumanity" should be consistent with virtual
suicide is unclear. Warren Beck, on the other hand, accounts for the
enigma of Flem's death as cowardice: "The impasse at which Flem
has arrived illustrates him as a flat character but also contributes to
his representativeness of all those whose aggressions can brave it out
only as long as their victims shrink from retaliating with equal force.
And that the fellow who seemed unbeatable has come to the point
where he cannot even spit marks the plainest of finalities."[21] Ironically, Beck misses the symbolic import of Flem's spitting. Until
Gavin brings him the news of Mink's release from Parchman, Flem's
spitting has signalled his disdain for, and rejection of, a situation. But
when Gavin confronts him, Flem does not spit, and even Gavin notes
the omission: " 'What else do you want me to do?' If he would just
spit once he thought. 'Nothing,' Snopes said. 'What?' Stevens said,
'Yes,' Snopes said, 'Much obliged' " (381). Flem's refusal to spit is
his acknowledgment of his imminent murder, which in turn signals
his acceptance of membership in the mortal round.

At least two of Faulkner's readers recognize Flem's final act
as something not easily to be dismissed. Michael Millgate says, specu-
latively, "Mink and Linda, it would appear, may actually have done
Flem a favor by killing him, and Gavin Stevens may once again have
trapped himself into playing Flem's game."[22] Vickery's doubts
about Flem are more subdued, as she describes the melancholy of
The Mansion: "So pervasive is the melancholy that it touches and
softens Mink, an old tired man moved by past compulsions and even
Flem Snopes, who had never asked for pity and perhaps had never
recognized that his was the most wasted life of all."[23] The qualifica-
tion of "perhaps" in this sentence reveals her difficulty with Flem's
death. Earlier she admits that "as part of the ritual, Flem, too,
transcends his nature, for as he waits for Mink to pull the trigger for
the second time, his characteristic impassivity is not without courage
and dignity as well."[24] But these are half-hearted and, one suspects,
puzzled attempts to account for Flem's demise.

To understand Flem's death, one must see it as part of Faulkner's ultimate strategy for the Snopes saga. Too many readers
demand of the trilogy exactly what the characters insist upon—an
explanation of events which will agree with the philosophical and
moral positions they hold personally. But Faulkner's vision is superior to the demand; it finally excludes no human being from kinship
with humanity. Consequently, Faulkner signals Flem's membership

among the "pore sons of bitches that have to cause all the grief and anguish they have to cause!" (*The Mansion*, 430), by having him essentially commit suicide. It must be particularly noted that "pore sons of bitches" is a verbal motif used by many characters, but when Ratliff picks it up, and repeats "Have to cause" presumably we discover his recognition that Flem has been, in his turn, as much a victim as those whom he exploited. As Popeye's biography, in *Sanctuary*, saves him from the readers' unqualified howls of execration, so Flem's acquiescence to his own death saves him. Flem's final act uncovers a depth of emotion which had not been suspected, and its import reaches all the way back to *The Hamlet*, requiring a reassessment of his character. Only those readers who have already made up their minds, and who are comfortable with the moral world of Jefferson, refuse the effort. But Faulkner has the last word, and the conclusion of *The Mansion* requires careful reading.

Alone in the collapsed cellar of the house in which he and his family had lived forty years earlier, Mink, having had his revenge on Flem, peacefully contemplates his own death. In the words of the narrator, Mink realizes that death leaves folks "all mixed and jumbled up comfortable and easy so wouldn't nobody even know or even care who was which any more, himself among them, equal to any, good as any, brave as any, being inextricable from, anonymous with all of them: the beautiful, and splendid, the proud and the brave, right on up to the very top itself among the shining phantoms and dreams which are the milestones of the long human recording— Helen and the bishops, the kings and the unhomed angels, the scornful and graceless seraphim" (435-36). The lyrical quality of this passage suggests that the "community" into which Mink is about to be admitted is an exalted and exclusive club. But closer attention reveals a progression from Helen—an obvious echo of Eula's mythic role—to "scornful and graceless seraphim." This vision of death echoes an earlier passage in *The Hamlet*. There, in the most lyrical episode of the three novels, it is part of a description of the earth which Ike Snopes walks upon: "He walks lightly upon it, returning, treading lightly that frail inextricable canopy of the subterrene slumber— Helen and the bishops, the kings and the graceless seraphim" (186). The notable difference between the two passages is the interpolation of "unhomed angels" and the qualifier "scornful" added to "graceless seraphim." In the earlier version, which concludes Ike's temporarily successful abduction of Houston's cow, the final term, "graceless seraphim," is certainly included to suggest Ike's membership in the human community. And in the final version, the noted additions are equally intended to suggest both the inevitable condition of

man—an "unhomed angel"—in an existential universe and the essential kinship every individual of the human species shares, even the
"scornful" who finally express their capitulation to their human-ness
by scornfully "watching the dull point of light in the cock of the
hammer when it flicked away" (410).

In making Mink—*and Flem*—equal with everyone at the end of
the trilogy, Faulkner does not make a joke of human faith in a "fundamental justice and equity" in human affairs; rather, he makes the
faith irrelevant, so that Fualkner's vision enfolds every one of "the
pore sons of bitches" as an equally valid member in the existential
experience. Warren Beck perhaps comes closest to an understanding
of Faulkner's trilogy by remarking, "The wheel of time, spun back
and forth with masterly control, turns up facets of the truth, appre-
hensions the more intense for never being reduced to conventional
definition, and forever struck across by the slanting light of irony."
It is unfortunate that Beck does not recognize the full import of his
statement, and that he goes on to say that "Ethical evaluation is
constantly evoked, never imposed, as plot feeds more than curios-
ity, implying that whatever the fate of individuals, for mankind, the
end is not yet, nor is the outcome assured."[25] It is true that an ethical evaluation is constantly evoked by the internal narrators, but that
it is Faulkner's evaluation cannot be claimed, for looming always on
the horizon of this Faulknerian world is the awesome figure of Flem
Snopes, a crazed mirror reflecting man's troubled nature.

Notes

[1]*The Hamlet* (New York: Vintage Books, 1956), p. 321. Page references
to *The Town* and *The Mansion* also are from Vintage editions, published in 1957
and 1965 respectively, and hereafter will be cited in the text.

[2]*The Town*, p. 134.

[3]Michael Millgate, in *The Achievement of Willaim Faulkner* (London:
Constable and Company, Ltd., 1966), p. 237, estimates that Ratliff's commentaries account for only eight percent of the second novel.

[4]In one notable instance, Will Varner sexually exploits even Mink

Snopes' wife, which competes with Flem's mere financial exploitation of Henry Armstid's wife for top billing in human vice.

See p. 240 of *The Hamlet* for an insinuation that Mink's wife sells her favors to Will Varner, and p. 140 for evidence that he is sexually exploiting the wife of one of his tenants—without even the civility of removing his hat!

[5]Cleanth Brooks strangely exults in Flem's impotence: "It is fitting that he should be impotent, unable to bed the wife for whom all the other men long, and with no love for, and no rapport with, the nature over which he exerts more and more control." *William Faulkner: The Yoknapatawpha Country* (New Haven: Yale University Press, 1963), p. 181. Brooks' remark, while unambiguous about his antipathy to Flem, suggests that he sees no causal relationship between Flem's character and his physical disability.

See also the views of Joseph Gold who ably develops his thesis regarding the source and quality of Flem's character ("The 'Normality' of Snopesism: Universal Themes in Faulkner's *The Hamlet,*" *Wisconsin Studies in Contemporary Literature*, 3 (Winter 1962), pp. 25-34). As his title indicates, however, Gold focuses upon only *The Hamlet*, which allows him to argue that "to see Snopesism as an alien and disastrous force of change in an otherwise sanguine world is to undermine the power of Faulkner's social criticism and the humanistic burden which I believe motivates the novel" (p. 25). But the events in the other novels of the trilogy, particularly Flem's passive suicide, substantially add to our understanding of Flem and seriously compromise Gold's notion of Faulkner's "humanistic burden."

[6]In *A Reader's Guide to William Faulkner* (New York: Noonday Press, 1964), p. 315, Volpe accounts for Ratliff's victimization by Flem as consistent with "the plan of the novel." He argues that "If he [Ratliff] is not bested by Flem, he too will remain beyond the pale of emotional fallibility in which everyone but Flem is gathered."

[7]Brooks, p. 214.

[8]Millgate, p. 251.

[9]Brooks, p. 173.

[10]Volpe, p. 307.

[11]Volpe, p. 309.

[12]Brooks, p. 215.

[13]*The Novels of William Faulkner* (Louisiana: State University Press, 1964), p. 192.

[14]*The Snopes Dilemma: Faulkner's Trilogy* (Coral Gables: University of

Miami Press, 1968), pp. 228-29. For an insightful evaluation of Watson's book, see John V. Hagopian's review in *American Literature*, 42 (May 1971), 304-305.

[15]Watson, p. 218.

[16]Watson, p. 98.

[17]*Man in Motion* (Madison: University of Wisconsin Press, 1963), p. 95.

[18]Vickery, p. 199.

[19]Vickery, p. 205.

[20]Watson, p. 216.

[21]Beck, p. 91.

[22]Millgate, p. 248.

[23]Vickery, p. 200.

[24]Vickery, p. 196.

[25]Beck, pp. 3-4.

Faulkner, Prufrock, and Agamemnon: Horses, Hell, and High Water

by

John M. Howell

Though Faulkner never publically acknowledged his debt to T. S. Eliot, readers have repeatedly noted echoes of "The Love Song of J. Alfred Prufrock" (1917) and *The Waste Land* (1922). They have pointed to echoes in the unpublished and published poetry (*The Marble Faun* [1924] and *A Green Bough* [1933]). And they have pointed to echoes in such fictional works as *Mosquitoes* (1927); *As I Lay Dying* (1930); "Carcassonne" (1931); *Sanctuary* (1931); *Light in August* (1932); *Pylon* (1935); *Absalom, Absalom!* (1936).[1]

Common to the poetic and narrative contexts in which these echoes appear is a persona betrayed by a romantic ideal which leads to either a physical or spiritual death. And common to this pattern of "dying" is a vision of horses in association with fire, waves, or fish. Critics have identified the horses in Faulkner's fiction as symbols of the male principle, of the life force, of mana, of sexual abnormality.[2] Though I find these interpretations illuminating and provocative, I believe they place too great an emphasis on the effect and not enough on the cause. I would like to suggest that much of the symbolism associated with horses was inspired by Faulkner's absorption of Prufrock's vision of the "sea-girls"; his periodic synthesis of Prufrock's vision with that of Phlebas, the "Death by Water" figure of *The Waste Land*; and his periodic synthesis of these visions of drowning with Agamemnon's vision of hell in *The Odyssey*.

Though Faulkner seems to have echoed, at one time another, virtually every line of "Prufrock," he was clearly most moved by the "sea-girls." They are the aggregate symbol of Prufrock's desperate need for illusion and the "drowning" realization of his defeated idealism. Like Guido da Montefeltro of the poem's epigraph from *The Inferno*, Prufrock is in hell. Prufrock has, as Grover Smith puts it, "allowed his ideal conception of woman (the sea-girls at the end) to dominate his transactions with reality. He has neither used human love nor rejected it but has cultivated an illusory notion of it which has paralyzed his will and kept him from turning desire into action."[3]

Faulkner's romanticists have a similarly idealized conception of horses which dominates their transactions with reality and denies life. In the paper I explore the tentative assertion that in most cases Faulkner's horses, like Prufrock's sea-girls, symbolize either a wish or ideal which the viewer and/or rider compulsively substitutes for a creative life—that Faulkner's horses, like Prufrock's sea-girls, ultimately symbolize the hell of spiritual suffering. Though I, like Prufrock, do not dare to commit myself fully, I do venture to say that the exploration of this hypothesis has, at the very least, something to reveal about the dynamics of Faulkner's creative process, something to reveal about the dynamics of his concern with the tragedy of romantic idealism.

As Richard P. Adams and others have shown, Faulkner often expands his theme of romantic idealism by alluding to Keat's "Ode on a Grecian Urn."[4] He does this no more extensively and significantly than when he personifies the "urn" in the title figure of *The Marble Faun*, who first appears in manuscript in the spring of 1919.[5] I emphasize the significance of this moment in Faulkner's career because it was at this time that he apparently first synthesized his personification of romantic idealism—the marble faun—with Eliot's personification of romantic idealism—Prufrock—and gave the faun Prufrock's vision of "sea-girls" in the form of "wave-ponies."

Just as Prufrock is not Hamlet, or John the Baptist, he is not, most certainly, that greatest of all heroes, Odysseus. The sirens do not sing their fatal love song to him:

> I have seen them riding seaward on the waves
> Combing the white hair of the waves blown back
> When the wind blows the water white and black.
>
> We have lingered in the chambers of the sea
> By sea-girls wreathed with seaweed red and brown
> Till human voices wake us, and we drown.[6]

Responding to the metaphor of "combing" the waves, and to the rhyme of "back" and "black," Faulkner gives his faun a vision of "wave-ponies," a fantasy which momentarily allows him to transcend his marble bonds which define, like Prufrock's impotent psyche, the perimeters of his spiritual hell:

> Soft the breeze, a steady flame . . .
> . . . comb[s] the wave-ponies' manes back
> Where the water shivers black . . . .[7]

This metamorphosis of "sea-girls" into "wave-ponies" would continue its sea-change in Faulkner's imagination. Though it would not always be so immediately recognizable, it would, as the following brief catalogue indicates, always be true to the tenor, if not the vehicle, of the "sea-girls" metaphor.

In the final lines of his one-act play, *Marionettes*, completed in the late fall of 1920,[8] Faulkner has the character Marietta say,

> "The wind smooths the sky's hair smoothly back,
> The wind combs the pines from grey to black . . . .
> . . . and the wind combs the sky grey and black."[9]

In the final lines of an unpublished poem entitled "Love Song," a 118-line paraphrase of "Prufrock," Faulkner wrote, sometime before the fall of 1921, that

> . . . darkness lays soft fingers on his eyes
> And strokes the lamplight from his brow,
>   to wake him, and he dies.[10]

Then in a poem entitled "Drowning," dated "2 April 1925,"[11] and later published in *A Green Bough*, Faulkner returns, as the title suggests, to a very literal transcription of the original "sea-girls" image:

> Where ribs of sunlight drown
> He joins in green caressing wars
> With seamaids red and brown . . . .[12]

Finally, in poem III of *A Green Bough* Faulkner comes almost full circle to a reincarnation of the faun's "wave-ponies" in suggesting that "Water-stallions/Neighing crest the foaming rush of tides."[13]

With poem VI of *A Green Bough*, however, Faulkner moves to a more original and at the same time more tragic view of the "horse" as metaphor, while extending, I suggest, the "sea-girls" metaphor with its emphasis on illusion, wish, and betrayal:

Man comes, man goes, and leaves behind
The bleaching bones that bore his lust;
The palfrey of his loves and hates
Is stabled at the last in the dust.
He cozened it and it did bear
Him to wishing's utmost rim;
But now, when wishing's gained, he finds
It was the steed that cozened him.[14]

But even more significantly, we see the same "palfrey," or "steed," or one very much like it, in Faulkner's prose-poem "Carcassonne," published in *These Thirteen* (1931), but "possibly written," Blotner notes, in the spring of 1926.[15] As in poem VI, the pony is the symbol of a wish. Articulate, though apparently not articulate enough, the persona of "Carcassonne" wishes to be a first-rate poet, an ideal role which he identifies with being a first-rate rider: "*I want to perform something bold and tragical and austere*, he repeated, . . . *me on a buckskin pony with eyes like blue electricity and a mane like tangled fire, galloping up the hill and right off into the high heaven of the world . . . .*"[16] But like Prufrock, with his interior dialogue between "you and I," the poet manqué realizes in a dialogue with his "bones," that his fantasy is a substitute for the creative act itself. And he moves from his fantasy of transcendence to a fantasy of drowning which echoes not only Prufrock's death by water but also Phlebas's in *The Waste Land*. Recapitulating the marble faun's Prufrockian vision of "wave-ponies," the poet manqué lingers among "waves" which are, as the following passage indicates, like "horses":

> Bones might lie under seas, in the caverns of the sea, knocked together by the *dying echoes of the waves. Like bones of horses* cursing the inferior riders who bestrode them . . . . But somebody always crucified the first-rate riders. And then it's better to be bones knocking together to the spent motion of falling tides in the caverns and the grottoes of the sea. (CS, p. 897, italics mine)

But like Prufrock, Faulkner's persona ultimately realizes that in dreaming of the ideal rather than acting, he has created his own spiritual "hell," a recognition dramatized by his allusion to Agamemnon's dying vision of Clytemnestra and Hades: "*where fell where I was King of Kings but the woman with the woman with the dog's eyes to knock my bones together and together*" (CS, p. 898).[17]

This juxtaposition of Agamemnon's dying vision with the poet manqué's drowning vision of horses and "hell" clearly parallels

Faulkner's use of the title "As I Lay Dying" for two unpublished stories about the spotted ponies in Frenchman's Bend. One version was rejected by *Scribner's* in November, 1928, only a few weeks after the completion of *The Sound and the Fury*. The other version—entirely in dialogue, Blotner records—seems not to have been submitted.[18] The title is taken from the speech of Agamemnon's ghost to Odysseus in Book IX of *The Odyssey*. In one of the many foreshadowings of Odysseus' imminent return to Penelope, Agamemnon speaks of Clytemnestra's betrayal on his return from the Trojan Wars—and her ultimate cruelty: "As I lay dying the woman with the dog's eyes would not close my eyelids for me as I descended into Hades."[19] Though the desire to illuminate the persona's vision of spiritual hell in "Carcassonne" may account solely for Faulkner's allusion to Agamemnon, perhaps Eliot inspired this association as well. Eliot, we will remember, compares Sweeney to Agamemnon in "Sweeney Among the Nightingales" (1920). Faulkner echoes the allusion to Agamemnon as well as the rhetoric of "Sweeney Among the Nightingales" in a poem dated 26 February 1926 and later published in *A Green Bough*.[20]

One thinks immediately, of course, of *As I Lay Dying*. More illuminating, however, in tracing the vagaries of Faulkner's imagination, is a brief look at the source of the two unpublished versions of "As I Lay Dying," the published story "Spotted Horses" (1931), and "The Peasants" section of *The Hamlet* (1940). All four variations were based on Faulkner's first venture into the world of Yoknapatawpha, "Father Abraham," apparently written in late 1926 or early 1927,[21] at which point Faulkner dropped it in favor of "Flags in the Dust"—or *Sartoris*, as it was called at the time of its first publication.

"Father Abraham" opens with a description of Flem Snopes as president of the Jefferson bank. Then it goes back to his beginnings, focusing on his return from Texas with Eula, her child, and the wild ponies which Flem's wrangler sells to the comically obsessed—and betrayed—men in Frenchman's Bend. On the verso of page eight of the twenty-five page manuscript Faulkner drew a picture of himself as a faun in a scene which, as Blotner observes, "might have illustrated a portion of *The Marble Faun*."[22] By the same token, one might suggest that the vision of the marble faun was present in the creation of not only "Father Abraham" and the works that it spawned, but in all those works where horses symbolize illusion and betrayal. Though the ponies which streak and whirl like fish about the corral in the manuscript and the typescript of "Father

Abraham"[23] had their experiential counterparts in the ponies which appeared in Oxford when Faulkner was a child, they have their symbolic counterparts, I suggest, in the marble faun's vision of the wave-ponies with their manes combed by the "steady flame" of the breeze.

One has only to look at the imagery of "The Peasants" in 1940 to see that the association of horses with hell, water, and fish was very much alive in Faulkner's imagination throughout his major years. When Flem first returns with the ponies to Frenchman's Bend the word "hell" is used as an expletive by one of the townsmen, and the association is developed not merely with Flem, who later outwits Satan, but with the ponies:

> "What in the hell is that?" one said.
> "It's a circus," Quick said. . . . Now they could see that the
> animals behind the wagons were horses. . . .
> "Hell fire," the first man—his name was Freeman—said.
> "It's Flem Snopes."[24]

Later, Faulkner uses fire imagery to describe the ponies' actions, and the association of "hell fire" with horses produces a thematic equation. The wrangler makes the mistake of trying to feed the ponies shelled corn, and the interior of the barn explodes "into mad tossing shapes like a downrush of flames. 'Hell fire,' one of them said" (H, p. 287). At the same time, Faulkner also seems to have "wave-ponies" in mind when, as in "Father Abraham," he compares the ponies to fish: "They whipped and whirled about the lot like dizzy fish in a bowl"; and later: "The ponies still streaked back and forth through the growing dusk like hysterical fish, but not so violently now" (H, p. 279).

Though comic rather than tragic, "The Peasants" has, like all great comedy, its tragic undercurrents. If we pause to reflect, we realize that there is an element of despair in the peasants' willingness to spend money they cannot afford to buy horses they cannot ride. They are, like Prufrock, romantic idealists, willing to embrace illusion because it takes their minds off reality. And they are, like Prufrock—and Agamemnon, whose dying vision inspired the titles of two versions of the same story—ultimately betrayed. They see a "hell," albeit a comic hell, when the ponies explode out of the corral, and when they realize they have been swindled by Flem Snopes.

As numerous critics have noted, Faulkner echoes Eliot

throughout *Mosquitoes* (1927), particularly "Prufrock" in the character of Ernest Talliaferro, who has trouble with women, and is getting "old" and getting "thin"—to name only a few of the more obvious echoes. It is perhaps more significant, however, that Talliaferro parallels the persona of "Carcassonne," as well as Prufrock, in that he listens to "his grumbling skeleton—that smug and dour and unshakable comrade who loves so well to say I told you so . . . ."[25] One should also note, more for purposes of continuity than anything else, that Faulkner repeatedly compares the wind to fire and the clashing hooves of centaurs.[26]

The centaur image is far more significant in *Flags in the Dust* and/or *Sartoris*. Indeed, it is used to establish the dominant theme of the novel: the tragedy of romantic idealism. Written initially in apparent alternation with "Father Abraham," which Faulkner seems to have dropped in the spring of 1927, *Flags in the Dust* focuses on the character Bayard Sartoris and his inability to deal with the past—the legacy of his ancestor "Carolina Bayard," the death of his brother, John. According to Bayard's Aunt Jenny, his ancestor had galloped to glory with Jeb Stuart's cavalry in the "thunderous coordination of a single centaur . . . ."[27] And he had died while galloping into a Union camp in search of anchovies, an association stimulated perhaps by the precedent of horses and fish in "Father Abraham," and its equally absurd effect.

Unable to forgive himself for his brother's death in an airbattle over France, Bayard emulates his galloping ancestor by riding an untamed stallion, which stands like "a motionless bronze flame . . ." but then bursts "like bronze unfolding wings . . ." (FD, p. 137). And though Bayard does not die when he is thrown from this horse, the horse's "wings" foreshadow Bayard's suicidal flight in an airplane whose wings fall off, giving him the death he has sought from the time of his brother's death. Perhaps, on the other hand, the death-wish was there in his mind from the moment he heard his Aunt Jenny's love song about the centaur and the anchovies. Playing on the theme that the past dominates the present of the Sartoris family, Faulkner manages to suggest that Bayard will inevitably succumb to the lure of this grotesquely romantic ideal.

Cleanth Brooks notes that "earlier versions of *Sartoris* (preserved in manuscript and typescript) show that originally Faulkner stressed even more heavily the themes and mood of Prufrock and the waste land."[28] One of the reasons that we are not more aware of the parallels is that Faulkner has split the Prufrockian persona in two. Bayard Sartoris, a man of action, hardly seems to resemble the virtually immobile Prufrock. Yet Bayard is a romanticist who is victimized by a vision which owes something, I believe, to an abstraction of the Prufrockian fantasy. Horace Benbow, on the other hand, comes very close to Prufrock in his emotional cowardice, his substitution of poeticisms for passionate involvement. Horace suffers, like Prufrock from his emotional isolation, and one is reminded of the poet manqué in "Carcassonne" when Faulkner describes how Horace lies on his bed

> while that wild fantastic futility of his voyaged in lonely regions of its own beyond the moon, about meadows nailed with firmamented stars to the ultimate roof of things, where unicorns filled the neighing air with galloping or lay supine in latent and golden-hooved repose. (FD. p. 187)

Though Horace dreams of unicorns rather than fiery-maned or drowning ponies, the theme of romantic illusion closely approximates Prufrock's vision of the "sea-girls" once again, and suggests a further abstraction of this metaphor.

Both Bayard and Horace are in love with the same woman, Horace's sister, Narcissa, though Horace seems more attracted to her at times than Bayard, particularly in the unpublished versions. Faulkner develops this incest motif in *The Sound and the Fury*, in Quentin Compson's fixation on his sister, Caddy. But he also incorporates the death-wish motif elaborated by Bayard's fixation on the death of his brother, John. For Quentin, Caddy's loss of innocence— her virginity—symbolizes the death of his own innocence, the death of his own egocentric universe. On the night she lost her virginity she sat in the branch, or creek, behind the Compson house, and they contemplated suicide. On his final day of life he carries out the death-wish of this moment, drowning himself in the Charles River, a bigger stream yet the same stream, a temporal symbol of the motion which he knows he cannot escape. Alluding to Saint Francis, Quentin thinks of Caddy, once his whole life, as "Little Sister Death."[29] Looking at the trout which hovers motionless in the Charles, Quentin makes it the personal symbol of Caddy in the branch, a symbol which calls him, siren-like, to the "caverns and the grottoes of the sea" (SF, pp. 111, 139), imagery which dominates his consciousness, just as it does the poet manqué's in "Carcassonne"—and, of course, the consciousness of Prufrock and Phlebas, which is so often one entity in Faulkner's imagination.

And like the tortured personae who precede him, Quentin's spiritual hell is identified with a horse. When he thinks of Caddy on the eve of her wedding he immediately associates the emotional agony he felt that night with the agony he felt when he fell from a horse and broke his leg—an agony compounded when he walked on it prematurely and it had to be reset: [Caddy:] "I've got to marry somebody. *Then they told me the bone would have to be broken again*" (SF, p. 139). Like Bayard, Quentin caused the fall through his own irresponsibility: "*Wait Wait just a minute through the sweat ah ah ah behind my teeth and Father damn that horse damn that horse. Wait it's my fault*" (SF, p. 140). And like the poet manqué of "Carcassonne," Quentin associates the horse with thoughts of drowning among "murmuring bones" (SF, p. 98). But unlike the poet manqué, Quentin carries out his fantasy. He is inspired, finally, by the large trout whose seeming immobility expresses the stasis that Quentin desires. Looking at the trout, Quentin says, "*If it could just be a hell beyond that: the clean flame the two of us more than dead. Then you will have only me then only me then the two of us amid the pointing and the horror beyond the clean flame*" (SF, p. 144).

In sum, like his spiritual predecessors, Quentin thinks of a horse, a fish, a death by water, a personal hell—associations firmly established by now in Faulkner's imagination. Through the projection of Quentin's troubled mind, Caddy becomes a "Little Sister Death," a siren appropriately identified with a fish if one has, as I think Faulkner did, Prufrock's "sea-girls" in the back of his mind.

As Blotner suggests, Horace Benbow of *Sanctuary* (1931) is "a distinctly Prufrockian figure."[30] But though there are not as many echoes of "Prufrock" and *The Waste Land* in *Sanctuary*, Faulkner still associates the horse and the fish with the siren figure, and the identification is worth at least briefly noting. In *The Sound and the Fury* it is Quentin who makes the motionless trout into a symbol of Caddy, and who dreams of drowning in the "caverns and grottoes . . . ." In *Sanctuary*, however, Temple Drake is a siren to the core. Though she is "as wild as a young mare . . . ,"[31] after Popeye introduces her to a surrogate lover named "Red," her destructive potential is symbolized, like Caddy's, by her comparison to a fish. Kept by Popeye from seeing Red, she effectively condemns him to death. Almost in Popeye's presence she hurls herself at Red, "her mouth gaped and ugly like that of a dying fish . . ." (S, p. 287). And this takes place, appropriately, at a nightclub called the "Grotto." Needless to say, Red "drowns" when Popeye discovers the truth. But truth is slippery in Faulkner's world. Temple has only to tell the truth in court to save Lee Goodwin's life. But she destroys Goodwin as well, by perjuring herself, with a face "quite pale," before a jury whose faces are as "pallid as the floating bellies of dead fish . . ."(S, p. 341).

A dead fish is similarly identified with Addie Bundren, the siren figure of *As I Lay Dying*, published in 1930, but written between the first and second drafts of *Sanctuary*. Yet Addie is also a Prufrockian visionary whose vision, as the title suggests, is compared to Agamemnon's, an allusion aligning her with the male romanticists who precede and follow her. As Sally R. Page says, "Addie is an idealist whose desire for the achievement of an inner vision of perfect union and fulfillment within reality drives her ultimately to a rejection of reality, of humanity, and of life itself."[32] And in rejecting her essential humanity Addie becomes an abstraction—to herself and, in death, to her youngest son, Vardaman, who says, ". . . *Jewel's mother is a horse. My mother is a fish.*"[33]

The horse which Jewel makes into a mother surrogate gallops straight out of "Father Abraham" and *Flags in the Dust*, echoing the stallion that Bayard rides, for example, in the imagery of its coat, "bunching, tongues swirling like so many flames," and its motion, a "glittering maze of hooves . . . an illusion of wings . . ." (AILD, p. 12). Like Bayard's stallion, Jewel's horse symbolizes a spiritual agony, the hell of being unable to love the remote figure of his mother. And like the ponies which whirl in Frenchman's Bend, the horse is compared to a fish. Unable to grasp the reality of his mother's death, Vardaman's traumatized mind fixes on the fish he has caught as a totem of her spirit. Then he compares the fish to Jewel's horse in a vision of her death made more terrible because the fish has been eaten: "I see him dissolve—legs, a rolling eye, a gaudy splotching like cold flames—and float upon the dark in fading solution; all one yet neither; all either yet none. . . . I am not afraid. 'Cooked and et. Cooked and et' " (AILD, p. 55).

This same image of a horse in water is repeated in association with Jewel's natural father, Reverend Whitfield. Once, early in her marriage, Addie thought she had found spiritual transcendence in Whitfield. But he merely sired Jewel and betrayed her idealism—a pattern of character and action summed up by Vernon Tull's comparison of Whitfield's voice to horses at Addie's funeral. In a description introduced by an echo from "Prufrock," Tull says:

> . . . the voices quaver away with a rich and dying fall. Whit-
> field begins. His voice is bigger than him. It's like they are
> not the same. It's like he is one and his voice is one, swimming
> on two horses side by side across the ford and coming into the
> house, the mud-splashed one and the one that never even got
> wet, triumphant and sad, (AILD, p. 86)

Again, we find a protagonist who is betrayed by a character who is
associated with horses and water. Whitfield is Addie's "Clytemnestra." Even as she lies dying, he betrays her. When he heard she was
about to die, he felt compelled to confess his sin to her husband,
Anse. Learning when he reaches Tull's house that she has died
already, he convinces himself that God will accept the "will for the
deed" (AILD, p. 171)—or a "dry" horse, if you will, for a "wet" one.

A similar vision of horses in water objectifies the romantic
idealism and death-in-life of Gail Hightower in *Light in August*
(1932). Throughout his life he has focused on the idealized and
absurd fantasy of his grandfather who was shot out of his saddle
while trying to steal chickens, an obvious echo of Carolina Bayard's
quest for anchovies. Ultimately, Hightower recognizes the spiritual
hell he has created by giving himself to a fantasy rather than to life,
when he has the illusion of "floating" and "dying" as cavalry sweep
past in his imagination "like a tide whose crest is jagged with the
wild heads of horses . . . ."[34]

In *Absalom, Absalom!* (1936) Wash Jones has a similarly
destructive illusion about Thomas Sutpen. For Jones, Sutpen is a
vision of "galloping hoofs," an "apotheosis," Quentin Compson says,
quoting his father, "lonely, explicable, beyond all human fouling
. . . ."[35] But the apotheosis falls suddenly to earth when Sutpen rejects the female child he has sired by Wash's granddaughter, Milly.
Earlier that morning Sutpen's prize mare, "Penelope," has given him
a colt. He reveals his true identity as what Rosa Coldfield calls a
"man-horse-demon" (AA, p. 8), when he tells Milly, ". . . too bad
you're not a mare too. Then I could give you a decent stall in the
stable . . ." (AA, p. 286).

Like Addie Bundren, Thomas Sutpen is both vision and visionary. Addie is destroyed by a vision of love; Sutpen, by a vision of
aristocracy. And like Addie, the persona of "Carcassonne," and

others, his spiritual hell is identified by allusions to Agamemnon. Though Sutpen has named his mare, "Penelope," he is more prophetic in naming his Negro daughter, "Clytemnestra"; for she, like her namesake, with the "dog's eyes," becomes the *"cold Cerberus of his private hell . . ."* (AA, p. 136). It is a hell which Sutpen, like the poet manqué, has tried to transcend, talking *"that which sounded like the bombast of a madman who creates within his very coffin walls his fabulous immeasurable Camelots and Carcassonnes"* (AA, p. 160).

A year earlier—1935—Faulkner had published *Pylon*, written, he said, because "I'd got in trouble with *Absalom, Absalom!* and I had to get away from it for a while . . . ."[36] But in writing *Pylon* Faulkner had not gotten away from Eliot. As in *Mosquitoes*, allusions to *The Waste Land* and "Prufrock" abound in a fashion which suggests that Faulkner lacked a profound imaginative commitment. Perhaps, in fact, as exemplified by his use of "Lovesong of J. A. Prufrock" for a chapter title, he was trying to create a poetic resonance that he felt the narrative lacked. Whatever the case, his obvious echoing of "Prufrock" between drafts of *Absalom, Absalom!* suggests that it was still very much alive in his imagination. And though by now the "sea-girls" may have been no more than a chorus, his equation of the "hells" of Agamemnon and "Carcassonne" with "galloping hoofs" and romantic idealism, suggests that their original metamorphosis, the "wave-ponies," was still a vital catalyst.

With his description of the fish-like ponies in "The Peasants" section of *The Hamlet* (1940), Faulkner came full circle to "Father Abraham." Though a three-legged racehorse wins races in *A Fable* (1954), and though the racehorse "Lightning" in *The Reivers* (1962) is inspired to gallop faster by the smell of sardines—in what might be called the final tribute to the marble faun's wave-ponies—the horses in both novels are optimistic symbols of life.

The symbolism of the fish is similarly attentuated, though recognizable in its association with death and idealism. This continuity of reference is largely the result, I believe, of its being associated with spiritual descendants of Quentin Compson: Harry Wilbourne in *The Wild Palms* (1939) and Ike McCaslin of "The Bear" in *Go Down, Moses* (1942). Harry's grotesquely idealized romance with Charlotte Rittenmeyer ends with her equally grotesque death. Quentin identifies Caddy with the trout which rises in the Charles River. Similarly, when Charlotte begins to die, Harry thinks to himself that it is "like

watching a fish rise in water—a dot, a minnow, and still increasing
. . . ."[37] Ike McCaslin—called Quentin Compson in "Lion: A
Story,"[38] the prototype for "The Bear"—even more closely recapitulates Quentin's vision of the trout. Just as Quentin idealizes Caddy and recapitulates her symbolic "death" in the stasis of the trout,
so also Ike idealizes the bear and foreshadows its death when he
watches the bear disappear:

> It faded, sank back into the wilderness without motion as he
> watched a fish, a huge old bass, sink back into the dark depths
> of its pool and vanish without even any movement of its fins.[39]

And though Ike does not, like Quentin, commit suicide, the death of
the bear marks the death of his commitment to life. Having lost the
perfect world of the bear, the wilderness, and the hunt, the rest of
his life is an anticlimax. He repudiates his farm—and with it, his
wife—and retreats to the kind of isolation that is anticipated by Hightower in *Light in August*. Though we are, at this point, perhaps too
far removed from Prufrock's vision of the "sea-girls" to even comment on the parallel, one can safely observe, I think, that Ike's spiritual ancestors in the Faulkner canon have all collectively anticipated
his romantic idealism, his inevitable betrayal, his spiritual retreat.

It is, as I have suggested throughout, the tragedy and the comedy of romantic idealism that link all the various personae in the
works I have discussed. Time and again Faulkner's characters give
themselves up to romantic visions. Grotesque in their rigidity, their
failure to adjust to the motion of life, they discover their own private hells when their visions fall to earth. Though I may have exaggerated the residual effect of that moment in 1919 when the marble
faun absorbed Prufrock's vision of transcendence, and though I have
no definitive answers as to what in each case Faulkner may have intended, I think there is some virtue at least in asking what Prufrock
would call "an overwhelming question."

Notes

[1]Though I am indebted to Joseph Blotner's discussion of Eliot's influence on the unpublished as well as published materials, in *Faulkner: A Biography*, 2 vols. (New York: Random House, 1974), I have also profited from reading the following studies: Richard P. Adams, "The Apprenticeship of William Faulkner," *Tulane Studies in English*, 12 (1962), 116-117; and *Faulkner: Myth and Motion* (Princeton: Princeton University Press, 1968), pp. 231-235; Cleanth Brooks, *William Faulkner: The Yoknapatawpha Country* (New Haven: Yale University Press, 1963), pp. 104-106, 130-131; Mary Jane Dickerson, "*As I Lay Dying* and *The Waste Land*—Some Relationships," *Mississippi Quarterly*, 17 (Summer 1964), 129-135; Frederick L. Gwynn, "Faulkner's Prufrock—and Other Observations," *Journal of English and Germanic Philology*, 52 (Jan. 1953), 63-70; Michael Millgate, *The Achievement of William Faulkner* (New York: Random House, 1963), pp. 144-145; Robert M. Slabey, "Faulkner's 'Waste Land': Vision in *Absalom, Absalom!*" *Mississippi Quarterly*, 14 (Summer 1961), 153-161; and Hyatt H. Waggoner, *William Faulkner: From Jefferson to the World* (Lexington: The University of Kentucky Press, 1959), pp. 13, 48, 74, 126-127, 265.

[2]See, respectively, Roma King, Jr., "The Janus Symbol in *As I Lay Dying*," *University of Kansas City Review*, 21 (June 1955), 287; Walter Brylowski, *Faulkner's Olympian Laugh: Myth in the Novels* (Detroit: Wayne State University Press, 1968), pp. 92-93; and Phyllis Hirshleifer, "As Whirlwinds in the South: *Light in August*," *Perspective*, 2 (Summer 1949), 234.

[3]*T. S. Eliot's Poetry and Plays* (Chicago: University of Chicago Press, 1956), p. 17.

[4]See Adams, "The Apprenticeship of William Faulkner," pp. 118-121, for the most detailed discussion.

[5]*Faulkner: A Biography*, I, 240-241.

[6]*T. S. Eliot: Collected Poems: 1909-1962* (New York: Harcourt, Brace and World, 1963), p. 7.

[7]See *Faulkner: A Biography*, I, 241; and *The Marble Faun* (1924; rpt. New York: Random House, 1965), p. 37.

[8]*Faulkner: A Biography*, I, 295.

[9]*Marionettes* (Oxford, Miss.: The Yoknapatawpha Press, 1975), pp. 48-49; see Noel Polk's discussion of this parallel in "Faulkner's *Marionettes*," *Mississippi Quarterly*, 26 (Summer 1973), 271.

[10]*Faulkner: A Biography*, I, 310.

[11]Ibid, Notes, p. 63.

[12]See *A Green Bough* (1933; rpt. New York: Random House, 1965), p. 41.

[13]Ibid, p. 18.

[14]Ibid, p. 24.

[15]*Faulkner: A Biography*, I, 502.

[16]*Collected Stories of William Faulkner* (New York: Random House, 1950), p. 899. Hereafter cited with the abbreviation CS.

[17]I am indebted to Blotner's discussion of these correspondences, in *Faulkner: A Biography*, I, Notes, p. 74.

[18]Ibid. pp. 596-597.

[19]See Blotner's account of how Faulkner quoted these lines when questioned about the title, in *Faulkner: A Biography*, I, 634-635. .

[20]See *Faulkner: A Biography*, I, 398-399, and *A Green Bough*, pp. 49-50.

[21]*Faulkner: A Biography*, I, 531.

[22]Ibid.

[23]I wish to thank the curator of the Arents Collection (New York Public Library) for allowing me to study the manuscript of "Father Abraham"; and the curator of the William Faulkner Collections (University of Virginia Library) for allowing me to study the carbon typescript.

[24]*The Hamlet* (1940; rpt. New York: Vintage-Knopf, n.d.), p. 275. Hereafter cited with the abbreviation H.

[25]*Mosquitoes* (1927; rpt. New York: Liveright Corporation, 1955), p. 346.

26Ibid, p. 338.

27*Flags in the Dust* (1973; rpt. New York: Vintage, 1974), p. 18. Hereafter cited with the abbreviation FD.

28*William Faulkner: The Yoknapatawpha Country*, p. 105.

29*The Sound and the Fury* (1929; rpt. New York: Modern Library College Edition, n.d.), p. 94. Hereafter cited with the abbreviation SF.

30*Faulkner: A Biography*, I, 614.

31*Sanctuary* (1931; rpt. New York: Modern Library, 1932), p. 262. Hereafter cited with the abbreviation S.

32*Faulkner's Women: Characterization and Meaning* (Deland, Fla.: Everett/Edwards, Inc., 1972), p. 112.

33*As I Lay Dying* (1930; rev. ed. New York: Vintage-Knopf. 1964), p. 187. Hereafter cited with the abbreviation AILD.

34*Light in August* (1932; rpt. New York: Modern Library College Edition, n.d.), p. 467.

35*Absalom, Absalom!* (1936; rpt. New York: Modern Library College Edition, n.d.), p. 136. Hereafter cited with the abbreviation AA.

36*Faulkner: A Biography*, I, 861.

37*The Wild Palms* (1939; rpt. New York: Vintage-Knopf, n.d.), p. 245.

38*Harper's Monthly Magazine*, 172 (December 1935), 67-77.

39*Go Down, Moses* (New York: Modern Library, 1942), p. 209.

Faulkner and His Reader

by

Carolyn Porter

In *The Pound Era*, Hugh Kenner comments on the "instinct
that applied brown varnish" to paintings, thereby simultaneously
aging them and "setting the object at a distance to make it interesting." Kenner goes on to suggest that this "instinct . . . as the nine-
teenth century progressed drew writing and painting closer and closer
together," yielding a critical vocabulary dominated by terms like
"structure . . . surfaces and depths and insight and outlook . . . round
and flat characters . . . point of view . . . perspective . . . foreground
and background."[1] Kenner is by no means the first to point this out;
as William Holtz has recently noted, "the analogy with painting is
persistent and long honored in the history of criticism."[2] Holtz himself makes this statement at the beginning of a "Reconsideration" of
Joseph Frank's concept of spatial form, a concept which has, since
the publication of Frank's essay in 1945, heavily influenced the way
in which visual and narrative modes of apprehension have been discussed by critics of the twentieth century novel.[3]

I refer to this issue not in order to enter the vexed debate still
going on about the relation between visual and narrative art, but in
order to focus on a particular aspect of the visual mode as it figures
in narrative, in particular, the narrative of William Faulkner.

Let me begin by suggesting that to confront a visual object,
whether an actual picture or a literary image, is to assume the status
of an observer, and so to accept a position separate from the picture
or image one confronts. According to John Berger, this position is
"the viewing point of Renaissance perspective, fixed and outside the
picture, but to which everything within the picture was drawn."
Berger suggests that this viewing point has disappeared in the cubist
painting, to become "a field of vision which is the picture itself."
Consequently, when looking at a cubist painting, we observe spatial

relations between visual forms, but the relation defined between any two forms "does not, as it does in illusionist space, establish the rule for all spatial relationships between all the forms portrayed in the picture." Berger depicts the viewer's eye repeatedly moving into the cubist painting and back to its surface, where it deposits each time the newly acquired knowledge before returning to discover yet another relationship. Thus the cubist painting acts as "an expression of the relation between viewer and subject," and the evaluative question appropriate to it is not "Is it true? or: Is it sincere?" but "Does it continue?" Berger is arguing, then, that the cubist painting's actual subject is "the relation between the seer and the seen."[4]

What such an argument implies, among other things, is that the cubist works that interest Berger radically undermine the detachment of the viewer, a detachment which we as literary critics continue implicitly to assume when we use visual metaphors to conceptualize our experience as readers. Of course, one cannot escape using visual terms altogether, as the ensuing discussion amply demonstrates. Nor do I wish to advocate dispensing with what is—particularly when dealing with the modern novel—indispensable.[5] Rather, I wish to suggest that in the case of Faulkner's works, the virtual identity between reader and viewer is called into question, and for important reasons. For just as the cubist painting may be seen as undermining the stable vantage point held by the viewer of a Renaissance painting, "fixed and outside the picture," Faulkner's experiments in narrative technique from *The Sound and the Fury* through *Absalom, Absalom!* may be seen as increasingly complex strategies to undermine the reader's detachment.[6] After describing the general line of this development, I want to focus on *Light in August*,* where its thematic implications become clear, and finally to discuss *Absalom, Absalom!*, where the reader's detachment is finally undercut radically.

The Sound and the Fury is actually Faulkner's simplest experiment in terms of technical conception. In its original form, without the appendix, the novel asks the reader to inhabit four successive points of view in order to construct for himself the story of the Compson family. The final section, moreover, offers a retroactive perspective on the events recorded which, while it may not present a

---

*To reinforce my comments here on *Light in August*, I have used some portions from my paper, "The Problem of Time in *Light in August*," as published in *Rice University Studies*, 61, i; 107-125.

single, privileged vision of the world of the novel, at least allows us to integrate all that we have seen from a single, detached point of view. *As I Lay Dying* is conceptually more complex. Instead of a gradually emerging group of characters set against a gradually emerging background, we have a field of interacting figures recurrently emerging out of a flux. Never allowed to settle for long into any character's consciousness, frustrated in our endeavor to form an image of more than passing instants, we are less confronted with the world of the novel than pulled through it along with the Bundrens. The novel imitates life not by recreating the world in the form of a painting, but by recreating experience as a flow of consciousness in which some images vividly remain to haunt us, but no sense of "foreground" and "background" is secure. In *Light in August*, Faulkner combines the interior monologue with an omniscient narrator and expands the scope of his fiction from the family to the town. Here the reader's disorientation derives from the multiplicity of plot lines rather than from the multiple perspectives of the earlier novels. While *As I Lay Dying* resists our desire for the single, fixable perspective of illusionist space by forcing us through a rapidly paced substitution of one point of view for another, *Light in August* resists the same desire by refusing to allow us to follow any single action through to its completion. Each story necessitates another, until plot lines seem to spread out indefinitely. Moreover, we are set down *in medias res*, so that as we move forward in time, we double back further and further into the past. In *Light in August*, it becomes clear that Faulkner's manipulation of perspective is intimately involved with his interest in time. If we compare this novel with *The Sound and the Fury*, we can begin to see the relation between time and perspective.

In *The Sound and the Fury*, time is an explicit issue for the Quentin Compson who begins his last day by twisting the arms off the face of his watch. But time remains more an explicit thematic concern than an implicit means of reader coercion. Within each section of the novel, a single perspective is developed through which we must fill in the events of the past. But once we begin to assemble the patches of time past revealed in the opening section, we are already engaged in the most complex activity the novel demands of us. Difficult though this task is, the stable and detached perspective afforded by the final section makes it possible to put the pieces of the puzzle together. Although *The Sound and the Fury* is the sort of puzzle capable of more than one solution, more than one assembled form, it is nonetheless a puzzle that *can* be assembled. *Light in August*, on the other hand, while it makes the issue of perspective thematically explicit in the figure of Gail Hightower, the willfully

detached observer seated behind his window, implicitly manipulates
the reader by casting the omniscient narrator in the role of roaming
listener and interpreter. That is, Faulkner refuses us a single, fixed
perspective here not by placing us in several minds successively, but
by moving us from one place and time to another as the narrator
focuses his attention on one character's story only to turn away to
another's.[7] This strategy is further complicated by the demand it
makes on the narrator to give each character a past.

In *The Sound and the Fury*, the present consists of three days
whose events are less important as episodes in plot development than
as retrospective references to events in the past, and serve primarily
to establish relations between the two. The world of the present
introduced in the opening section is provided with a history in the
course of the novel, and the appendix Faulkner later composed for
Cowley's selected edition of his works merely expands this history
into the past and the future; but history in either case functions to
deepen the meaning and elaborate the significance of these present
events. In other words, Sartre was right when he argued that this
novel has no future, because its present consists in events conceived
not as acts with as yet undetermined future consequences, but as
consequences already determined by as yet unrevealed previous
events.[8] As we read *The Sound and the Fury*, we are pulled forward
not by the desire to see what happens next, but by the need to
understand why this is happening now. In *Light in August*, the narrative pull encompasses both of these needs, a point which may be
demonstrated by looking at the way the two novels begin.

Our confusion at the opening of *The Sound and the Fury* derives from the uncertain meaning of the word "Caddy." We must
first learn its literal reference in the present, and eventually its symbolic reference to the past. Once this is done, however, the scene
takes on both clarity and significance. The opening pages of *Light in
August*, on the other hand locate us in a world in motion, and
present us not with a present scene whose meaning is flushed out
fully once we learn its relationship to the past, but with a moving
present capable of leading us virtually anywhere. Lena Grove's quest
to find the father of her unborn child, precisely by virtue of its
apparent hopelessness, promises to carry us on an endless journey.
The novel which proceeds from this beginning makes good on this
promise to the extent that its plots proliferate at an alarming rate.
But while forcing us to attend to the question of what will happen
next in a present always moving forward, Faulkner also meets the
demand which grows more urgent as this present grows more com-

plex, the demand to fill in the history of the characters whose actions we witness. The reader's need to explain the present events by reference to their history, therefore, coexists with (although by no means peacefully) his need to keep up with them as they pull him forward into an indeterminate future.

In *Light in August*, then, Faulkner denies not merely the ultimate validity of a detached perspective as he did in *The Sound and the Fury*, but the very possibility of one. For in *Light in August*, any fixed perspective we may hope to gain is disrupted by time's unceasing flow. In other words, the reader is compelled to order time *while* it is moving. I want now to explain more fully how and why Faulkner forces the reader of *Light in August* to engage in this struggle.

With the significant exceptions of Lena Grove and eventually Byron Bunch, the characters in *Light in August* are victims of ordering myths, or what Frank Kermode has called degenerate fictions.[9] The townspeople of Jefferson form a community devoted not to fostering life, but to worshipping death, an attitude demonstrated by that "Protestant music" with its "quality stern and implacable, deliberate and without passion so much as immolation, pleading, asking, for not love, not life, forbidding it to others, demanding in sonorous tones death as though death were the boon."[10] As the roles of Joanna Burden, McEachern, and Doc Hines make clear, the Protestant church supports and enforces that commitment to the rigid distinction between black and white which imprisons and destroys Joe Christmas. The church's capacity to redeem time, to provide that "peace in which to sin and be forgiven . . . is the life of man," derives from the paradigmatic fiction on which it was founded, a fiction constituting an organization of time in which a *kairos* fills all time before and after with meaning, and thus redeems history by providing man with a place in it (461). But this fiction has, in Kermode's terms, regressed into myth; the Christian ordering of time has ossified into an institution committed to vengeance rather than to love, devoted to death rather than to life.

It is Gail Hightower, a man who has first retreated from life into the shelter of the church, and then from the church to his seat behind a window, who finally provides us with this vision of the church, and he does so in terms which help to explain why Faulkner has situated him behind that window as a willfully detached observer. In Hightower's final revery, the church is seen as a failure not because of the "outward groping of those within it nor the inward groping of those without," but because of the "professionals who control it and who have removed the bells from its steeples" (461). The bells which ring the hours, ordering man's days in accord with a redemptive organization of time, are gone. Developing the metaphor further, Faulkner describes all the world's steeples as "endless, without order, empty, symbolical, bleak, skypointed not with ecstasy or passion but in adjuration, threat and doom" (461). Clearly enough, Faulkner's metaphor has sexual implications; the church is figured as "one of those barricades of the middleages planted with dead and sharpened stakes," its power marshalled not in the service of procreation but of violence. By removing the bells from the steeples, the "professionals" have rendered the church impotent to foster life and peace, but all the more rigid and powerful in its ability to enforce its rule, to support the "empty, symbolical" distinctions which remain dogma (461).

But to notice the phallic imagery here is only to begin to see the significance of this conceit, for the bells' removal is an instance not only of the novel's elaborate concern with sexuality, but also of Faulkner's use of sound as a means of referring to that realm of ongoing life which Lena Grove inhabits. The most obvious case of this technique is the insect noises which recur throughout the novel, particularly in reference to Hightower and Christmas. Faulkner reminds us repeatedly that "beyond the open window" at which Hightower sits, "the sound of insects has not ceased, not faltered," and that Joe Christmas moves through a world constantly "alive" with the sounds of "crickets" (370, 149). Joe, of course, is cut off from this world, as is clear from the fact that the crickets keep "a little island of silence about him" (216). Sounds are used to emphasize Joe's alienation not only from the natural world, but also from the human community, that community which, because the church has failed to unite it in the service of love and peace, has become devoted to death and vengeance. Sitting behind the "open door" of his cabin, Joe hears the "myriad sounds of . . . voices, murmurs, whispers: of trees, darkness, earth; people . . . which he had been conscious of all his life without knowing it, which were his life, thinking *God perhaps and me not knowing that too.*"

These recurring sounds, then, reinforce our sense of the alienation from life from which Hightower, willingly, and Joe, unwillingly, suffer. But Faulkner's technique consists not merely in the use of "sound imagery." Further, I do not mean to say that all sounds in the novel "refer" in this way to a realm of ongoing life; the case of the protestant music makes this clear, for it is associated with death and not life. Rather, I think the use of certain sounds to signal the ongoing life from which Joe is alienated is part of a larger strategy which allies hearing with that temporal dimension which Lena Grove embodies, the continual present which sustains ongoing life, but from which the church's ossified order has alienated it. This strategy can be seen in the novel's opening pages.

As Lena Grove sits beside the road watching Armstid's wagon approach, Faulkner describes the scene in terms of a contradiction between what she sees and what she hears:

> The sharp and brittle crack and clatter of its weathered and ungreased wood and metal is slow and terrific: a series of dry sluggish reports carrying for a half mile across the hot still pinewiney silence of the August afternoon. Though the mules plod in a steady and unflagging hypnosis, the vehicle does not seem to progress. It seems to hang suspended in the middle distance forever and forever, so infinitesimal is its progress (5).

Faulkner creates here the impression of constant change; the wagon's sound signals its motion, while its appearance is static. He is appealing to our predisposition to view immobility as permanence, but complicating our response by attributing that permanence to motion itself. Characteristically, Lena allies herself with the wagon's sound, so that

> in the watching of it, the eye loses it as sight and sense drowsily merge and blend . . . so that at last, as though out of some trivial and unimportant region beyond even distance, the sound of it seems to come slow and terrific and without meaning, as though it were a ghost travelling a half mile ahead of its own shape (6).

As we know, Lena embodies the natural, procreative realm from which Joe is alienated and Hightower has fled. What I want to emphasize is that the *way* in which Faulkner establishes Lena's alliance with the earth's motion is by suspending her sight of the wagon ("the eye loses it") as he pursues her hearing. In other words, it is by locating Lena from the start in the "realm of hearing" that he makes her embody time's ceaseless progression (440).

Further, if we recall that the only order Lena seems to require is that minimal one indicated by her single metaphysical profundity,

"My, my. A body does get around," the ease with which her hearing outstrips her seeing is hardly surprising (26). For Lena Grove—and this is essentially what undermines her credibility as character while heightening her value as mythic force—exists in a perpetual present, a realm in which "time has not stopped" and never does, because Lena has no need to stand back and order her life in relation to time: she quite simply *is* time, understood as the "long monotonous succession of peaceful and undeviating changes from day to dark and dark to day" (26,5).

By bringing us into the world of the novel through Lena's peculiar consciousness, then, Faulkner presents us with a world in motion, thereby introducing us to the task we must perform as we move through the novel to come. Beginning *in medias res*, recapitulating Lena's past in a brief four pages, and returning to the present where Lena has remained, waiting for the wagon, Faulkner then follows her progress until she comes in sight of the "yellow column" of smoke whose source both we and Lena are eventually to discover (26). But as the novel proceeds, proliferating plots and characters, we are not content with concluding, as Lena does once again on the novel's last page, that "a body does get around" (480). Unlike Lena Grove, we are incapable of inhabiting time without trying to order it. Set down *in medias res*, we need to stand back and find a way of encompassing the horrifying events we must witness. In this respect, we share with Hightower a need to retreat into the role of viewer, to secure a vantage point from which to integrate events, stories, and characters into a formal unity and so confirm our detachment from them and their implications. And like Hightower, we are forced in the end to accept defeat.

In contrast to Lena, whose slow and steady progress never stops, Gail Hightower is a man who, as we are repeatedly told, "has not moved" (80).[11] Terrified by the "hot still rich maculate smell of the earth," Hightower has long since fled from it, "to walls, to artificial light" (300,301). We need not review the details of his peculiar flight from life. For present purposes, what is important is the fact that his flight from the "harsh gale of living" has finally taken the form of a withdrawal behind his window (453). The view framed by that window, however, is peculiar indeed. Hightower sits here not to look out on the living world itself, but to await a vision of the instant of his grandfather's death. He no longer "looks at" his sign, "his monument," and "he does not actually see the trees beneath and through which he watches the street," for he is waiting to see his grandfather and his troops "with tumult and soundless yelling . . . sweep past" (55, 52, 466-67). In other words, Hightower occupies the position of the detached viewer, but he does so in order to see the dead, not the living. As we shall see when we come to *Absalom, Absalom!*, Faulkner's ghosts are chiefly seen, not heard.

It is only the "steady shrilling of insects and the monotonous sound of Byron's voice" which persist in relating Hightower tenously to the living world beyond his window (83). It is Byron Bunch—notably, the single major character in the novel who allows himself to break free of the regulated order by which he has protected himself from sin and responsibility—who brings to Hightower's ears the news of Lena and Joe, and who eventually ushers Joe's mother into Hightower's house and seeks his aid when Lena needs a doctor. In short, it is because of Byron's habit of visiting and talking with Hightower that he eventually finds himself again involved with the living, hearing "the treble shouts of the generations," a participant in that world of birth and death from which he has fled (385).

If we return now to Hightower's final revery we will find Faulkner revealing through Hightower why any vision which promises to encompass events and redeem time is doomed to failure. As Hightower watches himself, in mounting horror, act out his life, the "wheel of thinking turns on" and he is forced to realize that he is responsible for his wife's death, that even by becoming his dead grandfather "on the instant of his death" he has not been able to remove himself from the burden of membership in the human community, since even if he has become his grandfather, he is still "the debaucher and murderer of [his] grandson's wife" (464, 465). Having been drawn into the events going on outside his window, Hightower is now forced to confront what his entire life has been devoted to denying—his participation in the world of the living, with all the responsibility this entails.

When he first nears this realization, the wheel of thinking "begins to slow" and he "seems to watch himself among faces, always among, enclosed and surrounded by, faces" (462). Hightower's vision now takes the form of a "halo . . . full of faces" (465). The wheel of thinking which becomes a halo is the complex vehicle for a metaphor whose tenor includes "all the faces he has ever seen" (465). As wheel, the vehicle moves ceaselessly; as halo it appears to be static. The wheel/halo is Faulkner's version of Keats' urn, itself by this time translated from an emblem of Lena's eternal motion into both a womb and a tomb. For a moment, it seems that the faces "are peaceful, as though they have escaped into an apotheosis," but this peaceful vision breaks down, and for a reason similar to that which made Keats' urn turn into a "Cold Pastoral": death and historical time reassert their dominion (465). Joe's face is not clear, and as Hightower looks at it, he sees why: "it is two faces which seem to strive . . . to free themselves one from the other," the faces of Christmas and Percy Grimm (465-66). Most significantly, these faces strive "not of themselves striving or desiring it . . . but because of the motion and desire of the wheel itself" (465-66). It is, then, the motion of time itself, signalled at the novel's outset by the sound of the wagon's wheels, and now by the wheel of time itself eternally moving, which both demands and resists the effort to conceive a vision which will organize time within a redemptive vision.

It can now be seen why the "freed voices" of those singing the protestant hymns assume "the shapes and attitudes of crucifixions, ecstatic, solemn, and profound" (347). Like Joe Christmas, when his body is described as "a post or a tower upon which the sentient part of him mused like a hermit, contemplative and remote with ecstasy and selfcrucifixion," those within the church are imprisoned by a degenerate fiction and thereby cut off from each other and from life's motion (150). In other words, those trapped within this order mirror the man forced to live outside it because of their common alienation from each other and from that "peace in which to sin and be forgiven . . . is the life of man" (461). Joe Christmas and Percy Grimm are bound to each other in their common and unwitting enactment of a devotion to death. This is what Hightower understands when, foreseeing Joe's lynching, he thinks, "they will do it gladly, gladly" because "to pity him would be to admit selfdoubt and to hope for and need pity themselves" (348).

Yet when Christmas is finally indeed crucified, whatever the citizens of Jefferson say to each other by way of ritual celebration, Faulkner apotheosizes him. He rises "soaring into their memories" to become a face "musing, quiet, steadfast, not fading," while the siren screams on, mounting toward its "unbelievable crescendo, passing out of the realm of hearing" (440). To transcend the "realm of hearing" is to die; and in an unredeemed world, to die is to join the ranks of "all the living who ever lived, wailing still like lost children among the cold and terrible stars" (466). Those whose voices assume the "shapes of crucifixions" then, adhere to a dead faith which severs them from "all the living who ever lived," whose voices remain therefore "unheeded" (465). In other words, the bells having been removed from the steeples, the church has come to represent not merely a retreat from life, but a citadel from which the human race itself, the living as well as the dead, has been exiled.

Hightower's vision reflects the larger struggle of both reader and narrator, the struggle to appropriate the ceaseless flow of time into an ordered fiction within which man can find meaning. This struggle is necessitated by the relationship between the past and the ongoing present in the novel. From the moment we encounter Lena sitting in the ditch to the final moment in which the furniture salesman relates his comic story to his wife, time pushes forward, seeming never to stop despite the lengthy flashbacks into the past. Bergson's concept of memory as automatically preservative is crucial to an understanding of Faulkner's strategy here.[12] The paragraph leading into Joe's history, which constitutes the longest foray into the past if not the deepest penetration of it, works primarily on the principle that memory is not a system of pigeonholes, but simply a part of the flow of our consciousness, our "attention to life" from which we are artificially alienated. Accordingly, "memory believes before knowing remembers," because memory represents that intuitive awareness, that attention to life which never wanes but is only interrupted, so that "knowing," intelligence, must "remember," must search for and select those moments from the past which it deems relevant to the present. "Memory . . . believes longer than recollects, longer than knowing even wonders," and so represents a sustained subterranean flow, fundamentally unaffected by the interruptions imposed from above by the contingencies of survival (111). Accordingly, Faulkner modulates into the past without interrupting the flow of the present by referring the shift to a dimension which includes both past and present within the ceaseless flux of duration. He not only introduces the shift in this way, but repeats his appeal to memory as an enduring aspect of the present like a refrain throughout the following chapters, reinforcing our sense of the fundamental continuity of time.

Consequently, as the present of the novel flows on into an indeterminate future, we move simultaneously farther and farther into the past until, with Hightower's final revery, we reach a point before the Civil War. Moving farther into the past while at the same time moving ceaselessly on into the future, the novel appropriates larger and larger chunks of time into a structure which is constantly struggling to enfold them within a unified vision. The novel not only operates on this principle but calls attention to it by deliberately biting off more than it seems able to chew, as it were. As time moves on and plots proliferate, the novel sets itself an enormous task of assimilation: as the structure expands to encompass a lengthening history within an ordered whole, that order is continually revealing itself as inadequate to the larger demands for meaning posed by the continuously moving present. Thus there is a mounting tension in the novel between time's ceaseless motion and our attempt to impose a structure large enough to give that motion a meaning, to humanize it.

Light in August, then, enacts a struggle for a unified form which will encompass the events it records, a redemptive vision which will compensate for the inadequacy of the church's degenerate fiction. But just as Hightower's tragic vision of the human community as continuous and whole fails to encompass and redeem the events he has witnessed, and this because the wheel of time keeps turning, so the tension between the flow of time and the human endeavor to impose a plot, a redemptive order, on that monotonous succession of day and night persists unrelieved. The novel as a whole seeks to redeem a diminished world by making of Joe Christmas's death a *kairos* for which Hightower's vision can supply a context and reference, but fails ultimately because that world keeps on moving.

For the same reason, the reader must fail in his endeavor to find a fixed vantage point from which to integrate events, characters, and stories into an ordered whole, separate and detached from himself. Had Faulkner ended the novel with Hightower's final vision, this would not be so forcefully true. But by telling the story of Lena and Byron on the road out of Jefferson through an entirely new character, the furniture salesman, Faulkner reinforces the implications of time's incessant progression into the future. Lena Grove's story acts as both bracket and ellipsis, to enclose and relieve the tragedy of Joe Christmas, but also to extend and amplify its intensity. By virtue of her health, her communality, and the sheer humor of her simple responses to life, she acts as comic relief to an intensely horrifying drama; but by virtue of the persistent and endless motion she comes to embody, her story extends and sustains the horror it ostensibly circumscribes. In a sense, her statement, "My, my. A body does get around," is quite seriously a profound one.

In *Light in August*, Faulkner employs a narrative strategy which forces the reader to acknowledge the necessary disruption of any fixed perspective by the flow of time, but in *Absalom, Abslaom!*

he goes further. He implicates the reader in the "stream of event" by forcing him to share the burden of narrative construction actively.[13] That is, by casting the novel's central action as an exercise of the imagination in narrative construction, Faulkner implicates his reader as a participant in the telling of a story, a strategy which serves to alter the reader's relation to the novel much as a cubist painting alters the viewer's relation to illusionist space. We have been, I think, too distracted by the fact that Rosa, Mr. Compson, and Quentin/ Shreve produce different "versions" of Sutpen's story to pay sufficient attention to the medium out of which we extract these versions, the medium of conversation. For *Absalom, Absalom!* does not simply conduct us through a series of perspectives, calling attention to the limitations of each; it demands the reader's participation in the collective act of narrative construction of which it is constituted. In conventional terms, one could say that the reader becomes a narrator, and because the major line of action in the novel consists in narration itself, the reader is threatened with becoming a character as well. But it seems more accurate to say that the novel is itself one voice in a dialogue with the reader, who, like Quentin Compson, struggles in vain to secure a detached position from which to assemble and confront a chaotic and inexplicable set of events.

Quentin comes to us as an auditor who is forced to listen to Rosa Coldfield, to his father, to his roommate, but who tries to resist a narrative pull which threatens to engulf him. By remaining the passive hearer, Quentin tries to secure a detached perspective on the story of Sutpen, and so to free himself from the burden of history by which he is already, as a college freshman, enmeshed. But when Shreve assumes the voice of one of the "two separate Quentins" talking to each other "in the long silence of notpeople, in notlanguage" at the beginning, Quentin is forced to participate in the telling of Sutpen's story, a process which, for a brief hour in the novel's eighth chapter, issues in the "happy marriage of speaking and hearing," only to subside once again in the ninth, leaving Quentin again hearing "without listening or answering," because he is again absorbed in watching ghosts (9, 316, 374)

Quentin's position is established in the novel's opening chapter. Before Miss Coldfield ever speaks directly, we join Quentin as he listens to her

> talking in that grim haggard amazed voice until at last listening would renege and hearing-sense self-confound and the long-

dead object of her impotent yet indomitable rage would appear,
as though by outraged recapitulation evoked, quiet inattentive
and harmless, out of the biding and dreamy and victorious
dust (7-8).

Faulkner gradually shifts Quentin's mode of apprehension here from
hearing to seeing ("Her voice would not cease, it would just vanish")
until Quentin's mind is wholly absorbed by a vision of Sutpen: "Out
of quiet thunderclap he would abrupt (man-horse-demon) upon a
scene peaceful and decorous as a schoolprize water color" (8). A picture "abrupts" before Quentin like a slide projected on a screen, a
picture of Sutpen "immobile, bearded and hand palm-lifted," surrounded by the wild blacks and the captive architect (8). Then Quentin seems "to watch" as "out of the soundless Nothing," Sutpen's
Hundred is created, the *"Be Sutpen's Hundred* like the oldentime *Be
Light"* (8, 9). In this "soundless" vision even God's words have become objects, seen and not heard. Again, a few pages later, and "as
though in inverse ration to the vanishing voice," the "ghost . . .
began to assume a quality almost of solidity, permanence," an "ogre-
shape which, as Miss Coldfield's voice went on, resolved out of itself
before Quentin's eyes the two half-ogre children" (13). Ellen, "the
fourth one," joins the picture now, one in which "the four of them"
are "arranged into the conventional family group of the period," and
which finally becomes a "fading and ancient photograph . . . hung on
the wall behind and above the voice and of whose presence the
voice's owner was not even aware" (14). By page twenty-one, Rosa
herself as a child has joined the "musing and decorous wraiths"
whom Quentin keeps visualizing: "Quentin seemed to watch resolving the figure of a little girl, in the prim skirts and pantalettes . . . of
the dead time" (21).

Quentin visualizes the ghosts, then, in the same way that Ellen
Coldfield visualizes her family, once Bon has married Judith in her
imagination:

> She seemed to have encompassed time. She postulated the
> elapsed years during which no honeymoon had taken place,
> out of which the (now) five faces looked with a sort of life-
> less and perennial bloom like painted portraits hung in a vac-
> uum (75).

Just as Rosa's conception of Charles Bon "was a picture, an image"
because Rosa was "not listening" to "what Ellen told her," Quentin's
conception of Sutpen and his family is also a picture, because he is
not listening to Rosa, but instead watching ghosts resolve before him

out of the dust (74, 75). Most importantly, because Quentin is engaged in ghost-watching, he too seems "to have encompassed time," as he notices that "the sun seemed hardly to have moved" (22). The story Rose is telling has for him the "quality of a dream," occurring "still-born and complete in a second" even though he knows that "the very quality upon which it must depend to move the dreamer (verisimilitude) to credulity" is an "acceptance of elapsed and yet-elapsing time" (22). Because Quentin already knows "part of" the Sutpen story, "the talking, the telling" of it simply strikes "the resonant strings of remembering," issuing in pictures which "encompass" events but do not explain them (11, 213). And it is because they seem to deny, to stand beyond the realm of "elapsed and yet-elapsing time" that these pictures have a "quality strange, contradictory and bizarre; not quite comprehensible" (22, 14). In other words, Quentin detaches himself from "the telling," which goes on in time, and confronts the images beyond "the voice," the ghosts who manifest "an air of tranquil and unwitting desolation . . . as if" they "had never lived at all" (22, 14).

In the course of the novel, Faulkner develops this association between vision and the effort to "encompass" and indeed transcend time. It would require another essay to explore fully all the ways in which he carries this out. For my purposes here, it should suffice to note that there is an opposition at work in the novel between "light" and the vision it supports, on the one hand, and "moving air" and the talking and hearing it sustains, on the other—an opposition grounded in one more basic, that between transcendence of, and immersion in, the "stream of event" (158).

As his first appearance indicates, Sutpen inhabits a realm defined by light. He is imagined at the inception of his design as looking "ahead along the indivulged light rays in which his descendants who might not even ever hear his (the boy's) name, waited to be born," and again "after he would become dead, still there, still watching the fine grandsons and great-grandsons springing as far as the eye could reach" (261, 271). Moreover, he is remembered as if he *had* transcended time. For example, when he first arrives in Jefferson, he seems literally to be a "man who came from nowhere" (20): the men on the hotel gallery simply

> looked up, and there the stranger was. He was already half-
> way across the Square when they saw him, on a big hard-

ridden roan horse, man and beast looking as though they had
been created out of thin air and set down in the bright summer
sabbath sunshine in the middle of a tired foxtrot (31-32).

Sutpen, in short, is seen as a man who himself is primarily a seer, a
demonic visionary who set out once and forever to transcend time by
founding a dynasty, and he commands the visionary response he gets
precisely because of his remorseless dedication to transcendence, his
"indomitable spirit" (254). "He was the light-blinded bat-like image
of his own torment" according to Rosa Coldfield, who shares his
"impotent yet indomitable frustration," and accordingly mirrors his
typically rigid and upright posture (7).

Rosa's "impotent and static rage" results from what she describes at one point as the "final clap-to of a door between us and all
that was, all that might have been—a retroactive severance of the
stream of event" (158). Thomas Sutpen's affront leaves Rosa fixed
behind "a sheet of glass" from which she observes "all subsequent
events transpire as though in a soundless vacuum," leaving her "immobile, impotent, helpless" (151). That "might-have-been which is
more true than truth" then becomes "the single rock we cling to
above the maelstrom of unbearable reality" (143, 149-150). Thomas
Sutpen too confronts the "clap-to of a door," an affront which leads
to a design whose purpose and effect is to "shut that door himself
forever behind him on all that he had ever known" (261). Sutpen's
design is conceived in an experience of impotence, at the moment
when he hears himself saying of the plantation owner, *"I not only
wasn't doing any good to him by telling it or any harm to him by not
telling it, there aint any good or harm either in the living world that
I can do to him"* (238). As Sutpen himself admits, the "boy-symbol
was just the figment of the amazed and desperate child" who is sent
to deliver a message and finds that it *"cant even matter"* whether it
was delivered or not (261). To defy this impotence, Sutpen conceives
of a design which hypostatizes it, beyond "the living world." Like
Rosa Coldfield's "dream," Thomas Sutpen's innocence lifts him
above the "stream of event," from which the "severe shape of his
intact innocence" rises as a "monument" to transcend rather then
redeem the affront, to order his life in accord with a static design.

But Sutpen's design fails for the same reason that God's did;
to order time and thereby fill it with meaning, one must inhabit it.
God could amend the error by sending his son into the world, but
Sutpen remains to be "articulated in this world" (171). To appreciate Sutpen's failure, as well as his peculiar immortality, we need to

understand the principle which opposes transcendence in the novel.

The clearest explanation of this principle is to be found in Judith Sutpen's single recorded speech. When she gives Bon's letter to Quentin's grandmother, she contrasts her purpose with her father's in bringing home those two colossal tombstones to mark the family grave. The letter differs from the tombstone because the act of passing something on "from one hand to another" represented in the letter at least

> would be something . . . something that might make a mark on something that *was* once for the reason that it can die someday, while the block of stone cant be *is* because it never can become *was* because it cant ever die or perish (127-28).

The act of passing on a letter "from one hand to another" affirms the continuity of life from one generation to the next, and stands as the physical, palpable link between past and present. The letter functions like the churinga which Levi-Strauss describes as an object passed on from one generation to the next in certain tribes, to furnish "the tangible proof that the ancestor and his living descendants are of one flesh."[14] As Judith explains, it is a matter of making an "impression." You try at first to make it by weaving a pattern, but "you are born at the same time with a lot of other people," and they too are "trying to make a rug on the same loom only each one wants to weave his own pattern into the rug" (127). You know that "it cant matter," and yet "it must matter because you keep on trying," but then in the end "it doesn't matter" since you die and only the mute tombstone remains. So much for transcendence. Consequently, Judith responds to impotence—the failure to make an "impression" which led her father to build a static monument—with the simple physical act of passing something on to someone. Judith thereby allies herself with time as horizontal motion, while Sutpen asserts a vertical transcendence of time. Moreover, this point is underscored by the fact that the letter itself embodies the same principle as the act of passing it on; it is a message passed on from "one mind to another" (127). Bon's letter, as well as Judith's act, manifest physically the principle of social continuity at work in all the conversations in the novel. All the speaking and hearing, dominated as it is by a single narrative voice, represents an ongoing social act which, though it cannot found a dynasty, can create a community among the living as well as between the living and the dead.

In contrast to Judith's acceptance of membership in the

human community, Sutpen in effect abandons that community when he leaves his family for the West Indies. His discovery of his impotence as a boy prohibits him from discovering that his actions can matter in "the living world," with flesh and blood people who breathe the same air he does. He thus remains impervious not only to any possible pain he might cause that cannot be paid for legalistically, but also to the reasons for any possible damage done to his design by other people. What makes his actions so offensive to the citizens of Jefferson is that same innocence which makes his failure so inexplicable to Sutpen himself; just as he enters the town as a "man who came from nowhere," so the acts of those who frustrate his design seem to him to come from nowhere (20). He fails to understand that his actions have effects which outrun his intentions, that is, because he does not recognize intentionality in others. He is a "foe" who does not even know that he is "embattled." (63).

And yet it is because he is embattled that he endures; the counter-designs provoked by his affronts destroy his design, but insure his eventual articulation. The central irony of Sutpen's life is that he wins immortality not by achieving his design, which ends in the mocking figure of Jim Bond, but through the counter-design of one whom he affronts. For it is Rosa who, although she too has in mind revenge in doing so, initiates a dialogue with the youth Quentin, and so keeps Sutpen alive. Like the architect he impresses into his service, those whom Sutpen fails to acknowledge as social creatures create of "Sutpen's very defeat the victory which, in conquering, Sutpen himself would have failed to gain" (39).

It remains to note, before returning to Quentin, that the "moving air" from which Rosa's room is protected becomes Faulkner's vehicle for moving from present to past, and for referring to that stream of event moving on outside Rosa's blinds. Moving air serves the same purpose that the sound of the insects did in *Light in August*, but functions in a more complex way. It carries the smell of wisteria and the sound of the sparrows into Rosa's office, but it also carries the sound of human voices, and so acts as the medium in which all the novel's conversations exist. At the beginning of Chapter Two, the air "still breathed" in 1909 is the "same air in which the church bells had rung on that Sunday morning in 1833," providing Faulkner with a means of modulating into the past without calling attention to the shift, as did "Memory believes before knowing remembers" in *Light in August*. Air sustains life, the physical, palpable life of breathing, smelling, hearing, and even speaking, that physical life of which the stream of event is constituted. It serves to connect Mississippi to Cambridge; when Faulkner shifts the scene to Quentin and Shreve in their room at Harvard, he does so in terms of what the air carries, "the wistaria, the cigar-smell, the fireflies—attenuated up from Mississippi and into this strange room" (173). Even in the dark, air remains.

As we have seen, Quentin resists listening to Rosa, since, as he evenutally realizes, he has "had to listen too long" (193). The story of Sutpen is "a part of his twenty years' heritage of breathing the same air and hearing his father talk about the man Sutpen" (11). And so, when Shreve begins re-telling it in Chapter Six, Quentin thinks *"He sounds just like father,"* registering once again that growing realization that he has had to listen to too much (181). But as he hears Shreve tell it again, he is drawn out of his detached vantage point. Recounting his father's story of Sutpen's troops bringing the marble tombstones back to Mississippi during the war, Quentin at first follows his habit of viewing: "It seemed to Quentin that he could actually see them" (190). But when Sutpen is seen arriving home with the tombstones, Quentin's habit is undercut: "he could see it; he might even have been there. Then he thought *No. If I had been there I could not have seen it this plain"* (190). As the age of television has taught us, to be there, a participant in an event, is a vitally different experience from that of the viewer who looks through the camera eye. Once Quentin begins to speak, to share in the telling, he is in fact participating in the stream of event for the first time in the novel.

Once Quentin begins to speak, Shreve remarks, "Don't say it's just me that sounds like your old man," forcing Quentin now to stumble forth from his fixed detachment and acknowledge a relation to Sutpen other than that of seer and seen:

> Yes, we are both Father, or maybe Father and I are both Shreve, maybe it took Father and me both to make Shreve or Shreve and me both to make Father or maybe Thomas Sutpen to make all of us (261-62).

Quentin's image of pools attached to one another by a "narrow umbilical watercord" represents his attempt to conceptualize the community he is about to enter, a community not merely joining him to Shreve, but to his father, and Charles and Henry and Sutpen too (261). Like that "fierce, rigid umbilical cord" which joins Rosa

to Clytie at the moment when they touch, "the two of" them "joined by that hand and arm which held" them, Quentin's image represents the community of blood, "the immortal brief recent intransient
blood" shared by the two to whom they are soon to be joined, "riding the two horses through the iron darkness" of a Mississippi
Christmas eve, "sixty years ago" (140, 261, 295, 294). (The Mississippi River itself serves as yet another "umbilical" by which Quentin
and Shreve are "joined, connected . . . in a sort of geographical
transubstantiation" (258).)

Immersed with Shreve, then, in the process of communal telling, Quentin no longer stares at static pictures, but participates in
the stream of event, and in an act of love as well, that "happy marriage of speaking and hearing wherein each before the demand, the
requirement, forgave condoned and forgot the faulting of the other"
(316). But this impassioned telling finally subsides, and when it does
so Quentin must face what he saw behind that door, and so fulfill
the dust cloud's prophecy: that he will "find no destination but . . .
a plateau and a panorama of harmless and inscrutable night and there
will be nothing . . . to do but return" (175). All that Quentin testifies to learning from Henry Sutpen is that he has come home to die.
Having waited until the last chapter for this confrontation, the reader
is met with nothing more than a conversation which mirrors itself:

> *And you are—?*
> *Henry Sutpen,*
> *And you have been here—?*
> *Four years.*
> *And you came home—?*
> *To die. Yes*
> *To die?*
> *Yes, to die.*
> *And you have been here—?*
> *Four years.*
> *And you are—?*
> *Henry Sutpen.* (373)

What Quentin confronts here is death, the maddening rebuttal to all
designs for transcendence and immortality; and this, of course, is the
message of the dust-cloud as well. Born into time, man struggles to
deny his mortality by transcending the stream of event, but the
"dust" is "victorious," as the two rooms in which the novel's opening and closing conversations take place indicate (8).

From Rosa's room to this one at Harvard, from September on to December, Quentin has had to listen to himself and others, each one "trying . . . to weave his own pattern into the rug," using language itself to try to transcend and encompass time, and each one failing (127). Thus Quentin and Shreve's dialogue is "a good deal like Sutpen's morality and Miss Coldfield's demonizing," in that each represents the effort of the "prisoner soul" which "wroils ever upward sunward" to rise above the earth where time and death await them (280, 143). Yet, on the other hand, Shreve and Quentin, in their joint act of creation, have accomplished what no one else in the novel could have, and this because they do it together, in an act of love, not vengeance. They use language too, although not primarily to impose a design, but rather as

> that meager and fragile thread . . . by which the little surface corners and edges of men's secret and solitary lives may be joined for an instant now and then before sinking back into darkness where the spirit cried for the first time and was not heard and will cry for the last time and will not be heard then either (251).

Yet for a brief hour, Quentin and Shreve *do* hear and respond. Their act of telling, in other words, differs from those of Rosa Coldfield and Mr. Compson not merely because they imagine more creatively, and so "encompass" more than either, but because of what makes this more ambitious vision possible—their joint participation in telling, that "happy marriage of speaking and hearing" which not only allows each to forgive the other's faultings, but even enables each to take the other "up in stride without comma or colon or paragraph," voicing that relentless Faulknerian sentence which constitutes the stream of event in *Absalom, Absalom!* (316, 280).

But as we have seen, their immersion in this stream is brief and passing, like all events. At the novel's end Quentin is caught once more in the renewed and unbearable conflict between his two selves, the one which struggles to escape time and death, and the other for whom the very struggle has led to an immersion in "the fluid cradle of events (time)" where death lies waiting (66). Quentin can neither inhabit time nor transcend it as long as he lives; only death itself resolves this conflict, as *The Sound and the Fury* reveals.

At the novel's end, both Shreve and Quentin issue prophecies. Quentin's "Nevermore of peace," acknowledges his tormented realization that he will never exorcise his ghosts because he cannot escape history. Shreve's prophecy reveals, on the other hand, the attitude of those who presume to have done so. The reader, accordingly, is left with a choice between two positions: Shreve's, fixed and outside the picture, or Quentin's, fixed and inside it, doomed to participate in what we hoped to merely witness. So unbearable is Quentin's position that we are almost relieved by Shreve's. Nonetheless Shreve's position is contaminated, not only by his tone of aggression and mockery, but also and more significantly by the reductive logic he employs, mimicking Sutpen's legalism. For Shreve's "moral," the conclusion he articulates, is that "it takes two niggers to get rid of one Sutpen." This "clears the whole ledger," he thinks, except that "you've got one nigger left" whom you can't "catch" and "don't even always see," but you "still hear" (378). But even though Quentin, as he acknowledges, does still hear the howling of Jim Bond, Shreve proceeds to use him anyway, to prophesy that "the Jim Bonds are going to conquer the western hemisphere" (378). Whatever accuracy may be attributed to Shreve's prediction, the significant point is that Shreve's resolution provokes the question of accuracy in the first place. For Shreve has become not only the detached viewer, confronting and assembling the story of Sutpen, but almost a parodic case of the scientific, objective observer who quantifies and predicts. When Shreve then asks Quentin why he hates the South, moreover, he makes clear his re-asserted separate identity. In severing the bond created between the two of them, then, Shreve not only turns on Quentin himself, but withdraws from the community they have embodied in the "happy marriage of speaking and hearing," a community stretching back both to Mississippi and to the past.

Further, Shreve's summing up parodies the attempt on the part of the reader to stand off and assemble a final interpretation, to detach himself from the talking, the telling.

From the beginning, Faulkner has been immersing us in the stream of event which his sustained voice embodies. His strategy in this respect consists in telling us things before we can understand him, possessing us of information before we have yet learned where it fits in the story, while at the same time pulling us forward by withholding the crucial information about Bon's past, as well as the crucial scene in which we expect to have this information verified. By the end of Chapter One, for example, we actually know about the major events of Sutpen's life after his arrival in Jefferson, but we cannot make sense of them. As a result, when these events are related again and again in the ensuing chapters, we know "it already," so that what is said almost seems to strike, as it does for Quentin, "the resonant strings of remembering" (212-13). Further, as we read on, it is as if we, like Henry, had been brought into a room and experienced a shock at the sight of Sutpen abrupting before us, as if we "knew" but did not yet "believe" what we had seen (335). And because we, like Rosa, were "not there to see" these events, we visualize them for ourselves, much as we visualize the static picture of Rosa and Quentin in that vividly presented opening scene (30).

By the time we reach the end of Chapter Five, the events Rosa has conjured up before us have, thanks to Quentin's father, been placed in some sequence, but they remain for us, as for him, like Quentin's pictures, "contradictory and bizarre," because we still lack the information which will account for them, the facts about Charles Bon's past (14). "Something is missing," as Mr. Compson puts it, that something which our "chemical formula" has failed to include, so that when we bring the characters together "in the proportions called for . . . nothing happens" (101). This kind of scrutinizing of the events one has witnessed and the account one has made of them, as Mr. Compson describes it, consists in the effort to "re-read, tedious and intent, poring, making sure that you have forgotten nothing" (101), and it is this kind of activity in which we find Sutpen himself engaged in the second half of the book, in his second conversation with Quentin's grandfather,[15]

> sitting there in Grandfather's office trying to explain with that patient amazed recapitulation, not to Grandfather and not to himself . . . but trying to explain to circumstance, to fate itself, the logical steps by which he had arrived at a result absolutely and forever incredible, repeating the clear and simple synopsis of his history . . . as if he were trying to explain it to an intractible and unpredictable child (263).

It is precisely this motive for storytelling which is contaminated in Shreve's summing up, and which is undercut by the way in which Faulkner meets our expectations in the novel's final chapter.

As we enter the novel's second movement in Chapter Six, we are still waiting, like Bon once was, for the "answer, aware of the jigsaw puzzle integers . . . jumbled and unrecognizable yet on the point of falling into pattern," the answer which will "reveal . . . at once, like a flash of light," the meaning of the story (313). As we gradually discover the relation between Bon and Sutpen, and the reason for Sutpen's repudiation of Bon, the events of Sutpen's story begin to compose a coherent picture. But while investing Quentin with the knowledge of Bon's past, Faulkner withholds from us its source, the conversation between Henry and Quentin on that night in September at Sutpen's Hundred. Thus we still don't know "quite all of it," because there is still one thing missing, the verification of Quentin's knowledge about Bon. Accordingly, we await that scene which will allow us to believe what we already know by the time Quentin and Shreve have assembled the story for us, the scene, that is, which will provide proof of Quentin's claim that he learned this crucial "fact" on "that night" when he accompanied Rosa to Sutpen's Hundred (264, 266).

When the confrontation between Quentin and Henry is finally depicted, however, no "flash of light" comes. Further, this scene not only fails to meet our expectations for verification, but repudiates the very motives for such expectations. To seek an answer to the question left hanging since the end of Chapter Five, the question of what Quentin found at Sutpen's Hundred, in order to verify the information he seems to have acquired there, is to mimic Sutpen and Shreve at the end. It is to seek, in other words, to fulfill that need for a final explanation which will account for events by means of a "chemical formula" and this in order to sit back, satisfied with a completed picture from which we are detached.

But while it repudiates this motive for telling (and reading), this scene also generates in us the same sense of an irrevocable conflict which it epitomizes for Quentin. For by this time, the very endeavor in which we have been engaged, to assemble events into an ordered and completed whole, has drawn us into the role of participant in the same activity which constitutes the novel's major line of action, the telling of a story. Accordingly, when we find our expectations of an ending thwarted by the scene at Sutpen's Hundred, it is for the same reason that, as the dust-cloud warns him, Quentin "will find no destination but will merely abrupt gently onto a plateau and a panorama of harmless and inscrutable night" (175). For as participants in the same kind of activity which constitutes the stream of event for the participants in the novel's central line of action, we are in effect the inhabitants of the time we seek to order and transcend, and so, like Quentin, trapped within the very picture we have presumed to compose. Faulkner implicates the reader in the stream of event, then, by forcing him to share the burden of narrative construction while denying him the means to succeed at the task. For success would entail assembling a coherent and credible narrative.

But in the process of failing at this task, the reader, like Quentin Compson, is forced into history. In *Absalom, Absalom!*, as in life itself, by the time we understand what is happening, we are already participants in it.

Insofar as he can, then, what Faulkner tries to do in this novel is to work against not the inherent temporality, but the inherent spatiality, of the reader's experience, that spatiality, in other words, which endows the reader with the freedom to "re-read, tedious and intent, poring" over pages which he can turn backward as well as forward (101)[16]. This freedom derives from the simple fact that the reader holds a spatial object in his hand; he can not only re-read passages he has already read, he can actually put the book down, rise from his chair, and walk away, out of the talking, the telling. In this respect, the novel, any novel, can be "viewed" in the way that Berger says the cubist painting is viewed. But it is this material spatiality which Faulkner is trying to undermine, and this in order to make of the reader—that emblematic figure of detachment from the "real" world—a participant in the story he reads. The result is a novel in which the protagonist, or at least the only living, breathing one in the novel, sits for an entire evening, and for three chapters, "quite still, facing the table, his hands on either side of the open text book . . . his face lowered a little, brooding" (217-18).

Notes

[1]Hugh Kenner, *The Pound Era* (Berkeley: University of California Press, 1971), 25-27.

[2]William Holtz, "Spatial Form in Modern Literature: A Reconsideration," *Critical Inquiry*, 4 (Winter, 1977), 271.

[3]Joseph Frank, "Spatial Form in Modern Literature," *Sewanee Review*, 53 (Spring, Summer, Autumn, 1945), reprinted in *The Widening Gyre* (Bloomington: Indiana University Press, 1968), 3-62.

[4]John Berger, "The Moment of Cubism," *The Look of Things* (New York: Viking Press, 1974), 151-153.

[5]A term like "perspective," for example, is indispensable in part because

modern novelists have themselves been so conscious of it, and have so often ex-
perimented with it. One need only consider the work of Hnery James, where the
passion for seeing, ever more deeply, at times threatens the efficacy of the telling, to be reminded of how central is Conrad's desire "before all to make you
see." Indeed, part of what interests me in the stance of the observer is the way
in which not only critics of, but characters in, the modern novel have become
observers.

[6]I do not include *Sanctuary* (1931) and *Pylon* (135) in this discussion
because I think in these novels Faulkner was more intent upon gaining control
of his language than in experimenting with narrative structure. They are, therefore, essentially peripheral to the strategy that led, in *Absalom, Absalom!* to a
genuinely radical and major work, the strategy for relating past and present
means of techniques which thwart the reader's effort to remain detached from
the flow of time sustained in the novel. Moreover, the history of *Sanctuary*'s
composition, and the fact that Faulkner turned to writing *Pylon* because he was
stuck in the middle of writing *Absalom, Absalom!*, I would argue, support the
view that these two novels were not the major efforts for Faulkner himself that
The Sound and the Fury, Light in August, and *Absalom, Absalom!*, in particular,
were.

[7]The novel's first three chapters provide the most striking example of
this strategy. Faulkner turns from Lena, now in sight of Jefferson at the end of
Chapter One, to Byron's memories of Joe Christmas's arrival in Jefferson at the
beginning of Chapter Two. Not until we are five pages into the chapter do we
meet "Brown," (32), the man whom we would normally expect the author to
introduce in the next episode of a book which, so far, seems to be centrally concerned with Lena Grove. So while the confusion between "Bunch" and "Burch"
leads Lena to expect Burch to be at the mill when she arrives there, the reader,
for the same reason, expects a comic plot to develop. Instead, he is introduced
to a new character, Joe Christmas, whose story seems utterly irrelevant to the
one he thinks he is reading. By virtue of his name, however, Christmas cannot be
a minor character; so the reader adjusts his expectations to encompass the possibility of tragedy, only to meet in the next chapter still another character, whose
relationship to Lena and Christmas must now be encompassed somehow.

[8]As Sartre puts it, "In *The Sound and the Fury* everything has already
happened." Cf. "On *The Sound and the Fury*: Time in the Word of William
Faulkner," Robert Penn Warren, ed., *Faulkner: A Collection of Critical Essays*
(Englewood Cliffs, N. J.: Prentice-Hall, 1966), 87-93.

[9]The following discussion of *Light in August* is heavily indebted to discussion of fictions as representing "imaginative investments in coherent patterns
which, by the provision of an end, make possible a satisfying consonance with
the origins and with the middle." *The Sense of an Ending* (New York: Oxford
University Press, 1967), 17. I am aware that by identifying spatiality and vision
with the effort to constitute these "patterns," I am violating Kermode's stric-

tures against precisely such an identification, but I do so because I think Faulkner did so. For a discussion of this issue, see Joseph Frank's "Spatial Form: An Answer to Critics," in *Critical Inquiry* 4 (Winter, 1977), 242-252. See also Faulkner's statement to Malcolm Cowley on the subject of "trying to say it all in one sentence, . . . to put it all, if possible, on one pinhead," in Cowley, ed., *The Faulkner-Cowley File* (New York: Viking Press, 1966), 14.

[10]William Faulkner, *Light in August* (New York: Random House, 1968), 347. All references in text are to this edition.

[11]Cf. also pp. 298, 361, 365, 370.

[12]According to Bergson, the "past . . . is necessarily automatically preserved." The present is a "certain interval of duration" like a sentence now being pronounced. Our attention spans the interval defined by the sentence, which can be elongated or shortened, "like the interval between the two points of a compass." The interval represented by one sentence can be stretched to include two by a change in punctuation. Accordingly, "an attention which could be extended indefinitely would embrace, along with the preceding sentence, all the anterior phrases of the lecture and the events which preceded the lecture, and as large a portion of what we call our past as desired." The present, therefore, is a function of the extent of our "attention to life." The distinction between the present and the past is a result of our apparent inability to sustain that attention. The present becomes past only when it no longer commands our immediate interest. In other words, if we did not have to channel our attention toward the future, if our "attention to life" were not repeatedly interrupted by the urgencies dictated by the practical concern of accomplishing our particular ends, our present would include our "entire past history . . . not as instantaneity, not like a cluster of simultaneous parts, but as something continually present which would also be something continually moving." Cf. Henri Bergson, *The Creative Mind* (New York: Philosophical Library, 1946), 162-180.

[13]William Faulkner, *Absalom, Absalom!* (New York: Random House, 1936), 158. All references in the text are to this edition.

[14]Claude Levi-Strauss, *The Savage Mind* (Chicago: University of Chicago Press, 1966), 241.

[15]Notice the difference between Sutpen's habit of explaining events not to the man he ostensibly addresses, but to "fate," and the manifest need on Shreve's part, once he turns to the question of love, to meet Quentin's repeated complaint, "that's still not love." (328) For these climactic moments in their conversation, Quentin and Shreve are talking to and for each other, another point which distinguishes their motives for telling Sutpen's story from those of anyone else in the novel, not excepting Sutpen himself.

[16]It is important to understand that Faulkner's strategy cannot completely undercut the spatial dimensions of the reader's experience. In other

words, although I think it is clear that he is working against the reader's attempt to remain a passive observer, it is also clear that, in the end, he acknowledges, in Shreve's final response to the story he and Quentin have just tried to create, the impossibility of making the reader a full participant in the story which he and Faulkner have also just tried to create.

Faulkner and
His Carpenter's Hammer

by

Glenn O. Carey

> After all, there must be some things for which
> God cannot be accused by man and held
> responsible. There must be.
>
> *Light in August*

> If Jesus returned today we would have to crucify
> him quick in our own defense, to justify and
> preserve the civilization we have worked and
> suffered and died shrieking and cursing in rage
> and impotence and terror for two thousand years
> to create and perfect in man's own image; if
> Venus returned she would be a soiled man in a
> subway lavatory with a palm full of French
> post-cards—
>
> *The Wild Palms*

In *Knight's Gambit*, a Faulkner character says, "In fact, I
sometimes think that the whole twentieth century is a sorry thing,
smelling to high heaven in somebody's nose."[1] The reader of Faulkner's fiction often realizes that it is Faulkner himself who was
offended by the noisome smell of civilization. Throughout Faulkner's work one notices his deep emotional reaction whenever he
presented an aspect of civilization that he despised and that he
believed should and could be changed and improved. In dramatizing
this condemnation, Faulkner consistently underscored the evil in the
man-made world. As the old Negro preacher says in *A Fable*, "Evil is
a part of man, evil and sin and cowardice, the same as repentance and
being brave. You got to believe in all of them, or believe in none of
them. Believe that man is capable of all of them, or he aint capable
of none."[2] Faulkner's strong emphasis on evil caused some early
critics who superficially read his fiction to pronounce derogatory

judgments, saying that Faulkner was concerned with evil and violence too often, too much, and too shockingly. One of the answers
to these critics could begin with a reminder that the writers of the
greatest literature in English—Chaucer, Milton, Shakespeare, Fielding,
Melville, to name only a familiar few—were also concerned in their
writings with evil, not because of evil alone, but because they were
aware that through the dramatic presentation of evil the author often
can create a meaningful artistic achievement that will include the
writer's acknowledgment and acceptance of man's responsibility to
his fellow man. Thus it is with Faulkner.

At Nagano Faulkner was asked, "Can you please explain a
little about your works, in which things of evil or violence come in
and you have used them as material in expressing your ideas?" Faulkner's reply explains why he used evil and violence to dramatize his
social criticism.

> Yes—never to use the evil for the sake of the evil—you must
> use the evil to try to tell some truth which you think is impor-
> tant; there are times when man needs to be reminded of evil, to
> correct it, to change it; he should not be reminded always only
> of the good and the beautiful. I think the writer or the poet or
> the novelist should not just be a "recorder" of man—he should
> give man some reason to believe that man can be better than
> he is. If the writer is to accomplish anything, it is to make
> the world a little better than he found it, to do what he can, in
> whatever way he can, to get rid of the evils like war, injustice—
> that's his job. And not to do this by describing merely the
> pleasant things—he must show man the base, the evil things
> that man can do and still hate himself for doing it, to still
> prevail and endure and last, to believe always that he can be
> better than he probably will.[3]

In conjunction with this concern of Faulkner with evil, and in
answer to those who may still believe that Faulkner was writing
about evil and corruption only as it is found in the South, one should
remember that evil is universal and that the microcosm of Jefferson,
Yoknapatawpha County, Mississippi, can have acceptance as a universal symbol just as the Mississippi River has in *Huckleberry Finn*, the
lifeboat has in "The Open Boat," and the *Pequod* has in *Moby-Dick*.
Many of Faulkner's novels clearly have universal implications. As an
example, *The Sound and the Fury* has received much interpretation
of this kind. Irving Howe in a classic 1952 study wrote that it is not
only about "modern humanity in Mississippi" but modern humanity

in New York, Paris, and thus everywhere: "*The Sound and the Fury* seems a terrible criticism not of the South alone but of the entire modern world. The more severe Faulkner's view of the South, the more readily does one forget he is writing about the South."[4] Jean-Paul Sartre also readily perceived this universality in *The Sound and the Fury*: "We are living in a time of impossible revolutions, and Faulkner uses his extraordinary art to describe our suffocation and a world dying of old age."[5] A year earlier William Van O'Connor saw that Faulkner applied in this novel ". . . his most characteristic subject matter, his heritage as a southerner, and modern man in search of belief."[6] Relevant to Faulkner is what Herbert Read said elsewhere: "regionalism, in spite of its local origins, is always universal— that is to say, it appeals, not to the limited audience of the region in which it is written, but to mankind everywhere and at all time."[7] When Read's viewpoint is directed towards Faulkner's fiction, his regionalism achieves a universality that gives major importance to his criticism of civilization's effects and consequences. It seems further pertinent to refer those few remaining diehard doubters of Faulkner's use of evil to John Milton's "Areopagitica," in which he wrote that "the knowledge and survey of vice is in this world so necessary to the constituting of human virtue, and the scanning of error to the confirmation of truth . . . ." Finally, again to use some of Milton's own words, Faulkner can be called a truly universal "champion of truth."

Faulkner demonstrated in his writings and in his personal statements that he was profoundly disturbed by some of the actions of modern man and by what is called civilized progress. In his concern Faulkner said that some people,

> . . . the humanitarian in science and the scientist in the humanity of man, who might yet save that civilization which the professionals at saving it—the publishers who condone their own battening on man's lust and folly, the politicians who condone their own trafficking in his stupidity and greed, and the churchmen who condone their own trading on his fear and superstition—seem to be proving that they can't.[8]

Faulkner made true religion—sometimes, for convenience, he called it Christianity—or the acceptance of responsibility for one's fellow man an important element in his fiction. Once he was asked, "Does that mean an artist can use Christianity simply as just another tool, as a carpenter would borrow a hammer?" Faulkner's reply shows his panoramic social vision:

The carpenter we were speaking of never lacks that hammer. No
one is without Christianity, if we agree on what we mean by the
word. It is every individual's individual code of behavior by
means of which he makes himself a better human being than his
nature wants to be, if he followed his nature only. Whatever its
symbol—cross or crescent or whatever—that symbol is man's reminder of his duty inside the human race.[9]

Faulkner consistently reminded himself of his duty, his
responsibility to his fellow man. Interspersed in his fiction are observations and criticisms of civilized man, who is the "author and victim
too of a thousand homicides and a thousand copulations and divorce-
ments."[10] To Faulkner, modern man is drowning himself in *"this
seething turmoil we call progress."*[11] He called sharp attention to
man's spiritual dryness and self-designed destruction in his Nobel
Prize Speech. "Our tragedy today is a general and universal physical
fear so long sustained by now that we can even bear it. There are no
longer problems of the spirit. There is only the question: When will I
be blown up?"

As Faulkner watched what he called *"the miragy antics of men
and women,"*[12] one remembers that he described humanity in *Mosquitoes* as "a kind of sterile race: women too masculine to conceive,
men to feminine to beget. . . ."[13] Twenty years later he wrote that
modern life is "that agony of naked inanesthetisable nerve-ends
which for lack of a better word men call being alive."[14] He wrote in
*The Wild Palms, "you are born submerged in anonymous lockstep
with the teeming anonymous myriads of your time and generation;
you get out of step once, falter once, and you are trampled to
death."*[15] Again, in *Mosquitoes*, of relevance are Fairchild's final
words to Talliaferro, a vain, frustrated, unhappy man. First Fairchild
looked at Talliaferro, then he looked up, "O Thou above the thunder
and above the excursions and alarms, regard Your masterpiece!"
When Fairchild looked down again at Talliaferro, " 'Get to hell out
of here,' he roared. 'You have made me sick!' "[16] In *Absalom, Absalom!*, Faulkner wrote that two of the principal characters are symbolically "doomed to live," and that only a few of us in this world
are able "to make that scratch, that undying mark on the blank face
of the oblivion to which we are all doomed . . . ."[17] It is just as Judith Sutpen also says,

> . . . you make so little impression, you see. You get born and
> you try this and you don't know why only you keep on trying
> it and you are born at the same time with a lot of other people,

all mixed up with them, like trying to, having to, move your arms and legs with strings only the same strings are hitched to all the other arms and legs and the others all trying and they dont know why either except that the strings are all in one another's way like five or six people all trying to make a rug on the same loom only each one wants to weave his own pattern into the rug; and it cant matter, you know that, or the Ones that set up the loom would have arranged things a little better, and yet it must matter because you keep on trying or having to keep on trying and then all of a sudden it's all over and all you have left is a block of stone with scratches on it provided there was someone to remember to have the marble scratched and set up or had time to, and it rains on it and the sun shines on it and after a while they dont even remember the name and what the scratches were trying to tell, and it doesn't matter.[18]

On the other hand, especially in "Faith or Fear," Faulkner stressed the hopeful side of life as he described a list of those God-like men who are remembered century after century.

They are the long annal of the men and women who have anguished over man's condition and who have held up to us not only the mirror of our follies and greeds and lusts and fears, but have reminded us constantly of the tremendous shape of our godhead too—the godhead and immortality which we cannot repudiate even if we dared, since we cannot rid ourselves of it but only it can rid itself of us—the philosophers and artists, the articulate and grieving who have reminded us always of our capacity for honor and courage and compassion and pity and sacrifice.[19]

One could further note what that sensitive Faulkner character the Reverend Gail Hightower says about modern man in *Light in August*: "Poor man. Poor mankind,"[20] as well as what the gruff, perceptive Reverend Joe Goodyhay says in *The Mansion*, "Save us, Christ. The poor sons of bitches."[21]

We can see that Faulkner often condemned and yet pitied mankind. He also repeatedly said that man creates his own disasters and that he should try to rise above these self-created calamities:

Well, there are some people in any time and age that cannot face and cope with the problems. There seem to be three stages: The first says, This is rotten, I'll have no part of it, I will take death first. The second says, This is rotten, I don't

like it, I can't do anything about it, but at least I will not
participate in it myself, I will go off into a cave or climb a
pillar to sit on. The third says, This stinks and I'm going to
do something about it.[22]

Faulkner then added, "What we need are people who will say, This is
bad and I'm going to do something about it, I'm going to change
it."[23] In trying to change it, Faulkner included in his fiction much
about evil in society, and this is particularly evident in *Sanctuary*,
which is full of the "current trends" (Faulkner's term) of man's mass
compulsions to be famous, rich and successful, as well as calling
attention to our mechanized and specialized way of life where sex,
love, and personal involvement in life have become less a matter for
individual judgment and decision than a reflection of mass society's
current desires and pressures. In *Sanctuary* Faulkner, through the
main characters, etched the deformed body and spirit of modern
man. He not only depicted the moral confusion and the social decay
of the South, but he indicted contemporary man everywhere in modern life where people in their hurried and harried life consistently
minimize the worth of the individual and where many of us continue to remain unconcerned about the excessive loss and degrada-
tion of human life through drugs and suicide, the excessive highway
accidents, and the steadily rising crime and terrorism throughout the
United States and the world. Many of us today have learned to
accept the ever-present specter of mass murder as wars come and go
so quickly that an American born around 1910 can see in the retro-
spect of adulthood that his lifespan includes at least two world wars,
one so-called police action, the Vietnam conflict, and, by today, the
omnipresent threat of a worldwide holocaust that has the potential
to destroy man completely. The "current trends" of *Sanctuary*
emphasize man's debasement of his moral, ethical, and religious beliefs, as well as his reliance on hypocrisy as a routine way of life.

The motivating character in *Sanctuary* is Popeye, a big-time
Memphis gangster of the 1920's, a bootlegger who strongly affects
the lives of Temple Drake and Horace Benbow. Although some of
these changes are caused by the character traits of Temple and Benbow, Popeye ignites the fuse that sets off the upheavals in their already disturbed lives. Popeye is one of those Faulkner characters
who represent the mechanical civilization that has invaded and par-
tially conquered the South,[24] and Faulkner frequently describes
Popeye in "mechanical" terms. This kind of description comes in
swift order, for early in the novel Popeye enters wearing his stiff

straw sailor "like a modernistic lampshade," his eyes looked like "two knobs of soft black rubber," and his face had a "bloodless color, as though seen by electric light." He wore a tight black suit, had "doll-like hands," and "his skin had a dead, dark pallor. His nose was faintly aquiline, and he had no chin at all. His face just went away, like the face of a wax doll set too near a hot fire and forgotten." Popeye's whole appearance has "that vicious depthless quality of stamped tin."[25]

Popeye is a lost human being, Faulkner said, who became a symbol of evil in modern society only by coincidence.[26] Coincidence or not, Popeye represents evil in *Sanctuary*, and evil unadulterated with good. The only "good" action is Popeye's yearly trip to Pensacola to see his mother, but these journeys are more habit than filial concern.

This epitome of modern evil is depicted as the all-powerful gang leader who fears no one and who is feared by everyone he meets; but Popeye, if he has reached the zenith of underworld power, has also reached the nadir of physical and spiritual life. Popeye cannot enjoy his wealth because he has nothing he can do with it, and he cannot drink liquor because it poisons him (10, 370). He has "no friends and had never known a woman and knew he could never . . ." (370). Because he is impotent, he uses either a corncob as his sexual instrument (as he did once with Temple) or a substitute (his henchman Red) to obtain a vicarious sexual and emotional release. Popeye's heredity and inferior environment have given him an unusually sordid background. He was unable to talk and walk until he was four because of congenital syphilis from his father, who married Popeye's mother only because he was forced to after he had made her pregnant. His grandmother who lived with him and his mother was a pyromaniac, and his adult associates are gangsters, prostitutes, and morons, or as Ruby Lamar calls most of them, "crimps, and spungs and feebs" (8).

Remarkably, Popeye has one outstanding physical trait. He shoots with amazing accuracy, and he kills Tommy the feeb, and Red the handsome gangster who, following Popeye's orders, has had frequent intercourse with Temple while Popeye watched in ecstasy, making a "high whinnying sould like a horse" (191). The ironic justice of *Sanctuary* has Popeye arrested near Birmingham while on the way home from seeing his mother: "they arrested him for killing a man in one town and at an hour when he was in another town killing somebody else . . . and he said 'For Christ's sake . . .' " (370-71).

Loveless, hopeless, purposeless, and almost faceless—this is Popeye in *Sanctuary*— a monstrous embodiment of twentieth century man. Popeye could be called an end product of our spiritually sterile modern civilization, as one recalls that Faulkner said that Popeye is a symbol of evil in society, and that this incarnation of evil was born out of society's virulence. But, even so, Faulkner gives Popeye some redeeming qualities at the end—seemingly instinctive insights into the futility of his success and the emptiness of his life. In jail, after calmly hearing his death sentence, Popeye accepts the double irony of fate and justice by rejecting help from his high-priced Memphis lawyer.

Popeye then permits a minister to pray for him, saying, "Sure . . . go ahead. Dont mind me," and while the minister prays Popeye smokes. As an added note of rejection, Popeye says to the turnkey who wants to return the change from a $100 bill, "Keep it . . . Buy yourself a hoop" (378).

During his last living hours Popeye turns from many things modern-day society considers compellingly important: a powerful influence that can "fix" anything; an excessive abundance of money that seemingly can buy everything, including influence; and a calculated religious attitude, which in moments of need frequently becomes immediately important for the safety and comfort of one's present and future life. In these final scenes, Popeye's physical and mental rejection of what modern man too often considers overwhelmingly important—power, money, religion—symbolically separates him at the end of his life from the society that produced and shaped him.

In *Sanctuary* society left its stigma on Popeye in his twisted physical, mental, and spiritual growth, and Faulkner through exaggerated irony and satire presented Popeye as an extreme symbol of modern man. Yet, before he dies, Popeye significantly turns away from all that he had been conditioned by society to accept as success, as he impassively allows himself to be destroyed, seemingly because nothing he has achieved is worth living for.

Elsewhere in his fiction Faulkner chose other aspects of current trends and self-created destructiveness to underscore man's moral and ethical violations. In *Pylon, Requiem for a Nun, The*

Town, and particularly in *Intruder in the Dust* and *Sartoris*, Faulkner scathingly censures modern man's manic prostitution to the automobile, a mechanism daily destroying human, animal, and plant health and life.[27] The world's incessant obsession with war—"man's fatal vice" as Faulkner called it—is reprobated in *The Mansion, Light in August*, and impressively excoriated in *Soldiers' Pay* and *A Fable.*[28]

Faulkner in his writings used what he called his carpenter's hammer to design a superstructure of criticism and condemnation for certain aspects of civilization that he scorned and that he believed should and could be changed and improved. In his entire creative life Faulkner manifested his profound belief that "the whole twentieth century is a sorry thing."

Notes

[1]William Faulkner, *Knight's Gambit* (New York: Random House, 1949), p. 54.

[2]William Faulkner, *A Fable* (New York: Random House, 1954), p. 203.

[3]*Faulkner at Nagano*, ed. Robert A Jeliffe (Tokyo: Kenkyusha Ltd., 1959), pp. 13-14.

[4]Irving Howe, *William Faulkner: A Critical Study* (New York: Random House, 1952), p. 6. (Available in a third and expanded edition, University of Chicago Press.)

[5]Jean-Paul Sartre, *Literary and Philosophical Essays* (New York: Criterion Books, Inc., 1955), p. 87.

[6]William Van O'Connor, *The Tangled Fire of William Faulkner* (Minneapolis: University of Minnesota Press, 1954), p. 41.

[7]Herbert Read, *The Tenth Muse* (New York: Grove Press, Inc., 1957), p. 69. Of interest in a consideration of Faulkner's attacks on civilization is his attitude towards primitivism. Important in any discussion of primitivism in Faulkner's work would be the early criticisms of Ursula Brumm and R. W. B. Lewis. See Brumm, "Wilderness and Civilization: A Note on William Faulkner,"

Partisan Review, 22 (Summer 1955), 340-350; and Lewis, "The Hero in the New World: William Faulkner's 'The Bear,' " *Kenyon Review*, 13 (Autumn 1951), 641-660.

8William Faulkner, "On Privacy: The American Dream: What Happened to It," *Harper's Magazine*, 211 (July 1955), 38.

9Jean Stein. "The Art of Fiction XII: William Faulkner," *Paris Review*, 4 (Spring 1956), 42.

10William Faulkner, *Absalom, Absalom!* (New York: Random House, 1936), p. 89.

11Ibid., p. 147.

12Ibid., p. 162.

13William Faulkner, *Mosquitoes* (New York: Liveright Publishing Corp., 1927), p. 252.

14William Faulkner, *Intruder in the Dust* (New York: Random House, 1948), p. 26.

15William Faulkner, *The Wild Palms* (New York: Random House, 1939), p. 54.

16*Mosquitoes*, p. 345.

17*Absalom, Absalom!*, pp. 132, 129.

18Ibid., p. 127.

19William Faulkner, "Faith or Fear," *Atlantic Monthly*, 192 (August 1953), 54.

20William Faulkner, *Light in August* (New York: Random House, 1932), p. 87.

21William Faulkner, *The Mansion* (New York: Random House, 1959), p. 282.

22*Faulkner in the University*. ed. Frederick L. Gwynn and Joseph L. Blotner (Charlottesville: University of Virginia Press, 1959), pp. 245-246.

23Ibid., p. 246.

24See Malcolm Cowley, "Introduction," *The Portable Faulkner* (New

York: The Viking Press, 1967). Cowley was among the first to make this observation.

[25]William Faulkner, *Sanctuary* (New York: Random House, 1932), pp. 2-5. Further references will be included in the text.

[26]*Faulkner in the University*, p. 74.

[27]See Glenn O. Carey, "William Faulkner on the Automobile as Socio-Sexual Symbol," *The CEA Critic*, 36 (January 1974), 15-17.

[28]See Glenn O. Carey, "William Faulkner: Man's Fatal Vice," *Arizona Quarterly*, 28 (Winter 1972), 293-300.

Notes On Contributors

MELVIN BACKMAN teaches at C. W. Post College, Long Island University and is a former chairman there of the Department of English. Along with his many articles here and abroad on Faulkner and Hemingway he has published *Faulkner: The Major Years*, which has been translated into French under the title *William Faulkner: de "Sartoris" a "Descends, Moise."*

HARRY MODEAN CAMPBELL is Professor Emeritus at Oklahoma State University and is a former chairman there of the Department of English. He has published a large number of articles on English and American literature, and he and Ruel E. Foster collaborated on *William Faulkner: A Critical Appraisal.*

GLENN O. CAREY, editor of this volume, is a professor of English at Eastern Kentucky University. He has edited a collection of modern short stories, *Quest for Meaning*, and has published articles on Faulkner, Coleridge and Samuel Butler.

WILLIAM P. CUSHMAN teaches at the Baylor School in Chattanooga where he is chairman of the Department of English. Besides his journal publishing, he has also been active in film making and film study.

JERRY A. HERNDON teaches at Murray State University where he is also Director of Graduate Study in English. Besides publishing articles on Whitman, Frost, Emerson, Hawthorne, Melville, Hemingway, and Robert Penn Warren, he has interviewed authors such as Jesse Stuart and Harriette Arnow.

JOHN M. HOWELL teaches American literature at Southern Illinois University at Carbondale. He is the author of *Hemingway's African Stories*, a monograph on Hemingway's "The Short Happy Life of

Francis Macomber," and *John Gardner: A Bibliography*. He has published articles on Faulkner, Salinger, Hemingway and T. S. Eliot.

DUANE J. MACMILLAN teaches English at the University of Saskatchewan. He has published papers on Faulkner and other American authors in various Canadian and American journals and has edited a *Festschrift* volume in honor of Marston La France, *The Stoic Strain in American Literature*.

RICHARD A. MILUM teaches English at The Ohio State University at Lima. He has published numerous papers on Faulkner and has a book-in-progress, a cross-cultural study of Faulkner and modern French criticism.

EDWIN MOSES teaches English at Kansas State University. He has published articles on Faulkner, Camus, and F. Scott Fitzgerald, among others.

SANFORD PINSKER teaches English at Franklin and Marshall College. He has published these books — *The Schlemiel as Metaphor: Studies in the Yiddish-American Novel; The Comedy that "Hoits": An Essay on the Fiction of Philip Roth; Between Two Worlds: The American Novel in the 1960's; The Languages of Joseph Conrad*; and two books of poetry—*When Ozzie Nelson Died and Other Tragedies of our Time*, and *Still Life and Other Poems*. He has published articles on Faulkner, Conrad, and Bellow, and his poems have appeared in numerous periodicals.

CAROLYN PORTER teaches English at the University of California at Berkely, has published articles on Faulkner, and now has a book-in-progress—*Man Thinking, Man Working: Detachment and Participation in American Literature*.

ELIZABETH D. RANKIN teaches English at Auburn University and has published criticism on the fiction of John Fowles.

PATRICK SAMWAY, S. J., teaches at Le Moyne College in Syracuse where he is chariman of the Department of English. His articles have appeared in a variety of periodicals in the United States and France, and he has recently co-edited an anthology, *Stories of the Modern South*.

P. P. SHARMA teaches English at the Indian Institute of Technology, Kanpur, India. He has published in Indian and American journals on Faulkner, Charlotte Bronte, Virginia Woolf, and modern American dramatists such as Arthur Miller and Tennessee Williams.

WOODROW STROBLE teaches English at the State University of New York at Cortland where he also was Director of Tutorial Services for Project Opportunity, a program for disadvantaged students. His professional experience includes seven years of teaching in secondary schools.

EDMOND L. VOLPE has taught English at New York University and the City College of New York, and now is President of The College of Staten Island, City University of New York. He has published widely in literary and educational journals on Henry James, Nathanel West, James Jones, Norman Mailer, and aspects of higher education. Among his numerous books (as editor or co-editor) are *A Reader's Guide to William Faulkner, Eleven Modern Short Novels, Grammar in Action, An Introduction to Literature, Twelve Short Stories, Essays of Our Time, Reading and Rhetoric from Harper's*, and *The Pulitzer Prize Reader*.

A